THE EXPERIMENT OF FAITH

Matthew J. Ramage

THE EXPERIMENT OF FAITH

Pope Benedict XVI on Living the Theological Virtues in a Secular Age

The Catholic University of America Press   Washington, D.C.

Copyright © 2020

The Catholic University of America Press

All rights reserved

The paper used in this publication meets the minimum requirements of American National Standards for Information Science—Permanence of Paper for Printed Library Materials, ANSI Z39.48–1984.

∞

Library of Congress Cataloging-in-Publication Data

Names: Ramage, Matthew J., author.

Title: The experiment of faith : Pope Benedict XVI on living the theological virtues in a secular age / Matthew J. Ramage.

Description: Washington, D.C. : The Catholic University of America Press, [2020] | Includes bibliographical references and index.

Identifiers: LCCN 2019059110 | ISBN 9780813232690 (paperback) |

Subjects: LCSH: Benedict XVI, Pope, 1927–Teachings. |
Christian life—Catholic authors. | Theological virtues.

Classification: LCC BX1378.6 .R36 2020 | DDC 248.4/82—dc23

LC record available at https://lccn.loc.gov/2019059110

To those who have given me life—and new life

And to those with whom I have been blessed to run "the experiment of faith"

But we have this treasure in earthen vessels....

We are afflicted in every way, but not crushed; perplexed, but not driven to despair; persecuted, but not forsaken; struck down, but not destroyed; always carrying in the body the death of Jesus, so that the life of Jesus may also be manifested in our bodies.

Though our outer nature is wasting away, our inner nature is being renewed every day. For this slight momentary affliction is preparing for us an eternal weight of glory beyond all comparison, because we look not to the things that are seen but to the things that are unseen; for the things that are seen are transient, but the things that are unseen are eternal.

2 Corinthians 4:7–18 (RSV)

CONTENTS

Preface   ix

1. Nietzsche's Challenge to the Faith and Benedict XVI's "Existentialist" Response   1

Part 1: Core Concepts of the Christian Faith Life

2. Putting out into the Deep: Christian Spirituality and the Call to Holiness   17
3. Rules of the Game: Obedience and True Freedom   33

Part 2: Benedict XVI on the Theological Virtues

4. Faith (I): Seeking Understanding and Taking a Stand   53
5. Faith (II): Obedience to What Precedes Us and What Being a Christian Really Means   84
6. Hope (I): The Church's Vision of Cosmic Transubstantiation and Redemptive Suffering   100
7. Hope (II): The Mysteries That Make Hope Possible and Their Implications for Our Lives   121
8. Charity (I): God's Love and Our Response in Truth   143
9. Charity (II): Integral Ecology and Man's Place in Creation   169

Part 3: Benedict XVI in Dialogue with Other Contemporary Thinkers

10. Salvation by Allegiance, Not Certainty: How to Believe Biblically — 197
11. "Ironic" Belief: The Christian Story and Apologetics in a Secular Age — 217
12. Conclusion: The Beauty of Life in Christ: Faith's Ultimate *Apologia* — 239

Bibliography — 267
Index — 279

PREFACE

The present volume might be thought of as the third in what a friend of mine called with tongue in cheek the "darkness trilogy of CUA Press." Like my previous two books, *Dark Passages of the Bible* and *Jesus, Interpreted*, this book is for me a deeply personal affair. It is not just a piece of focused scholarship on the thought of Benedict XVI/Joseph Ratzinger—though it is that. Nor is it merely an in-depth exploration of the meaning of the theological virtues—though it is that as well. This is a book of academic theology, but it is also the story of my own endeavor to "run the experiment of faith," to put it in the words of Pope Benedict XVI that will recur often over the course of the following pages.

My fascination with the emeritus pontiff's thought over the years is at bottom driven by my quest of the truth of existence—which I happen to think the humble man who now goes simply by "Fr. Benedict" articulates better than anyone else I have ever read or met. My hope is that, by sharing some of my own spiritual and intellectual journey in the context of laying out Benedict XVI's overall vision of the Christian faith, you the reader may find greater strength to "fight the good fight of the faith" (1 Tim 6:12) in today's postmodern world. Ours is a society which sees Christianity as merely one option among other lifestyles at best, or—as Friedrich Nietzsche and many others allege—as an ideology that is positively antithetical to authentic human flourishing. If this book helps any readers struggling in the faith to live it more deeply and with greater joy within our contemporary cultural context, I will be a very content author.

Among the many individuals who deserve my gratitude for their contributions to this book, pride of place of course goes to our emeritus pontiff Benedict XVI, whose thought has helped me more than anyone else to "see through the glass" (1 Cor 13:12) with a great deal more of clarity than I would have had if left to my own devices. I also owe a debt of gratitude to my colleagues at Benedictine College whose conversations helped refine many of the ideas in this manuscript, as well as to those at my institution who proofread it. In particular, I wish to think Raphael Imgrund and the students of my fall 2018 Christian Moral Life class who were among the first to read the text and provide feedback. I am further indebted to the outstanding staff of the Catholic University of America Press with whom it has been a joy to collaborate on three projects now, in particular John Martino, Brian Roach, and Louise A. Mitchell.

Most importantly, I have been able to write this book (and do anything meaningful in this world) only because I first received the gift of life and the gift of the Catholic faith from my parents. Without them, I obviously would not be here, and I almost certainly would not have the privilege of having a career as a Catholic theologian. But I also would not be here today without the support of my wife and love of my children and friends—especially the donation of a kidney that I recently received from my dear friend, Christopher Barnard. If my parents gave me the gift of life in the first place, then Chris's generosity has given me a second chance at life, a new lease on this amazing reality that is God's to give or take away at any moment he chooses. I dedicate this book to all of those who have given me life and to all of those alongside whom it has been my privilege to run "the experiment of faith" over my life's course thus far.

THE EXPERIMENT OF FAITH

1

INTRODUCTION

Nietzsche's Challenge to the Faith and Benedict XVI's "Existentialist" Response

What If the Truth Were the Other Way Around?

You really ought to know better. More and more enlightened people are casting off the Christian faith with every passing year, so why go on embracing the unprovable claims of an outdated religion that arose before the advent of modern science? Why bow to an authority that requires you to submit to someone else's repressive rules that impede your happiness? Why let old, power-hungry men in Rome deny you the freedom to seek fulfillment through sexual self-expression? Why continue belonging to an institution that no longer speaks to men and women living in today's world?

I did not come up with the above questions on my own. They are questions I have run across time and again, articulated always in slightly different ways, over the course of my adult life as a Christian. But these challenges we encounter so often today find much of their inspiration in the work of a pivotal figure who lived over a century ago, Friedrich Wilhelm Nietzsche. Widely considered history's greatest critic of Christianity, Nietzsche is crucial for Christians today because he raises the big question: is the Christian moral life justifiable, or should we give up and go home to enjoy the comfort of our instinctual desires freed from the artificial constraints of an authority whose glory days passed away centuries ago?

Over the years I have entertained countless questions and concerns about the Christian faith, to some of which I feel like I have arrived at a relatively satisfactory response, others not. Like so many others, I have had to ask: Does God exist, or is the divine merely our own projection? Is Jesus God in the flesh, or is his story really just ancient myth at its best? Are Christian moral teachings true to our biology and psychology, or are they relics of a human past out of which we are now rightly evolving? But one of the things about Nietzsche that interests me most is the focus of his questioning and criticism. While many skeptics attack this or that Christian belief, Nietzsche saw that the heart of Christianity was not its doctrines but rather something else much more intimate. I can think of no concise text that better captures his plan than this:

> So long as Christian *morality* is not felt to be a *capital crime against life*, its defenders have the game in their hands. The question of the mere "truth" of Christianity—be it with regard to the existence of its God or the historicity of its origin legend, not to mention Christian astronomy and natural science—is a matter of secondary importance so long as the value of Christian morality goes unquestioned.[1]

For Nietzsche, it goes without saying that Christianity's core doctrinal claims are scientifically unviable. And he recognized that mock-

---

1. Friedrich Nietzsche, *Nachgelassene Werke: Ecce homo; Der Wille zur Macht* (Leipzig: Kröner, 1922), 327, no. 251 (my translation, emphases in Nietzsche's original). For an English translation of the complete work, see Friedrich Nietzsche, *The Will to Power* (New York: Vintage Books, 1969), 145. Benedict XVI cites a portion of the text in his book *Jesus of Nazareth: From the Baptism in the Jordan to the Transfiguration* (New York: Doubleday, 2007), 97. As indicated in his bibliography, the pope based his own reflection here—as he does elsewhere at various points throughout this corpus—upon the work of Henri de Lubac. For the specific Nietzsche source discussed above, see de Lubac's *The Drama of Atheist Humanism* (San Francisco: Ignatius Press, 1995), 115.

ing the faith for its ostensible incompatibility with the best of modern thought will only get him so far. Since people will go on believing Christianity's outrageous truth claims so long as its morality remains intact, Nietzsche concluded that the Christian moral life is the point at which a critique must strike.

By the way, when we speak of Christian "morality," we should refrain from thinking that Nietzsche merely intends to assault a collection of controversial moral teachings. He hopes, rather, to collapse the entire Christian moral edifice, the Christian way of life as such. It is not just that the Church tells you what you can and cannot do in your bedroom that is at issue for Nietzsche. The problem is that, at every turn, the Christian faith blows the whistle on *joy*. "The most specific issue," writes Nietzsche in his *On the Genealogy of Morality*, "was the worth of the 'unegoistic,' the instincts of compassion, self-denial, self-sacrifice." This basic moral premise is, according to Nietzsche, "the great danger to mankind."[2]

In an ironic move, Nietzsche calls the Christian ethos nihilistic, insisting that it stifles our natural drives and asks us to profess what we all instinctually know to be false. For, who really thinks that it is good to be poor, sick, ugly, and powerless? Yet this is precisely what Christianity ludicrously asks us to accept. Accordingly, Nietzsche considers Jesus of Nazareth "seduction in its most sinister and irresistible form," his bearing the cross a "ghastly paradox" and his issuing of the Beatitudes (Mt 5:1–12; Lk 6:20–26) the "the greatest sin on earth so far."[3] In reality, asserts Nietzsche, the allegedly unegoistic posture of the Christian is only a mask for his hypocrisy. Hell is invented for the wicked because we hate them and pine for revenge. Heaven is contrived for the "blessed" because it makes them feel better, but they would not act as they do had they the power and money to change

---

2. Friedrich Nietzsche, *On the Genealogy of Morality* (Cambridge: Cambridge University Press, 2007), 7.

3. Ibid., 18; Nietzsche, *Thus Spake Zarathustra: A Book for All and None* (New York: Modern Library, 1940), LXXIII, 16.

their lot in life. Countless Christians thus continue to live under their delusion of bourgeois doctrine and morality, but what if the truth were the other way around?

What, indeed, if the truth were the other way around? I mean, is it not the case that we sometimes make ourselves feel better by playing the moral superiority card? And have not many of us wondered whether heaven is really just a coping mechanism, and hell either a projection of our hatred or a pragmatic invention of priests to instill good behavior in the uneducated by means of fear? Like many other people, I have often pondered whether Nietzsche might be right and the Christian wrong after all. But how would one even begin to go about answering this question? The task of the present volume is to do precisely this by enlisting the help of Joseph Ratzinger/Pope Benedict XVI.[4] While many recognize him as one of the past century's most important ecclesial figures, relatively few realize how serious a consideration this Roman pontiff gives to the thought of Christianity's great challengers throughout his corpus. In fact, given how frequently Nietzsche's name comes up in his writings, I think it is not a stretch to say that Benedict considers this nineteenth-century German philosopher to be Christianity's greatest critical interlocutor, his philosophy the faith's most serious alternative.

And I think that the emeritus pontiff does not just view Nietzsche's arguments as interesting historical artifacts. Rather, I believe he is so concerned with the latter because his criticisms are representative of our secular culture's now default view that there is no objective reality behind our faith and that Christian morality is an oppressive relic of the past that needs to be jettisoned together with its foundational myth. Nearly two centuries ago, Alexis de Tocqueville said that Americans are all Cartesians without ever having read Descartes. We might

---

4. To the extent that it is possible to do so while retaining its readability, this book at times refers to the one man Ratzinger/Benedict by his surname and at other times by his papal name in the effort to distinguish writings composed during his pontificate from those preceding it.

say something similar with respect to Nietzsche today: it is increasingly becoming the case that the Western mind is Nietzschean even if most people have never read a word of Nietzsche.

If Nietzsche's critique of Christianity centers not merely on its doctrines but on how its entire moral system is a mere construct that stifles authentic human flourishing, then Benedict thinks that the antidote to such a claim must be a response in kind. If the faith is to be seen as true, it must be able to craft an intelligent critique of Nietzsche's philosophy, showing how nihilism consistently lived prevents human flourishing, and reducing to the absurd the view that morality is a mere social construct. You can think of this as the "negative" side of the argument that Christianity has to be able to make in today's world. More important, though, is the "positive" side of the case that Benedict thinks we need to be making. Nietzsche proposed an alternate way of life to that of the bourgeois society in which he lived, a society that went by the name of Christian. If it is to survive Nietzsche's critique, the Christian faith will have to stand out from and challenge the bourgeois morality of our own age. It will need to be experienced neither as stifling nor as a mere affirmation of the status quo but as a call to greatness that is supremely life-giving and liberating precisely because of the demands it places upon us. This Christian faith will have to be intelligent, but not just an intellectual affair. Christianity will need to not merely proclaim itself good, but give people reason to see *why* it is good.

In order to do this, the Church will have to not merely propose different truths but craft a rival story, an alternate way of life to that which our secularized world offers. Accordingly, the aim of this book is to offer a response to the Nietzschean criticism of our Christian ethos. This *apologia* or argument in favor of the faith will consist in painting a picture of what authentic Christian moral living looks like according to Benedict XVI.

The Structure of This Book

My means to achieve this end which gives rise to the structure of this book will consist in chapters aimed at showing forth the goodness of Christian faith as especially evident in Benedict's robust understanding of the theological virtues of faith, hope, and charity, and illustrating how one fully appreciative of Nietzsche's critique can continue to live them in our secular society.[5] As we will be spending most of this book on these virtues which are means to our final goal in life, I will begin with a preliminary section (chapters 1–3) that discusses the core concepts and aims of the Christian faith life. This includes a chapter articulating what, precisely, it means for the goal of our life to consist in the pursuit of holiness and how we can, in Benedict's words, run the "experiment of faith" in our spiritual lives. Following this initial chapter is another preliminary one on the "rules of the game" of faith—specifically the nature of human freedom and its relationship with truth, a reality necessary to get right if our reflections on faith, hope, and charity are to be grounded in an authentically Christian worldview. The second section at the heart of the book (chapters 4–9) is comprised by several chapters dedicated to expounding Benedict's approach to the theological virtues. In the third and final section

---

5. For another text on Benedict and the theological virtues, see Thomas Rausch, SJ, *Faith, Hope, and Charity: Benedict XVI on the Theological Virtues* (New York: Paulist Press, 2015). Rausch's volume is very helpful, with sections on the reception, positive and critical, of each of Benedict's virtue encyclicals. However, providing an overview of the encyclicals' content and documenting is not my concern here. My aim is not just to present Benedict's thought but rather to use it to help us address a particular problem: how to live "through the glass, darkly"—how to live an intelligent Christian faith in today's secularized world. For another shorter piece that deals with Benedict on the theological virtues, with a particular emphasis on their necessity within modern societies and political communities, see Rachel Amiri and Mary Keys, "Benedict XVI on Liberal Modernity's Need for the 'Theological Virtues' of Faith, Hope, and Love," *Perspectives on Political Science* 41, no. 1 (2012): 11–18. For a pair of valuable texts surveying Benedict's thought as a whole, see Tracey Rowland, *Ratzinger's Faith: The Theology of Pope Benedict XVI* (Oxford: Oxford University Press, 2008); and Aidan Nichols, *The Thought of Pope Benedict XVI* (New York: Burns & Oates, 2007).

(chapters 10–11), we will put Benedict into dialogue with other contemporary figures whose thought is congenial to that of the pontiff and who are invaluable to the project of articulating what a rational, biblically grounded faith looks like in our secular context. Finally, the book will conclude in chapter 12 by detailing Benedict's conviction that the greatest *apologia* in favor of the Church today is to be found in the experience of holiness and beauty that comes only through the wholehearted exercise of the theological virtues—by living the "experiment of faith." In this chapter, I will share some of my own existential reflections on why I follow Christ in a world where he is often seen as merely one option among many others.

Based on the extent to which Benedict deals with Nietzsche's thought, I will be referencing his work here and there throughout the book, as I have done here in chapter 1. In the central middle section of the book (chapters 4–9), I will lay out how Benedict responds to Nietzschean criticisms whenever he brings them up while spending most of the chapter expounding Benedict's unique take on the theological virtues. Finally, I will conclude these chapters (and chapter 3) by suggesting ways to run "the experiment of faith." This will echo the final chapters of the book in which I will recount how I have sought to apply the truths we are discussing in my own life—how I spend my whole life searching, praying, doubting, engaging in friendships, living marriage, and the like—which have enabled me to better grasp the truth of Christianity's claims. My hope is that this culminating section's applied existential reflections on why I myself profess the Christian faith will prove beneficial to those readers who find themselves struggling with acceptance of one or more of Christianity's core doctrines.

A Few Disclaimers

First, I want it to be clear from that start that this is not a work of apologetics in the sense often intended when referencing St. Peter's line, "Always be prepared to make a defense [*apologia*] to anyone who calls you to account for the hope that is in you" (1 Pt 3:15).[6] While it is a noble enterprise to do so, I am not trying here to defend a particular doctrine or moral teaching of the Catholic Church. I certainly hope that I will help people navigate concrete issues here and there in this book, but the sort of *apologia* I am making here—following Benedict XVI's lead—is actually much more expansive. My argument will be that the best account of the Christian faith's truth—in the particulars and as a whole—is best seen through the practice of Christian living in its fullness.

Second, as you can probably already tell, neither is this book primarily a work of academic scholarship that adopts an elevated "third-person viewpoint" on Benedict XVI's thought, purporting to present a comprehensive grasp of some question pertaining to the theological virtues in contemporary scholarly discourse. Rather, my aim in this volume is to engage in an in-depth intellectual exploration of one prominent theologian's response to the challenge of Christian discipleship in our secular age. My colleagues in the academy, especially moral theologians, should therefore be aware that the theological virtues serve here not so much as objects of analysis in themselves but rather as lenses for the exploration of the real-life questions which I consider to be of primary significance for Christians in the world today. Although this is a book of academic theology and aims to advance scholarly understanding of Benedict's vast corpus, my ultimate aim is to help people like myself—whether academics, college students, or ordinary people in the pews interested in life's tougher questions—to live their faith more deeply in today's world.

A third point related to this concerns the role played by Nietzsche in our exploration. Though his name will come up from time to time, as it already has, this book is not a work of comparative scholarship between Benedict and Nietzsche, nor does it aspire to a craft a fully developed critique of Nietzsche. The role Nietzsche plays in this book mirrors the role he plays in Benedict's own thought: Nietzsche stands

---

6. English Bible translations in this volume will be taken from the RSV unless otherwise noted.

out as our book's ideal periodical interlocutor and reference point for two reasons: he is the critic most often engaged by Benedict, and he represents a broad tradition of criticism which he manages to transmit with unique precision and gusto. I think it is also worth noting that I do not wish to present a straw-man caricature of Nietzsche as our "enemy" in this volume. Indeed, Nietzsche would not be such a powerful critic of the faith if there were not important truths in his observations and thought. Henri de Lubac, for instance, argues that there may be more points of contact between Nietzsche and Christian orthodoxy than commonly assumed.[7] Nevertheless, my aim in this work does not involve defending anything in Nietzsche's corpus but rather addressing some of his criticisms that Benedict finds relevant to the question of whether Christian faith is viable in today's world.

Fourth, I ought to say a few words about my use of a term from the book's title which I have already begun to deploy and will continue to use throughout the book. We find ourselves today inhabiting an age described by Charles Taylor as "secular." Indeed, ours is a very secular society in the sense that discourse about God and expression of our Christian faith in the public square are often characterized as an affront to other people's freedom, a danger that must be tightly curtailed in the name of tolerance. However, this is not the precise meaning of the word "secular" that I have in mind within this book. In Taylor's parlance, "secularity" refers to our present condition in which the path of faith is seen to be just one lifestyle option among others and is no more obviously true than its alternatives. As James Smith puts it in his helpful book distilling Taylor's much longer work *A Secular Age*, "Faith is fraught; confession is haunted by an inescapable sense of its contestability. We don't believe instead of doubting; we believe while doubting. We're all Thomas now."[8]

---

7. Lubac, *Drama of Atheist Humanism*, 17–129.
8. James Smith, *How Not to Be Secular: Reading Charles Taylor* (Grand Rapids, Mich.: Eerdmans Publishing Co., 2014), 4. See Charles Taylor, *A Secular Age* (Cambridge, Mass.: Belknap Press of Harvard University, 2007).

Our present condition of secularity is characterized by Taylor as being "cross-pressured." It is a life in which we often find ourselves caught between agnosticism and devotion, between faith and questioning. It is one in which we have become aware that any claim to a completely objective hold on the truth is hauntingly problematic. Accordingly, people inhabiting a secular age are skeptical not only of religious claims but toward meta-narratives broadly speaking, questioning the status of our epistemic justification for matters that people throughout most of prior history took for granted.[9]

Nietzsche is one of the key figures of our secular age, for he irreverently asks of Christian morality: Are you *really* sure your faith is right? Could it not be the other way around? One of my own key contentions in this book is that, yes, those of us inhabiting this secular age must admit that Nietzsche theoretically could be right. Do not get me wrong: I do not think that he actually is right or that you or I should leave the Catholic faith and become a nihilist. What I mean is that the Christian living cognizantly in a secular age is aware that Nietzsche cannot be answered in a definitive, objective, foolproof way. Accordingly, I think that the Christian must begin his response to the skeptic by admitting the limitations of our proofs on the one hand and the presence of any goodness in opposing positions on the other. Sure, we can and should answer objections to the faith posed by non-believers, but we are probably not going to argue "secularized" people (including ourselves) into faith. In other words, I think we have to let faith be faith—a total way of life that is rational but also *more* than rational. Articulating what this "more than rational" is will be a key feature of this book. In brief, for Benedict XVI the reasonableness of the Christian faith is seen precisely to the extent that we embark on the quest of *living* it.

---

9. Taylor, *A Secular Age*, 14.

One Final Clarification

Throughout this book, I will also be describing Benedict's perspective that I have just laid out as "existentialist." Given the standard meaning assigned to it over the course of the modern age, this term must of course be used with circumspection and preceded by some commentary. Dogmatic theologian and pope though he was, the focus of Benedict's writings as a whole is overwhelmingly concerned with faith in the concrete details of our daily existence—as a personal relationship with God who discloses himself in Jesus Christ through the mediation of his Church. Christoph Cardinal Schönborn captures this well in writing, "Inherent to Joseph Ratzinger, besides his immense conceptual clarity, is always a very true-to-life and existential approach to the questions he addresses." Schönborn suggests that the combination of his intellectual depth, deep piety, and connectedness with real life account for the sustained success of the emeritus pontiff's works over the years.[10] After characterizing Benedict's approach with the adjective "existential," Thomas Rausch, likewise, helpfully remarks, "In the end, [Benedict's virtue encyclicals] focus not on doctrinal or on moral issues ... but rather on what it means to live in God's love, the reality that our knowledge of God is dependent on our love of him and of his creatures."[11] Of course, we must also add that the emeritus pontiff would be the last to claim that living in God's love can contradict the doctrines and moral teachings of the Church; the point here is that our contemplation of these truths is ultimately at the service of fostering what Benedict calls "existential communion with God," a relationship that illumines all aspects of our existence.[12]

---

10. Christoph Schönborn, "The Reflections of Joseph Ratzinger Pope Benedict XVI on Evolution," in *Scientific Insights into the Evolution of the Universe and of Life*, ed. W. Arber, N. Cabibbo, and M. Sánchez Sorondo (Vatican City: Ex Aedibus Academicis in Civitate Vaticana, 2009), 20.

11. Rausch, *Faith, Hope, and Charity*, 102, 129.

12. Benedict XVI, homily for the Easter Vigil (April 15, 2006); Benedict XVI and Francis, *Lumen Fidei*, §4.

Another pair of reasons why I employ the provocative term "existentialist" to describe Benedict's project are that he regularly interacts in his writings with many of the authors commonly regarded as the first existentialists (for example, Kierkegaard, Dostoevsky, and Nietzsche), and that even when not referencing them he often reflects on their main areas of concern (for example, the angst and despair that ensue from living in what appears to be an absurd world, the need for an authentic encounter with others therein, the limits of human reason to account for meaning and offer direction in our lives). Commenting on the connection of Ratzinger's thought with that of Christian existentialist Kierkegaard, Emery de Gaál notes that, for these two thinkers, "Christianity is not first and foremost a teaching but an existence that needs to be communicated to others so that this form of existence can be lived."[13]

Thomas Merton is certainly correct when he clarifies that the sort of existentialism vital to the Church today is not the commonplace sort that assumes the only meaning in life is that which we as individuals assign to it.[14] Neither is it to be equated with the sort of "ex-

---

13. Emery de Gaál, *The Theology of Pope Benedict XVI: The Christocentric Shift* (New York: Palgrave Macmillan, 2010), 30.

14. Thomas Merton, *Mystics and Zen Masters* (New York: Farrar, Straus and Giroux, 1967), 258, 270. My point in referencing Merton here is not to assert a uniformity of dogmatic convictions across the board between him and Benedict. Rather, my observation is that the former's comments—written more than four decades before Benedict was elected pope—offer the best description I have come across of the fundamental approach that governs the pontiff's encyclicals on the theological virtues. If one does not find the term "existentialism" a helpful way to describe what Benedict is up to in his theology, then other formulations can be proposed, but for the purpose of this volume I will be sticking with the term as understood here by Merton. For example, Gabriel Marcel, the great pioneer of Christian existentialism in the twentieth century, eventually ceased describing his thought as "Christian existentialism" and suggested "Christian Socratism" in its place. The background to this change is that existentialist philosophy was sharply criticized in 1950 by the reigning pope who wrote that it "denies the validity of reason in the field of metaphysics" and that it is either atheistic or "concerns itself only with existence of individual things and neglects all consideration of their immutable essences." Pius XII, *Humani Generis* (1950), §§6, 32, http://w2.vatican.va/content/pius-xii/en/encyclicals/documents/hf_p-xii_enc_12081950_humani-generis.html. I would certainly agree with Merton that the pope's critique does not apply to Christian existentialism properly understood, but in its wake Marcel nevertheless thought it better to adapt his vocabulary.

perientialism" that regards our inner subjectivity as the source of all knowledge and dumbs down the faith to make it accessible through appeals to emotion and common experience. As Bishop Robert Barron well observes, our Christian existence cannot be reduced to a single grounding intuition such as the experience being ethically duty-bound (Kant), absolutely dependent (Scheliermacher), ultimately concerned (Tillich), or standing in the presence of the absolute mystery (Rahner).[15] Benedict's authentically Christian existentialism is much more robust than these. For him, the experience of Christian faith is bound up with the entire worldview and way of life revealed by Jesus Christ and lived out in the community of his Church. Our inner experience is not the arbiter of divine revelation: on the contrary, Benedict is always saying that revelation "precedes us." His point is that experiencing life in the Church in its totality is not just a general feeling that everyone has; it comes precisely through seeking understanding of and living out the Church's teachings. When we take this path or embark upon this "experiment," it becomes a veritable highway into the divine mystery which, while eminently rational, ultimately transcends reason and can be understood only from the inside. To use an image that we will return to later in the book, in Benedict's view the Catholic Church is a lot like a Gothic cathedral with its stained-glass windows. From the outside it looks dark and dreary—it is only *from the inside*, through a deeply lived experience of Catholicism, that the radiance of its truth can rightly be seen.

One of the key features of what I am calling Benedict's "existentialist" approach to the faith, a point reflected in Merton's comments above, is that finding beauty and happiness in the Christian life is not the same as being able to prove its truth definitely to others or even to arrive at perfect certitude for ourselves. To put it in the words of St. Paul, this is the bottom line: "For now we see through a glass, dark-

---

15. Robert Barron, *The Strangest Way: Walking the Christian Path* (Maryknoll, N.Y.: Orbis Books, 2002), esp. 18–24. Also illuminating on this point is Barron, "Evangelizing the Nones" (Erasmus lecture, Union League Club, New York, October 30, 2017).

ly; but then face to face: now I know in part; but then shall I know even as also I am known. And now abideth faith, hope, charity, these three; but the greatest of these is charity" (1 Cor 13:12–13).[16] What it means to see through the glass darkly or dimly—what the experience of authentic Christian faith, hope, and charity looks like within a secular age—that is what this book is about.

> 16. In this verse, I have taken the expression δι' ἐσόπτρου ἐν αἰνίγματι ("through a glass, darkly") from the KJV for its poetic quality and familiarity to most Christians. The RSV for its part translates the same prepositional phrase, "in a mirror dimly." As Gordon Fee observes, the saying is not intended by St. Paul in a pejorative sense—as if to say that our knowledge of God through divine revelation is distorted. Taken thus, the statement would be quite an affront to the Corinthians, who in Paul's day were famous for producing some of the finest bronze mirrors in antiquity. The point of the saying, rather, is to emphasize the *indirect nature* of our vision of God in this life, akin to how we today would contrast looking at a photograph of someone with seeing the person face to face. Gordon Fee, *The First Epistle to the Corinthians*, ed. Ned B. Stonehouse et al., rev. ed., The New International Commentary on the New Testament (Grand Rapids, Mich.: Eerdmans Publishing Co., 2014), 718.

Part 1

Core Concepts of the Christian Faith Life

2

PUTTING OUT INTO THE DEEP
Christian Spirituality and the Call to Holiness

Not Your Conventional Experiment

In the introduction to this volume, we have just considered Nietzsche's accusation that Christian morality is a capital crime against life whose very foundation needs to be toppled. According to Nietzsche, Christians invented their moral system as the only way they could enact revenge against their oppressors. Thus construed, Christianity is essentially a power play that purports to bestow meaning upon a meaningless world—there is no objective truth behind the religion's fanciful claims. Nietzsche crafted an alternate story about how we got our morals, and he furthermore offered a rival way of life to that of the bourgeois Christian society in which he lived. As I said in the introduction, I think that the Christian response to Nietzsche's criticism must follow along the same lines: if the faith is to be seen as true, it must stand out from and challenge the bourgeois morality of our own age. Moreover, the faith must propose not merely different truths but tell a rival story, offer an alternate path that is supremely life-giving and liberating.

Our quest to answer Nietzsche's critique of the faith will consist in painting a picture of what authentic Christian faith and life looks like, specifically by articulating a robust understanding of how one can live the theological virtues of faith, hope, and charity while fully appreciative of Nietzsche's critique in today's secularized society. But before diving into the virtues themselves, I think it is important to pause first and meditate with Benedict XVI on the reality toward which all of these virtues are ordered: the good life. In other words, if we will be spending most of this book on virtues which are means to our final goal in life, then it is only proper that we begin by articulating in what, precisely, our life's purpose consists—the goal of the "experiment" that the emeritus pontiff is asking us to carry out. We could follow the ancients and call this end happiness, or we could emphasize its nature as eschatological fulfilment and call it heaven or the beatific vision. In this chapter, I will be following the lead of Benedict's writings on the spiritual life and describe it as charity, incorporation into Christ, divinization, and, above all, holiness.

Holiness is a topic that many people in our secular age find useless or even abhorrent, and for this reason it is all the more important to discuss here at the outset of our journey in this book. Whereas there are countless atheists walking the face of our planet whom we would identify as morally upright individuals who want the good life such as they conceive of it, how many of these individuals would deem holiness a virtue? And who would regard Christian prayer as a true encounter with the divine, a healthy practice that immerses one more deeply into the truth of things? Yet this is precisely what Christianity professes. We believe that prayer really unites us to God, that we have a personal encounter with the divine in the exercise of prayer. In accord with the vision I laid out in the introduction, I will not be aiming here to disprove the atheist's view that Christian prayer is a delusion, a coping mechanism, or whatever else it may be construed as. As I will emphasize in later chapters, I do not think that the Nietzschean perspective on Christianity can be disproven in an utterly objective manner. Rather, my contention in this volume is that the ultimate answer to Nietzsche can only come through the laboratory of life. Benedict calls on us to undergo what he terms *the experiment of faith*. It is of this journey that he writes, "Only by entering does one experience; only by cooperating in the experiment does one ask at all; and only he who asks receives an answer."[1] Without further ado, we will now consider the step of that experiment that consists in prayer and the call to holiness.

The Goal of Holiness, Achievable through Charity in the Simplicity of Ordinary Life

In sitting down to pen this section detailing the core features of the Christian "experiment of faith," I thought that a helpful way to begin would be to craft a preliminary definition of holiness to set the stage for Benedict's portrait of its various contours. As I was reviewing my myriad notes and highlights from the pontiff's books in my home library, I came across the following text in which, to my great delight, I discovered that Benedict had already done the work for me. In his characteristic manner, Benedict poses the question directly: what is the soul of holiness? His answer, based on the words of the Second Vatican Council, is: "Christian holiness is nothing other than charity lived to the full."[2]

If the above language sounds too solemn, Benedict continues, we might frame the question slightly differently: at the end of the day, what is essential to holiness, to Christian existence in our world?

The essential means never leaving a Sunday without an encounter with the Risen Christ in the Eucharist.... It means never beginning and never ending

---

1. Ratzinger, *Introduction to Christianity*, 2nd ed. (San Francisco: Ignatius Press, 2004), 175–76; Joseph Ratzinger, "Why I Am Still in the Church," in *Fundamental Speeches from Five Decades* (San Francisco: Ignatius Press, 2012), 132–53.

2. Benedict XVI, "Holiness," general audience (April 13, 2011). This translation is from the Vatican website. It and other catecheses from January 13, 2010, to April 13, 2011, cited hereafter are contained in the collected volume Benedict XVI, *Holy Men and Women of the Middle Ages and Beyond* (San Francisco: Ignatius Press, 2012).

a day without at least a brief contact with God. And, on the path of our life it means following the "signposts" that God has communicated to us in the Ten Commandments, interpreted with Christ, which are merely the explanation of what love is in specific situations.[3]

Benedict's summary of holiness's path is concise and simple, something that every human being realistically can live. We encounter the risen Lord every Sunday, we take time to meet him at the beginning and end of each day, and we follow his commandments, which are simply articulations of how to live in specific situations or, as he immediately proceeds to add, "forms of charity."

At the same time as he notes that observance of the commandments is a crucial component of holiness, Benedict adds that constant reference to the law is not necessary for him who loves to the full. As Augustine has it, *Dilige et fac quod vis* ("Love and do what you will"). Far from being intended as a rationalization for evil or a claim that noble intentions suffice to justify our actions, this classic statement reveals the great freedom in which a life of pursuing holiness consists. Christians do not need to get hung up on whether or not we precisely adhere to the letter of the law at every moment, on whether our actions and thoughts are always correct. Sometimes we are going to be wrong. When we discover our error, we then repent and seek to amend our lives in light of our newfound knowledge or desire for excellence. Augustine's wise dictum is a reminder that, while we will inevitably fail throughout our life, God's mercy is unfailing. Our effort to love comes with no guarantee of immediate success. Nevertheless, it remains the case that we can have confidence of being on the right path—the path of holiness—if we live a life of love.

Is a life lived completely in love even possible? Benedict follows up his reflection on Augustine's saying with this very question, and the basis for his affirmative answer to it lies not in theoretical speculations but in people: the saints. The saints (*sancti* literally means the

---

3. Benedict XVI, "Holiness."

"holy ones") show us by their very lives that it is indeed possible to walk the path of holiness. And when he speaks of the saints, the pontiff does not have primarily in mind the canonized men and women of history who worked miracles or experienced extraordinary mystical phenomena:

> I would like to add that for me not only a few great saints whom I love and whom I know well are "signposts," but precisely also the simple saints, that is, the good people I see in my life who will never be canonized. They are ordinary people, so to speak, without visible heroism but in their everyday goodness I see the truth of faith. This goodness, which they have developed in the faith of the Church, is for me the most reliable apology of Christianity and the sign of where the truth lies.[4]

To be sure, the canonized saints have a pivotal role to play in confirming and deepening our faith. As we see here for Benedict, however, it is above all the non-canonized saints—the "simple" or "ordinary" people we know—who are the truest sign of where the truth of the faith lies. For while some souls may be granted a profound spiritual encounter with a canonized saint of ages past, for most of us it is our direct and intimate experience with a living member of the communion of saints that proves life-changing. In our encounter with a living witness of the faith, we find encouragement to aim high, to be not afraid that God will ask too much of us, to lay our entire lives on the line for love of God and so become a small piece in the great mosaic of holiness that God is continually creating in history.

Conformity to Christ: Adoption and Divinization

Benedict's commonsense approach to holiness finds another great expression in his catechesis on St. John of the Cross. One of the loftiest mystics of Church history, John's life easily could be viewed as irrelevant to the Christian living in today's secularized society. Well

---

4. Ibid.

aware of this objection, Benedict asks the question point-blank: does this saint have anything to say to the ordinary Christian who lives in the circumstances of our life today, or is he a model for only a few elect souls? To arrive at an answer, says Benedict, we have to remember that John's life was anything but a "float on mystical clouds." He had an incredibly hard life, one that was very concrete and practical. As a reformer of his religious order, John came under such opposition that he was imprisoned and abused both physically and mentally by his own confreres.

So what is John's doctrine of the spiritual life? The audacious end game of spiritual perfection, says John, is *divinization*—the transformation of the creature into God. Lofty as the goal may be, the way we get there is actually quite simple: it happens when we let ourselves be loved by God in Jesus Christ. Holiness, then, is not the result of our completing very difficult actions but rather the opening of our soul's windows to let in God's light. It is not reserved for the elite who can cite the Bible by chapter and verse or for those who are inclined to spend extensive hours in the chapel.[5]

When I read Benedict's catecheses a handful of years ago, I was at first a little disappointed. Is this really all holiness is, Holy Father? Is holiness really as simple as remembering God a couple times a day, commemorating the Resurrection on Sunday, keeping the Commandments, and letting ourselves be loved? I had wanted the pope to insist that we ought also to be doing a weekly holy hour, praying an evening family rosary, frequenting the sacrament of confession on a monthly basis, and the like. Of course, he and the other popes do recommend those devotions, and rightly so. But I think Benedict wants us to understand above all that living a life of holiness is very simple, something anybody of any time, place, or circumstance can achieve.

Moreover, persistently performing the above observances is not as easy as it may first appear. This is especially the case if we read the

---

5. Benedict XVI, "Saint John of the Cross," general audience (February 16, 2011).

Ten Commandments in light of the Sermon on the Mount: few of us have killed another human being, but it is incredibly hard not to kill spiritually by being angry at our brother (Mt 5:22). Likewise, it is fairly easy for most of us not to commit adultery on any given day, but avoiding lust tends to prove remarkably difficult (Mt 5:28). Above all, the difficulty of the other key element to holiness mentioned by Benedict—letting ourselves be loved by God—is easy to underestimate. It is indeed a simple concept, but it is far from easy to execute. It entails letting ourselves truly be forgiven by God, acknowledging our littleness before God, letting our past wounds heal, picking up and moving on after tragedy and sin. A lot of us have great trouble pulling off this feat, but Benedict considers the effort to do so one of the few key ingredients of a holy life.

In a catechesis on the "Abba" with which believers address God (Gal 4:6–7; Rom 8:14–17), Benedict articulates at greater length what the Christian's goal of holiness means, especially with respect to divinization. As the Fathers of the Church have it, holiness consists in a specific belonging to God wherein we become adopted "sons in the Son." Over the course of our earthly pilgrimage, we are called increasingly to become by grace what Christ is by nature, to be ever more deeply inserted into the ineffable relationship of love that is God: Father, Son, and Holy Spirit.[6] This, in fact, is "the essence of God's will," according to Benedict—that we be drawn out of ourselves and into Christ's divine nature so that all things may be united in him.[7] How, exactly, we are supposed to become Christ is very simple. It happens as we learn to stop seeking merely our own good and identify with Christ, imitating him in his life and in his death. In Pauline language,

---

6. Benedict XVI, General Audience (May 23, 2012). Translations from this and other audiences dating from May 2011 through October 2012 are taken from the Vatican website. They are also compiled and published in the terrific volume Benedict XVI, *A School of Prayer: The Saints Show Us How to Pray* (San Francisco: Ignatius Press, 2012).

7. Benedict XVI, "God Reveals His 'Benevolent Purpose,'" general audience (December 5, 2012); Benedict XVI, General Audience (February 1, 2012); Eph 1:10.

this entails letting ourselves be crucified with Christ so as to rise with him (Rom 6:3–11). Like the above teachings on holiness, this is a very simple doctrine and achievable by all, but this is by no means to say that it is easy. Conformity to Christ does not just happen. It requires constant vigilance, perseverance, trial and error, and the humility to get back up when we inevitably find ourselves desperately in need of divine mercy.

As a final point on the subject of divinization, I would like to emphasize an important point that helps us to avoid a misunderstanding of the doctrine. Benedict describes our divinization as a "mutual compenetration between Christ and the Christian." We are in Christ, and he is in us.[8] But when we become Christ—when we become God—it is not as if we get absorbed into the divine abyss and lose our individuality. On the contrary, Benedict emphasizes that the Christian doctrine of divinization upholds the distinction between us and God. As in marriage the two spouses become one while each retains his or her identity, so the person nuptially conjoined to Christ remains distinct from him. Recalling the patristic theology of St. John of Damascus, we read that Christians can truly be called "gods"—not because they are so by nature, but through the gift of God's grace. Just as the red-hot iron takes on the properties of fire through its insertion into the fire, so the human who participates in God takes on his very wisdom, love, and life.[9] The creature is not simply equivalent to God in this analogy. In becoming fire, the iron is not identical to that in which it is immersed. The two are distinct, yet not separate. Similarly, the divinized person is distinct but not separate from God—at least not

---

8. Benedict XVI, "St. Paul's New Outlook," general audience (November 8, 2006); Rom 8:1–2, 39; 12:5; 16:3, 7, 10; 1 Cor 1:2–3; Rom 8:10; 2 Cor 13:5; Gal 2:20.

9. Benedict XVI, "John Damascene," general audience (May 6, 2009); Ps 82:6; Lv 19:2; Mt 5:48. This and other catecheses from March 2008 to December 2009 are contained in the collected volume by Benedict XVI, *Church Fathers and Teachers: From Saint Leo the Great to Peter Lombard* (San Francisco: Ignatius Press, 2010). On the union of husband and wife as an analogy for the union of Christ and his Church, which are utterly one while remaining distinct, see Joseph Ratzinger, *Called to Communion* (San Francisco: Ignatius Press, 1996), 39.

separate so long as the will perseveres in God's grace. The oneness of the human person with God, then, is best understood not in terms of the solitary atom but rather on the plane of relationship. As we will read Benedict saying later in this volume, the unity that we discover through relationship is a higher form of unity than that enjoyed by the individual as a solitary atom.

Lectio Divina and the Three Expressions of Prayer

As I said above, Benedict's description of the life of holiness seemed too simple to me when I first read it. I had expected the pontiff to require more of us than that we keep the Commandments, celebrate the Sunday liturgy, let ourselves be loved by God, and remember him at the beginning and end of each day. After a lot of reflection, and perhaps a little more spiritual maturity gained over the past decade, I think that Benedict's summary does nicely capture the essential components of a Christian life. At the same time, he does highlight the importance of other spiritual practices, among which prayer with Scripture holds pride of place.

Throughout his catechetical works on the saints, we find Benedict articulating and instantiating an approach to Scripture grounded upon the latter's fourfold sense. As expressed by Hugh of Saint-Victor nearly a millennium ago and embraced in the *Catechism of the Catholic Church*, these senses are the literal or historical, the allegorical, the anagogical, and the moral.[10] The foundational sense of Scripture is the literal—or, perhaps better, literary sense. This is the original intended meaning of the text, whose correct exegesis in turn makes possible true and proper theology. The other three senses comprise the spiritual sense, whose manifold layers concern how the ancient biblical text

---

10. Benedict XVI, "Hugh and Richard of Saint-Victor," general audience (November 25, 2009); *Catechism of the Catholic Church*, trans. United States Conference of Catholic Bishops (Washington, D.C.: Libreria Editrice Vaticana, 1994), §§115–19.

finds perennial expression in the life of Christ (allegorical), our life on earth (moral), and our life in Heaven (anagogical).[11]

Benedict advocates a particular spiritual discipline, *lectio divina* or "divine reading," which builds on this framework of Scripture's four senses. Remarkably, in his apostolic exhortation on the Word of God, the pontiff sets aside time to walk us through the key steps of *lectio*. Though these steps admit of some variation among the writings of Catholic spiritual masters across the centuries, they essentially boil down to five. We begin our prayer with *lectio*, itself, the reading of a text from the Bible or a spiritual author with an eye to determining the content of its literal sense, what the text says in itself. Next comes *meditatio*, in which we "ruminate" on the word, chewing on it as long as it takes to ascertain what it means for us today. Closely related is the third step, *oratio*, in which we converse with the Lord and offer to him our response to his word. Fourth comes *contemplatio*, in which we ask God what kind of concrete conversion of mind, heart, and life he is asking of us today. Finally, we must translate our discernment into *actio*, a concrete resolution whereby we make a gift to others in charity.

Without this last step of action, St. Francis de Sales says that our prayer risks being not only useless, but even harmful.[12] The reason for this is that it is easy for the person who prays to think that he has become holy simply because he has recited the Church's prayers or taken the time to stop by the chapel for a visit. Important as these acts of devotion are, by themselves they do not make one holy. Our prayer has to be translated into action if it is to really achieve its end. In accord with what Benedict said above, holiness is evinced not by the depth of

---

11. For the understanding of Scripture's senses and the relationship of the literal or literary sense with theology, see Vatican Council II, *Dei Verbum* (1965), §12, http://www.vatican.va/archive/hist_councils/ii_vatican_council/documents/vat-ii_const_19651118_dei-verbum_en.html; and Matthew Ramage, *Jesus, Interpreted: Benedict XVI, Bart Ehrman, and the Historical Truth of the Gospels* (Washington, DC: The Catholic University of America Press, 2017), 56–100.

12. Benedict XVI, *Verbum Domini*, 86–87; St. Francis de Sales, *Introduction to the Devout Life* (New York: Image Books, 1989), 90.

our thoughts or feelings in prayer, but by the courage of our charity. It is not that our prayer will conclude every time with the revelation of some heroic action that God is beckoning us to perform, but Benedict wants our prayer to be of such a kind that it inculcates in us the daily habit of asking God how he wants us to transform our lives and the world around us.

Having laid out the five steps of *lectio* as summarized by Benedict, I now would like to add a few words of precision. The *Catechism* helpfully speaks of there being three expressions of Christian prayer: vocal, meditative, and contemplative. Something not discussed by Benedict above, vocal prayer is what most Christians think of when they employ the expression "saying our prayers." Vocal prayer is a pivotal part of the spiritual life, for through the spontaneous prayers expressed in our own words we lay our interior state before God so that he might purify and transform our entire existence. Moreover, the memorized, formulaic prayers we often say (for example, Our Father, Hail Mary, Creed, etc.) are given to us by the Church with a view to training our thoughts, sentiments, and actions to accord with those of Christ. But vocal prayer is really just the tip of the iceberg, the least profound expression of prayer. Meditative prayer leads us much deeper into the mystery of God, and the *Catechism* understands it very similarly to how Benedict does above.

On the subject of contemplation, I would note that Benedict's above description does not quite capture the essence of what contemplation is across the broader spiritual tradition of the Church. As the *Catechism* explains well, contemplation is the simplest expression of prayer. Benedict, for his part, speaks of contemplation as the time in prayer when we ask what concrete action God wants of us. This is not wrong, but I would place the accent differently as Benedict himself does elsewhere. I think that contemplation is best understood as the time when we put down our book, set aside our thinking, and just rest in the presence of God. To adapt Benedict's language from his catechesis on St. John of the Cross above, contemplation is the time when we let ourselves be loved by God, let him take the keys and do the driving. As the pontiff does well to observe in his catechesis on the spiritual master St. Francis de Sales, contemplation is the point where reason, having ascended all its steps, "closes its eyes" and becomes one with love.[13]

In another catechesis on the subject of contemplation, Benedict expands upon the crucial role played by silence in our spiritual lives. Notwithstanding all its strengths, the pontiff laments that our technological age discourages silent recollection. Many today fear silence, or at least do not know what to do with it. Indeed, now that I have had a smart phone for a couple of years, I find myself increasingly bothered by the very silence that God uses as an instrument to bring about our holiness. It is not that we need to be silent all day, or go on silent retreats. Such exercises often prove helpful for people, but it does not have to be as complicated as that. What we need to do is to carve out small periods of silence in our day to stop the noise that prevents God from more profoundly penetrating within our soul. All too often, we find ourselves preoccupied with productivity, the practical results we achieve throughout our day. While results are not irrelevant, they are not sufficient causes of our happiness and holiness taken on their own. Says Benedict: "Without daily prayer lived with fidelity, our acts are empty, they lose their profound soul, and are reduced to being mere activism which in the end leaves us dissatisfied."[14] Prayer is the breath of the soul, and if the lungs of prayer and God's word do not nourish that life, it will gradually be choked out.

Having treated of the three expressions of Christian prayer and the steps of *lectio* as described by Benedict, it should be noted that these descriptions could easily be amplified or given greater nuance.

---

13. Benedict XVI, "Saint Francis de Sales," general audience (March 2, 2011).
14. Benedict XVI, General Audience (March 7, 2012); Benedict XVI, General Audience (April 25, 2012). For an outstanding book that warns against the danger of what its author calls "the activist heresy," see Dom Jean-Baptiste Chautard, *The Soul of the Apostolate* (Trappist, Ky.: Abbey of Gethsamani, 1946).

For example, in his catechesis on St. Anthony of Padua, the pontiff mentions that the first step of prayer is *obsecratio*, the placing of ourselves in God's presence before we begin to read or talk to him. In St. Anthony's schema, this first step is followed by *oratio*, an affectionate dialogue between our soul and God. Finally, St. Anthony adds the *postulatio*, placing our needs before God, and *gratiarum actio*, thanking God for the many benefits we have received from him. As the reader begins to see, the number of steps to *lectio* can easily add up to eight or more. But here again, the Church is offering these steps as a means to simplify our lives, not complicate them. If the steps of *lectio* do not work for you today, try something different. Benedict's overarching concern in this regard is that Christians develop the habit of reading the Scriptures with a prayerful disposition that precedes, accompanies, and completes our study of them. No matter what form it ends up taking in our lives at any given time, the aim of Christian meditation is for us "to entrust ourselves increasingly to the hands of God, with trust and love, certain that in the end it is only by doing his will that we are truly happy."[15]

As a final word on the subject of *lectio divina* and the three expressions of prayer, I would like to follow up with a few thoughts on a particularly excellent text that Benedict suggests we employ as the basis for our prayer: the Book of Psalms. This book occupies a unique niche in the Bible, for, unlike other books, the Psalms do not have an easily identifiable narrative or plot. The purpose of the Psalms is not to teach us history, though they surely do include historical data. Their goal, says Benedict, is to teach us how to pray:

The Psalms are given to the believer exactly as the text of prayers whose sole purpose is to become the prayer of the person who assimilates them and addresses them to God. Since they are a word of God, anyone who prays the Psalms speaks to God using the very words that God has given to us, address-

---

15. Benedict XVI, "Monastic Theology and Scholastic Theology," general audience (October 28, 2009); Benedict XVI, "Meditation," general audience (August 17, 2011).

es him with the words that he himself has given us. So it is that in praying the Psalms we learn to pray. They are a school of prayer.[16]

One of the most interesting features of the Psalms is that they collectively express the entire gamut of human experience. There are psalms of thanksgiving for times when things are going great in our lives (for example, Ps 116), penitential psalms for those times when we have really lost our way (for example, Ps 51), lamentation psalms for when we are desperately suffering (for example, Ps 88), even cursing psalms for when we are mad at God or other people (for example, Ps 137). I could go on and on about the depth of the psalter, but the best thing Christians can do in this regard is to take our Bibles and begin prayerfully reading them.[17] Or, perhaps even better, develop the habit of praying the Psalms within their native context by reciting the morning, evening, or night prayer of the Liturgy of the Hours. In short, the Psalms teach us to let God have it all, that nothing we are experiencing is unimportant to him or beyond his reach. Like a child learning to talk, those who seek holiness must gradually learn how to speak and let ourselves be spoken to by God. Meditation with the Psalms is an exceptional path unto this end.[18]

---

16. Benedict XVI, General Audience (June 22, 2011). Benedict mentions that there is no narrative to the Psalms, but I think the case can be made that there is an overarching narrative to them, even though it is not strictly linear. For a helpful, readable entry point to this topic, see Michael Barber, *Singing in the Reign: The Psalms and the Liturgy of God's Kingdom* (Steubenville, Ohio: Emmaus Road, 2001).

17. On praying with passages in the Book of Psalms that have their author doubting the existence of an afterlife, see Matthew Ramage, *Dark Passages of the Bible: Engaging Scripture with Benedict XVI and Thomas Aquinas* (Washington, D.C.: The Catholic University of America Press, 2013), 256–73. For a series of wide-ranging meditations on how to pray with the Psalms, I highly recommend C. S. Lewis, *Reflections on the Psalms* (London: Harvest Books, 1964).

18. On a related subject that I do not address here, Benedict's comments on the family—the "domestic church"—as a school of prayer are well worth pondering. See Benedict XVI, "The Prayer and the Holy Family of Nazareth," general audience (December 28, 2011); and Benedict XVI, "How to Speak about God?" general audience (November 28, 2012).

Conclusion: Holiness through Liturgy and Incorporation into the Ecclesial "We"

If the spirituality that Pope Benedict is directing us towards is based in meditation on the word of God, we would be remiss not to emphasize a locus of this prayer which is very dear to the pontiff and likewise ought to be for all Christians seeking holiness: the liturgy. As described by Benedict, the liturgy is "a privileged context in which God speaks to each one of us, here and now, and awaits our answer."[19] A good liturgical celebration involves prayer punctuated with silence, which makes possible a conversation with God: first through listening and then responding to what we hear. The sacred liturgy offers us God's words, into which we are called to enter, attuning ourselves to them and making them our own. It is in this way, says Benedict, that we become children of God, that we are divinized. Citing a favorite line from the Rule of his patron St. Benedict, the pope teaches that the words of the liturgy precede our thought, and in uttering the words given to us by Mother Church, our minds are trained to accord with our voice: *mens concordet voci*.[20]

In addition to its vertical dimension of helping us to harmonize our mind with the mind of Christ, the liturgy also has a profoundly human or horizontal element that the believer cannot neglect if we wish to experience the fullness of Christian spirituality's beauty. The liturgy incorporates us into the universal "we" of Christ's mystical body. In receiving Christ's body, we become one body with him— and with all who share in his sacrifice (1 Cor 10:17). The Christian spiritual life is thus not an esoteric affair "just between me and Jesus." To be sure, we are meant to experience a profound intimacy with the ineffable divine mystery, but this is not possible without love of our brothers and sisters (1 Jn 4:20). In this and a multitude of other areas,

---

19. Benedict XVI, "The Liturgy, School of Prayer—The Lord Himself Teaches Us to Pray," general audience (September 26, 2012).
20. Ibid.; Benedict of Nursia, *Rule* (New York: Vintage Books, 1998), chap. 19.

Christian spirituality is a balancing act. The liturgy is Christ's sacrifice, but it is also a communal meal. The liturgy concerns my soul's relationship with God, and it also concerns my relationship with other believers, all people, and indeed (as we will see later) all of creation. In this regard, there is one point that Benedict wishes to emphasize to us time and again: the liturgy is not a "self-manifestation" of our community. It ought not to become a "closed circle" where we focus merely on our own concerns, celebrating our own greatness and confirming our preexisting expectations of God. Rather, liturgy's role—like that of God's word and of prayer in general—is to call us out of ourselves, leading us to make an ever greater gift of self to our neighbor in imitation of him who laid down his life for us.[21]

Of course, the person who assists devoutly at the liturgy or prays consistently with Scripture is by no means guaranteed to attain a level of certitude that amounts to a disproof of the Nietzschean skepticism that this book aims to address. Rather, cultivating the habit of prayer and a liturgical spirituality ought to be viewed as core features of the Christian "experiment of faith" described by Pope Benedict. If we want to truly understand and appreciate the beauty of Christianity, our religion's core truths and practices have to be integrated into the fabric of our daily lives. Seeking the good life of holiness through prayer, especially liturgical prayer, is an essential component of this quest.

21. Benedict XVI, General Audience (October 3, 2012); Joseph Ratzinger, *The Spirit of the Liturgy* (San Francisco: Ignatius Press, 2000), 21–23.

3

RULES OF THE GAME

Obedience and True Freedom

Why Getting Freedom Right Is So Important

The broad strokes of this chapter germinated while I was watching a news program a couple of years ago. We were visiting my parents in Illinois, and as I passed by the TV in the living room, I happened to overhear a self-professed Catholic political strategist misrepresenting the U.S. bishops on a subject related to healthcare ethics. At the end of the interview, it was pointed out to the woman that "your own bishops don't agree with you." In reply, she smirked and sarcastically laughed, "Well, the *bishops*, that's a whole other issue." Anyone watching this interview could tell that this individual, despite claiming to be Catholic, had little respect for the authority of the Catholic hierarchy. In her view, the bishops were just a bunch of old men out of touch with reality and refusing to get with the times. Regrettably, this attitude is enshrined in the words and deeds of many well-known Catholic media figures and politicians. Even worse, it colors the way countless Catholics in the pew perceive reality.

As many of us have had ample occasion to observe, the mentality sketched above has emerged all too commonly in recent years among those who profess the Christian faith. Both in the media and in my own career as an educator, I have consistently witnessed people parroting a narrative that paints ours as a time when we are finally casting off the shackles of tradition and truth claims that have long held us back from true societal progress—from following Nietzsche's exhortation to create our own values. Referencing a different interlocutor, Benedict XVI says that many have unwittingly adopted what he calls a Marxist analysis of the Church. As Ratzinger observed many years before being elected pope, Marx's fundamental law of history—the class struggle—rears its head time and again in the efforts of those who portray the hierarchical Church as opposed to the laity, who seek emancipation from centuries of discrimination and abuse of power.[1]

Regardless of whether we have read Marx himself or not, we are all living in an age dominated by this narrative; and our thought is shaped by it. In a word, Benedict believes that a *crisis of trust* looms under the surface of the many problems we face in contemporary society and within the Church in particular.[2] Moreover, he notes that this crisis coincides with our culture's increasingly absolutized notion of freedom which in its own turn "has become an almost magical word" and "the absolutely highest good, to which all other goods are subordinate."[3] Freedom and rights—it is axiomatic in our culture that nothing should stop us from exercising our freedom to do what we "feel" is right. It is practically axiomatic in contemporary Western culture that

---

1. For an incisive critique of the Marxist interpretation of Christianity, see the Congregation for the Doctrine of the Faith, instruction "On Certain Aspects of the 'Theology of Liberation,'" §§VII–VIII. Also insightful are Cardinal Ratzinger's comments in Ratzinger and Vittorio Messori, *The Ratzinger Report* (San Francisco: Ignatius Press, 1987). Here he explains the attractiveness of liberation theology and its hermeneutic of Church history: "If one accepts the fundamental assumptions which underlie liberation theology, it cannot be denied that the whole edifice has an almost irresistible logic." Ibid, 185.

2. Among the many places in which Benedict alludes to this, one of the most poignant is his essay "Why I Am Still in the Church," 133–53.

3. Ratzinger, *Church, Ecumenism, and Politics* (San Francisco: Ignatius Press, 2008), 175; Ratzinger, "Truth and Freedom," *Communio: International Catholic Review* 23, no. 1 (1996): 16.

the good life consists in doing what you want as much as you want, with whomever you want.

In accordance with the goal of this book as a whole and of this introductory section, in this chapter I will continue to develop an alternate narrative to that of the typical secular story about human freedom. In this instance, our task will be to develop a concise but robust account of what the Church teaches concerning the nature of human freedom, especially its relation to truth, the virtue of obedience, and the total gift of self required for freedom's attainment. In particular, I will show how Pope Benedict offers both a pointed diagnosis of our society's fatally flawed understanding of freedom and provides clear principles for how to live the "experiment of faith" with a freedom that runs counter-culturally to the standard assumptions of our secularized world. Like the previous chapter which dealt with holiness or divinization as the goal of our entire existence as human beings, this chapter is not yet directly focused on the heart of this experiment which takes place through the exercise of the theological virtues, but rather on a reality necessary to get right if our reflections on faith, hope, and charity are to be grounded in an authentically Christian worldview.

On the Virtue of Obedience to the Truth and Diagnosis of a False Freedom

Benedict's theology of human freedom is intimately bound up with the exercise of a particular virtue that is often underappreciated nowadays. I am talking here of the pontiff's emphasis on the "obedience of faith" of which St. Paul speaks (Rom 1:5; 16:26). While once a common virtue emphasized in the Church, today the importance of filial obedience is highly underestimated, viewed as a relic of an oppressive past or at best as an embarrassing subject that pastors fear broaching. (Just think: when was the last time you heard a homily that underscored the need for obedience to the Church?) Granted that preaching on the subject of obedience must be done with prudence, an attentive reader of Benedict will notice that he is always inviting us to rediscover the beauty of this discipline best described by St. Peter: "Having purified your souls by your obedience to the truth for a sincere love of the brethren, love one another earnestly from the heart" (1 Pt 1:22). For St. Peter as for the Catholic Church today, authentic happiness and love are impossible without purification of our own souls, and in particular that purification which comes through a sincere love of the truth and the courage to live in accordance with the moral truths of the Church—in other words, obedience to the truth.

In John 8:32, Jesus tells us that the truth will make us free. However, the prevailing mentality I mentioned above is one that fears the demands of truth. It holds either that truth is a relative category, or that the truth claims of the Church are not liberating but rather enslaving. Addressing this problem, Cardinal Ratzinger wrote that Christians today need to counter the skeptics' question, "What is truth?" with a pair of our own questions: "What is freedom?" and "What do we actually mean when we extol freedom and place it at the pinnacle of our scale of values?"[4]

Taking up Ratzinger's call, we in the Church need to find new modes of communicating the true nature of freedom in a way to which contemporary people can relate. Having taught a college-level introduction to moral theology course dozens of times over the past decade, I find that an excellent way to initiate a conversation on freedom is to deploy a distinction made by Benedict but perhaps developed most eloquently by the renowned Dominican theologian Servais Pinckaers. Pinckaers differentiates "freedom of indifference" on the one hand and "freedom for excellence" on the other. In my experience, I think freedom of indifference is the prevailing view today, wherein freedom is thought to be greater when we have more options on the table and fewer rules to obey. On this view of freedom, exterior constraints such as civil laws, Church teachings, and even the natural

---

4. Ratzinger, "Truth and Freedom," 17.

moral law are forces that detract from our fulfillment.⁵ The implications of a freedom of indifference mentality vis-à-vis the Magisterium (official teaching office of the Church) are described well by Ratzinger. He says that the true nature of the papal office has become incomprehensible to modern people because of the way we have shifted our perspective on the relationship of freedom and authority. Rather than a bridge between the person and the truth, everything which does not come from the person himself is considered an external imposition and, consequently, not binding.⁶ For the remainder of this particular section, I will be concerned with this stance on freedom and proceed afterwards to paint the contrasting picture of freedom for excellence, its positive alternative.⁷

As Ratzinger articulated at various points throughout his career, the allergic reaction many modern Catholics have to ecclesiastical authority is symptomatic of our culture's much broader buy-in to the freedom of indifference model, as a result of which we feel repulsed by any restraints which would make us dependent upon an external authority, stifling our instinctual desires: "Modern man, who presupposes the opposition of authority to subjectivity, has difficulty understanding this. For him, conscience stands on the side of subjectivity and is the expression of the freedom of the subject. Authority, on the other hand, appears to him as the constraint on, threat to, and even the negation of, freedom."⁸ The opposition between authority and

---

5. Ratzinger, *Church, Ecumenism, and Politics*, 176. See also Vatican Council II, *Gaudium et Spes* (1965), §17, http://www.vatican.va/archive/hist_councils/ii_vatican_council/documents/vat-ii_const_19651207_gaudium-et-spes_en.html.
6. Ratzinger, "Conscience and Truth," *Communio* 37 (2010): 536. See also a similar thread concerning the relationship of freedom, theology, and the Magisterium in the encyclical co-written by Benedict and Francis, *Lumen Fidei*, §36.
7. For an in-depth exploration of these rival visions of human freedom, see Servais Pinckaers, *Sources of Christian Ethics*, trans. Sr. Mary Thomas Noble, OP (Washington: Catholic University of America Press, 1995), 327–78.
8. Ratzinger, "Conscience and Truth," 530. For an insightful discussion of the modern notion of freedom and "progress," see Benedict XVI, *Spe Salvi* (2007), §18. See also his pointed discussion of freedom in relation to moral relativism: "Here we come in contact with the really

freedom of conscience is especially evident in the way our society increasingly tends to approach sexuality. These days, people are often told that they ought to feel free to act upon this or that sexual inclination because they did not, after all, freely choose to have the urge in question. While it is certainly the case that our various drives often arise in us instinctually apart from our having chosen them, it nevertheless misses something very important about the human person if we simply tell people that their actions ought to be governed by feelings irrespective of wisdom from broader channels of knowledge such as science, philosophy, religion, our family, and our community.[9]

In the second volume of his *Jesus of Nazareth* trilogy, Benedict XVI specified our society's broader crisis of trust in authority, a culture in which the isolated individual is the arbiter of right and wrong for himself, as a crisis of trust in God: "Through sin," he writes, "man comes to sense that his freedom is compromised by God's will and that consenting to it is not an opportunity to become fully himself but as a threat to his freedom against which he rebels."[10] In the third volume of the same series, Benedict adds, "God Himself is constantly regarded as a limitation placed on our freedom that must be set aside if man is

---

critical issue of the modern age. The concept of truth has been virtually given up and replaced by the concept of progress. Progress itself 'is' truth.... There are no directions in a world without fixed measuring points. What we view to be direction is not based on a standard which is true in itself but on our decision and finally on considerations of expediency." Ratzinger, "Conscience and Truth," 532.

9. Ratzinger also offers an incisive example of the desire for unbridled freedom in relation to abortion: "What is at stake is the right to self-determination. But is it really the case that the woman who aborts is making a decision about her own life? Is she not deciding precisely about someone else—deciding that no freedom shall be granted to another, and that the space of freedom, which is life, must be taken from him, because it competes with her own freedom? The question we must therefore ask is this: exactly what sort of freedom has even the right to annul another's freedom as soon as it begins?" Ratzinger, "Truth and Freedom," 27. Benedict returned to the theme of freedom and natural law at many points in his pontificate. For one important example concerning the reality that "man is not merely self-creating freedom," see the speech from his visit to the Bundestag in Berlin on September 22, 2011.

10. Benedict XVI, *Jesus of Nazareth: Holy Week: From the Entrance into Jerusalem to the Resurrection* (San Francisco: Ignatius Press, 2011), 160.

ever to be completely himself. God, with his truth, stands in opposition to man's manifold lies, his self-seeking, and his pride."[11]

Given all that has just been said, it is important to step back for a moment to recall that the analysis of freedom which we are undertaking here is not just about "those people" who are not living an authentically Christian life. On the contrary, its primary target is actually us—me as author and you as reader. My emphasis in this book is on Benedict's existentialist approach to theology, so it is important that we insert ourselves into the discussion and do some introspection with regard to how we approach the Church's teaching in our own lives. Devout believers may think that we are innocent of the rebellion I have just described, but if you think of your "favorite sin" you will realize that you likely refrain from doing it often merely out of duty, shame, or some other motive lesser than love of God (following what Pinckaers calls a "morality of obligation"). I am speaking first to myself here but also to all who read this: if you look around the world and even in your own heart, it is very easy to see the phenomenon that Pope Benedict observed when he remarked that the God who is love is hated when he challenges people to transcend themselves.[12] As far as Benedict is concerned, this out-of-control passion for the arbitrary ability to do anything and everything we want has an idol as its model and not God.[13]

---

11. Benedict XVI, *Jesus of Nazareth: The Infancy Narratives* (San Francisco: Ignatius Press, 2013), 86. This is a theme that the pontiff returned to many times while speaking to a variety of audiences. For an illuminating discussion of freedom and its limits in relation to technology, see his encyclical *Caritas in Veritate* (2009), 70. For an application to international relations and regulations, see Benedict's address to the United Nations in New York on April 18, 2008.

12. Benedict XVI, *The Infancy Narratives*, 86.

13. Ratzinger, *Church, Ecumenism, and Politics*, 255. See also a discussion where he describes the quest for unbridled freedom as a fallen response to Satan's temptation to "become as gods." Ratzinger, "Truth and Freedom," 28.

Sacrificial Service and the Total Gift of Self as the Pathway to True Freedom and Divinization

Having summarized Benedict's diagnosis of the truncated view of freedom so prevalent in our society today, at this point I would like to turn to the more positive side of the story and paint a picture of that in which true freedom consists, the crucial piece of "good news" that Benedict wishes us to exude and share with everyone we meet. If unbridled freedom is an idol, then what is God's idea of human freedom? In the Greek New Testament, the term *eleutheria* which we translate as "freedom" is a concept that can only be understood in light of its opposite: slavery. As Paul tells us in Galatians 5:1, "For freedom Christ has set us free; stand fast therefore, and do not submit again to a yoke of slavery." Freedom of indifference, doing whatever we want, is slavery when it leads to sin. Shortly thereafter in the same Letter to the Galatians, Paul exhorts us: "Only do not use your freedom as an opportunity for the flesh, but through love be servants of one another" (5:13). Pope Benedict comments on these texts, "[Paul] explains what freedom is—namely, *freedom in the service of good*, freedom that allows itself to be led by the Spirit of God. The law of Christ [a term used earlier in Gal 6:2] is freedom—that is the paradox of Paul's message in Galatians."[14]

In many places Benedict notes that people tend to mistake what Paul is actually saying here for what they want him to say. They want him to say that Christ has moved beyond the Old Testament and its "rules-based morality," because such a move in turn would appear to justify our desire to move beyond the Church's retrogressive rules. In his third volume on the life of Jesus, Benedict tells us:

In some portrayals of Jesus, the emphasis is placed almost exclusively on the radical aspect, on his challenge to false piety. Thus Jesus is presented as a liberal or a revolutionary. It is true that Jesus did introduce a new phase in man's

---

14. Benedict XVI, *From the Baptism in the Jordan to the Transfiguration*, 100.

relationship with God ... but this was not an attack on Israel's piety. Jesus' freedom is not the freedom of the liberal.... As Son, Jesus brings a new freedom: not the freedom of someone with no obligations, but the freedom of someone totally united with the Father's will, someone who helps mankind to attain the freedom of inner oneness with God."[15]

And who is this person who helps mankind to attain the freedom of inner oneness with God? According to Benedict, it is the saint. In the *Jesus* trilogy as well as in his masterful weekly catecheses, Benedict illustrates the true nature of freedom through the medium of the lives of the saints. For example, he writes of Francis of Assisi that "this extreme humility was above all freedom for service, freedom for mission, ultimate trust in God."[16] Meanwhile, for saints such as the Jesuit Francis Xavier, true freedom and renewal in the core of their being came through the total gift of self they made in martyrdom.[17] Benedict's words here resonate clearly with the words of the Second Vatican Council so often quoted by his predecessor, John Paul II: namely, the biblical notion of freedom in which man finds himself only through a sincere gift of self.[18]

Whether or not we are called to be blood martyrs for the faith, Benedict tells us that our search for true freedom and happiness will mean being constrained to undergo a crucifixion—a putting to death of our own selfish desires and favorite sins so as to make room for Christ to live in us: "To live the law of Christ means, therefore, to live according to the ontological status of the spiritual man, in the way of the Spirit. This means crucifying the flesh 'with its passions and desires' (Gal 5:24).... Therefore this freedom is not without its demands; neither is it arbitrary. It constrains to such an extent that it can be called a 'crucifixion.'"[19] For Benedict, the cross of Jesus Christ

---

15. Benedict XVI, *The Infancy Narratives*, 120.
16. Benedict XVI, *From the Baptism in the Jordan to the Transfiguration*, 78.
17. Ibid., 163, 166.
18. Vatican Council II, *Gaudium et Spes*, §24.
19. Ibid.

demonstrates in the most profound way possible that authentic freedom comes through sacrifice: through obedience to good laws, through the renunciation of the "rights" we claim for ourselves, and ultimately through the gift of our very selves even to the point of death. And, lest we think that this call to martyrdom is only for the privileged few of times past, Benedict issues the stark notice that our preaching of the gospel will inevitably require suffering for its sake if we are doing it right:

> Because life often appears more comfortable lived in the lie or simply without regard to truth than according to the demands of truth, men often get angry about the truth. They want to suppress it, repress it, evade it.... Whoever commits himself entirely to the truth ... will always approach the vicinity of martyrdom. He will become a sufferer. To proclaim truth without becoming a fanatic or dogmatist—that would be the great task.[20]

For those who wish to be effective as evangelists, Benedict reminds us that it is not brilliant rhetoric or sophisticated strategies that win people over. Rather, we will find strength to succeed in our mission as ambassadors for Christ to the extent that we imitate St. Paul in letting ourselves be wounded in service of the gospel.[21] And part of that vulnerability means proclaiming the whole truth no matter what its cost. In short, writes Benedict, "Suffering and truth belong together. Paul was resisted because he was a man of truth. His words and life still have meaning today because he served truth and suffered on its behalf. Suffering is the necessary authentication of truth, but only truth gives meaning to suffering."[22]

Benedict further describes the Christian's path of suffering and death as one of *theiosis* (being made like God) or, as the Church Fathers such as St. Athanasius put it, *theosis* (being "God-ized," or "becoming

---

20. Ratzinger, *Images of Hope: Meditations on Major Feasts* (San Francisco: Ignatius Press, 2006), 26.
21. Ibid., 26; 2 Cor 10:10.
22. Ratzinger, *Images of Hope*, 27.

God" as sharers in Christ's divinity through grace). Benedict expounds: "The pedagogy of freedom is guidance in ontological dignity, education for being, education for love, and thus guidance in divinization.... To be like God means to be like the Trinitarian God. Therefore, it means to be like Christ crucified. The pedagogy of divinization is necessarily a pedagogy of the Cross."[23] Neither Christ nor Pope Benedict tells us that this process will *feel* good: "It is not a romantic 'good feeling.' Redemption is not 'wellness,' it is not about basking in self-indulgence; on the contrary it is a liberation from imprisonment in self-absorption. This liberation comes at a price: the anguish of the Cross."[24] To use the language of Paul's famous hymn in the Letter to the Philippians, *kenosis* or the self-emptying that comes through obedience to death on the Cross, is alone the path that leads to *theosis*, being filled with the fullness of God (Phil 2:7–8; Eph 3:19). Riffing off of the Mass's offertory prayer and anticipating a point that I will make later in our chapters on hope, we need to hold up for men in our secular age the lofty goal of becoming sharers in the divinity of Christ through humbling ourselves to share in his humanity—especially by bearing our share in his Cross. This message we need to convey is best summarized by Ratzinger when he says, "We all thirst for the infinite: for an infinite freedom, for happiness without limits.... Man is not satisfied with solutions beneath the level of divinization."[25] Concealed within the heart of every human person is the yearning for perfection, but at the end of the day the path to true happiness and liberation lies in placing our freedom at the foot of the Cross. Like any authentic Christian teaching, this is nothing new, but what I am aiming to do here is look at this fundamental truth from a different angle that will help us to better evangelize, namely the angle of preaching to modern man the good news that an obedient submission of our freedom is precisely the gateway to perfect freedom and fulfillment.

23. Ratzinger, *Church, Ecumenism, and Politics*, 188.
24. Benedict XVI, *The Infancy Narratives*, 86.
25. Ratzinger, address to catechists and religion teachers (December 12, 2000), https://www.ewtn.com/new_evangelization/Ratzinger.htm.

Freedom for Excellence: The Harmony of Man with Truth and Law

Having just described authentic freedom as a life lived in self-sacrificial service that leads to divinization, at this point I would like to elaborate more on Benedict's thought concerning the relationship between truth, freedom, and law—and in particular those ecclesiastical norms to which so many today find it hard to submit. The pontiff summarizes the same key point in various places: "Truth and freedom belong together. There is no courage of freedom when there is no truth, and truth does not manifest itself except by dint of the courage of freedom."[26] With a slightly different emphasis, he elsewhere writes, "Fidelity to man requires fidelity to the truth, which alone is the guarantee of freedom (Jn 8:32) and of the possibility of integral human development."[27] For Benedict, it is clear that human beings become free and attain happiness to the extent that we appropriate the truth and live with excellence or virtue based on it. This is what Pinckaers calls freedom for excellence. Benedict is a lover of Blessed John Henry Newman's writings, and at one point he shows his agreement with the latter in emphasizing that, in Christianity, truth has priority over consensus, over the accommodation of groups.[28] Why is this the order of things? Truth and law, in particular the doctrines and norms of the Church, protect us from "the whim of the majority" and from the "dictatorship of relativism" that dominates the way many modern people think. Change is not a good in itself, Benedict reminds us, but conformity to the truth is.[29]

26. Ratzinger, *Church, Ecumenism, and Politics*, 190.
27. Benedict XVI, *Caritas in Veritate*, §9.
28. Ratzinger, "Conscience and Truth," 531.
29. Ratzinger, "Crises of Law," Address to the LUMSA Faculty of Jurisprudence in Rome (November 10, 1999), https://www.ewtn.com/library/Theology/LAWMETA.HTM; Ratzinger, homily to the College of Cardinals for the election of the Roman pontiff (April 18, 2005), http://www.vatican.va/gpII/documents/homily-pro-eligendo-pontifice_20050418_en.html; Ratzinger, "Truth and Freedom," 35.

The following is a very simple, real-life illustration of the proper relationship between truth, freedom, and law. The truly free basketball player is he who freely submits to the law of practicing his free throws outside of games. Why is this player truly free and not the guy who went out partying instead? Because of his obedience to the nature of basketball playing, which requires practice, he is then able to consistently excel in his shooting even in the fourth quarter of a grueling game. It is not better for the shooter to neglect practicing free throws in favor of some semi-related option such as perfecting behind-the-back shots from halfcourt. This example simply serves to point out that in life there are objective truths and goods and that our happiness as human beings is commensurate with our ability to align ourselves with them. We did not invent the reality that practicing free throws makes one able to make free throws in a game. This is simply the reality to which the athlete has to conform.

In a similar way to the basketball player learning to conform his own practices to the objective rules of the game, we would do well to conform our lives to the Church's dogmas and moral teachings as "rules of the game" of faith that we ourselves do not invent but rather seek to enter into and align ourselves with ever more deeply in the pursuit of victory, the crown of eternal life. Seen from this perspective, the Church's teachings have been given to us by God through revelation and through nature which he created. Our happiness, accordingly, consists in discerning these truths and lovingly embracing them. Once a person comes to terms with this reality, he will come to see the beauty of Fr. Pinckaers's statement that "Catholic moral teaching is not a mere code of prescriptions and prohibitions.... Catholic morality is a response to the aspirations of the human heart for truth and goodness."[30] To put this in Pope Benedict's terms, "Freedom is bound up with the existence of law; the law is not the opposite of freedom,

---

30. Servais Pinckaers, OP, *Morality: the Catholic View* (Notre Dame, Ind.: St. Augustine's Press, 2003), 1.

but rather its prerequisite.... Anyone who wants freedom, therefore, cannot strive for lawlessness, but rather must strive for good law."[31] As Benedict puts it elsewhere in a text that almost reads like a textbook definition of freedom for excellence, "This is true freedom: actually to be able to follow our desire for good, for true joy, for communion with God and to be free from the oppression of circumstances that pull us in other directions."[32]

Benedict masterfully turns today's freedom of indifference mentality on its head by showing that it, rather than the Church, is negative and gloomy. When the Christian accepts the invitation to embark on the life of the Spirit, he certainly must recognize that in doing so "a clear limit is placed upon arbitrariness and subjectivity," yet he consents to this precisely because of an awareness that an "absence of obligation and arbitrariness do not signify freedom, but its destruction."[33] As he explained elsewhere: "This much has become clear: *constraints are an essential*, formal part of human freedom. No type of actualization of freedom can escape this fact. It is certain, furthermore, that indeterminacy does not constitute the essence of human freedom.... *Freedom must be defined positively* if it is to be something positive."[34] What is this positive definition of freedom we need to offer in order to reach modern Western man? I contend that we who love the Church need to make a priority of emphasizing that the moral truths of the Church are here to make us free and *happy*. I think that we need to preach the good news of freedom for excellence, which consists precisely in becoming an excellent human being, an end which can only be achieved through humble obedience to reality. This is the Catholic Church's morality of happiness.

---

31. Ratzinger, *Church, Ecumenism, and Politics*, 183.
32. Benedict XVI, General Audience (May 16, 2012).
33. Benedict XVI, address to representatives from the World of Culture in Paris (September 12, 2008).
34. Ratzinger, *Church, Ecumenism, and Politics*, 182.

Obedience to the Truth Proclaimed by the Magisterium Leads to True Freedom

In talking about the Christian faith with all kinds of people over the course of my adult life, I have found that most if not all of the issues that Catholics have with the Church boil down to a fundamental mistrust of her authority. This is a freedom of indifference mindset wherein people think that, deep down, the Church's doctrines and discipline are not there for our happiness. It is also a view informed by more than a hint of the Nietzschean notion that the Church's moral codes are part of some broader power play, invented by ecclesial authorities for their own gratification. Christians today must be equipped to diagnose and address this deep authority issue with which so many people—including practicing Catholics, perhaps including me and you—need help. The following statement from Newman helps to achieve this end in a positive way. In it, Newman articulates how a simple existential shift from jaded skepticism to loving trust in the "deposit" of divine revelation grants even the simplest of believers access to the entirety of Christian faith and life:

> He who believes in the *depositum* of Revelation, believes in all the doctrines of the *depositum* ... whether he knows little or much, he has the intention of believing all that there is to believe whenever and as soon as it is brought home to him, if he believes in Revelation at all. All that he knows now as revealed, and all that he shall know, and all that there is to know, he embraces it all in his intention by one act of faith; otherwise, it is but an accident that he believes this or that, not because it is a revelation.[35]

---

35. John Henry Newman, *An Essay in Aid of a Grammar of Assent* (Garden City, N.Y.: Image Books, 1955), 130. See also Newman's *An Essay on the Development of Christian Doctrine* (Notre Dame, Ind.: University of Notre Dame Press, 1989), 86, where Newman states that "the essence of all religion is authority and obedience." Concerning the importance of assent to the Magisterium as the foundation of all other beliefs, Newman adds: "That the Church is the infallible oracle of truth is the fundamental dogma of the Catholic religion." Newman, *An Essay in Aid of a Grammar of Assent*, 131.

A skeptic could go on and on raising challenges against the Church while we respond with reasoned and charitable answers, but we need to follow Newman and press people more on the issue of ecclesial authority broadly speaking. For Newman, the Catholic faith is by its very nature comprehensive, meaning that, by assenting to the authority of the Magisterium as such, a believer assents to the whole deposit of revelation. Accordingly, even if a person has never studied a page of theology, he can still have access to the substance of its entirety simply by trusting in the Lord through his Church.

The negative corollary to the above quote, however, is that by dissenting from a definitive teaching a person is in effect rejecting the Magisterium itself. As Newman puts it, if a person does reject a key defined teaching of the Church, then it really had been only an "accident" up to that point that his views had aligned with the Church's profession of faith. Interestingly, Newman's thought was eloquently applied in *Lumen Fidei*, the encyclical on faith co-written by Francis and Benedict: "Since faith is one, it must be professed in all its purity and integrity. Precisely because all the articles of faith are interconnected, to deny one of them, even of those that seem least important, is tantamount to distorting the whole.... To subtract something from the faith is to subtract something from the veracity of communion."[36] As Francis and Benedict indicate, people today find it hard to conceive of a unity in truth. They fear that assenting to the Church, putting all our chips on the table, will lead to the destruction of our freedom. In reality, however, this is precisely how we walk the gospel's paradoxical path of free-

---

36. Benedict XVI and Francis, *Lumen Fidei*, §48. Although Francis officially promulgated this document, in the body of this book I will be referring to its author as Benedict for simplicity's sake. More importantly, I have chosen to do this because, after comparing the encyclical's motifs and vocabulary to Benedict's corpus as a whole, I have confidence that the sections I am excerpting from it were penned by Benedict. That the present paragraph should sound so much like Newman can be explained by the fact that Joseph Ratzinger had a passion for the great convert's thought ever since he was a graduate student. Evidence enough for Newman's influence on Ratzinger can be seen in that the latter quotes him frequently. For more on the history of Ratzinger's affinity with Newman, see Rowland, *Ratzinger's Faith*, 1–16.

dom. Ironically, if we choose not to follow the path of total obedience, we end up locked within our own mind. What results is the oxymoron of what Ratzinger once called "a faith of one's own devising ... a self-made faith [which] would only vouch for and be able to say what I already am and know anyway."[37] In other words, if we do not completely buy in to the Magisterium, we are left with no faith at all but rather a mere ratification of what we already thought to be true anyway.

Conclusion: Some "Experiments" to Run

In the previous chapter, I introduced Benedict's way of discussing our Christian faith life as an "experiment" that we must personally embark upon if we wish to fully grasp its truth and respond to criticisms along the lines posed by Nietzsche. I would like to conclude this chapter with a suggestion—an experiment—that any Catholic can perform by way of encouraging "whole hog" obedience in the Church. One of the Christian's most timely tasks is to encourage people not to simplistically reject the Church's teaching before sincerely learning what that teaching actually is. And the good news is that extending an invitation to people in this regard is easier now than it has ever been before. If you are laity and someone has a problem with the Church's teaching on contraception, email to them a link to Pope Paul VI's *Humanae Vitae* or to one of Janet Smith's works. If someone keeps pestering you about the issue of women's ordination, kindly print them a copy of John Paul II or the CDF on the question from the Vatican website. If a Catholic living in America does not understand why the Church teaches what she does about the morality of homosexuality or other gender-related issues, point them to the United States Conference of Catholic Bishops (USCCB) or to any number of outstanding popular Catholic media outlets which have valuable information just waiting to be shared with those who seek.

---

37. Ratzinger, "Why I Am Still in the Church," 147.

Finally, as Christians living in a rapidly secularized world indifferent to the dictates of religious authority, our "experiment" must involve cultivating a culture of freedom for excellence, putting into practice the words of the Second Vatican Council which teaches that our true freedom as children of God comes through sincere dialogue with and obedience to our spiritual shepherds.[38] But this has to be an experiment we strive to live first in our own lives and in our own families. Christ said that people will know we are his disciples by our love (Jn 13:35). If we radiate the love, freedom, and *joy* that comes through this obedience to the truth of the Church, then perhaps our witness will be an instrument of the Holy Spirit to bring another person closer to the authentic freedom that comes through following Jesus. Pope Benedict summarizes this missionary vision of Christianity in one line: "This remains the mission of all Christ's apostles in all times: to be his fellow workers in true joy."[39]

---

38. Vatican Council II, *Lumen Gentium*, §37.
39. Benedict XVI, "Saint Paul's Concept of Apostolate," general audience (September 10, 2008).

Part 2

Benedict XVI on the Theological Virtues

4

FAITH (I)

Seeking Understanding and Taking a Stand

What Do You Really Want: Truth or Happiness?

"If you wish to strive for peace of soul and happiness, then believe; if you wish to be a disciple of truth, then inquire." Benedict XVI recalls these pointed words, penned by a young Friedrich Nietzsche in a letter to his sister Elizabeth, at the outset of his encyclical on the virtue of faith.[1] Why does the pontiff refer to one of the greatest skeptics of all time at the start of a document intended to promote the Christian faith? Nietzsche's challenge casts into relief a question that burns in the hearts of countless people in our secularized world: is faith indeed a light of truth given to man from above, or is it rather an illusion from here below that blocks our path to freedom and authenticity?

We might pose the question in this way: is sincere truth-seeking compatible with belief? Or, rather, is Nietzsche right that belief is merely the refuge of those unwilling "to venture on new paths, at odds with custom, in the insecurity that attends independence, experi-

---

1. Friedrich Nietzsche, letter to Elizabeth (June 11, 1865), quoted in Julian Young, *Friedrich Nietzsche: A Philosophical Biography* (Cambridge: Cambridge University Press, 2010), 60. See Benedict XVI and Francis, *Lumen Fidei*, §2.

encing many mood-swings and even troubles of conscience"? Can a Christian claim to be "totally indifferent to what the result of his inquiries might be," as Nietzsche states one ought to be? Is the person of faith willing with Nietzsche to face the brute truth "even though it be in the highest degree ugly and repellent"?[2] From the starting point of these questions, Nietzsche would go on to develop his forceful critique of Christianity as a tradition that diminishes the full meaning of human existence and strips life of freedom and adventure.[3]

The point of the present chapter and the one that follows it is to deepen our response to the challenge represented in the person of Nietzsche by looking to the alternate narrative of man's path to fulfillment that Benedict XVI paints in his writings directly on the theological virtue of faith. This is not to say that I intend to demonstrate Nietzsche's position to be baseless, much less to cast him as an enemy whom Christians ought to attack. Indeed, I think that Nietzsche makes good points here and elsewhere in his writings. After all, I have met my fair share of Christians who have leaned on faith as a happiness crutch, an excuse to avoid facing the tough questions of our day. I am sure that I even do this myself sometimes.

As a Christian, it is very easy to keep doing what we are doing and living the way we are living simply because it is comfortable or at least a known reality. Likewise, it is easy to reply to those who challenge us, "Well, the Church has always said so" or "Because the Bible says so," and letting our intellectual curiosity stop there. So, instead of trying to disprove Nietzsche or deny that his critique hits home in important ways, my goal here is a positive one: while acknowledging what Nietzsche has right, to respond to him by painting a picture of what an authentic, vibrant, and intellectually engaged Christian faith looks like on the basis of our tradition's fundamental assumptions. I do not expect to convert

---

2. Nietzsche, letter to Elizabeth, quoted in Young, *Friedrich Nietzsche*, 59.

3. In his encyclical on love, Benedict also addresses Nietzsche's incisive claim that Christianity poisoned *eros*. This critique will be addressed in later chapters dedicated to the virtue of charity.

the atheist, but rather I offer my work here primarily to fellow believers in the hopes that some will set out on the "experiment of faith" which ultimately is what allows it to be seen as a compelling account of how an intelligent faith can be fervently affirmed in our secular age.

Does Faith Yield Real Knowledge, or Is It Just Useful?

It is not the case that Nietzsche entirely dismisses the value of faith. On the contrary, it may surprise some readers to learn that one of history's greatest skeptics actually lamented the loss of religion in his own day. Yet this sadness had nothing to do with religion's truth—only its power to constructively spur human greatness, creativity, and love.[4] Indeed, Nietzsche denies that any objective reality lies at the other end of one's act of faith. As he informs his sister, the blessings that accrued to him through his family's faith in Jesus equally could have been bestowed by means of the religion of Islam:

It is the faith that makes blessed, not the objective reality that stands behind the faith. I write this to you, dear Lisbeth, simply with the view of meeting the line of *proof usually adopted by religious people, who appeal to their inner experiences to demonstrate the infallibility of their faith. Every true faith is infallible*, it accomplishes what the person holding the faith hopes to find in it, but that does not offer the slightest support for a proof of its objective truth.[5]

Is Nietzsche right that faith itself—of whatever kind—is what makes man blessed? At the end of the day, does it really matter whether one is a Christian, Muslim, Jew, Hindu, Buddhist, or Taoist? Does it even matter if one affirms the existence of God, so long as one affirms

---

4. Nietzsche, *On the Use and Abuse of History* (New York: Macmillan Publishing Company, 1988), 42–44.

5. Nietzsche, letter to Elizabeth, quoted in Young, *Friedrich Nietzsche*, 59–60. Immediately preceding this citation, Nietzsche speaks of salvation coming "from Mohammed," which as we know today evinces a misunderstanding of Islam. Muslims view Muhammad as Allah's prophet, but not as a savior.

something transcendent of himself? Cannot one achieve happiness through any number of paths whose truth claims radically contradict one another?

While harboring no pretension of offering an exhaustive reply to Nietzsche on this matter, it is worthwhile to say something about what he gets right and wrong in the above passage. To begin, I think he does well to insinuate that a person's faith may indeed yield good fruit even if that person's beliefs fail to correspond fully to reality. After all, we have all met someone of a religion we know to be irrational in important respects while at the same time having to admit that the person in question is truly virtuous and happy. This significant admission admits of competing interpretations. For Nietzsche, this is merely evidence that there is no objective truth behind our religious beliefs.

Contrary to Nietzsche's position (as well as that of some strident Christians), the Catholic view acknowledges that there is often some truth behind the odd or even irrational beliefs among people we encounter. It might sound strange to say, but perhaps one way of putting it is that some believers may be right accidentally. What I mean by this is that a person may hold an important conviction incorrectly—for example, that Allah dictated the Qur'an (Islam), that one's innermost self or atman is God or Brahman (Hinduism), that the Bible is sole rule of faith (Protestantism), that Jesus appeared and preached to the Native Americans (Mormonism)—and yet still remain fundamentally in contact with the one true God and his moral law. This admission by no means entails the conclusion that we ought to be indifferent to the question of what religion one ought to profess, but it does mean that the Catholic Church holds no monopoly on truth and holiness. As the Second Vatican Council teaches, other religious traditions can participate in the fullness of truth that resides in the Catholic Church.[6]

---

6. Vatican Council II, *Nostra Aetate* (1965), http://www.vatican.va/archive/hist_councils/ii_vatican_council/documents/vat-ii_decl_19651028_nostra-aetate_en.html; Vatican Council II, *Lumen Gentium* (1964), §16, http://www.vatican.va/archive/hist_councils/ii_vatican_council/documents/vat-ii_const_19641121_lumen-gentium_en.html.

Indeed, the extent that these traditions are able to effect beauty and holiness among their adherents is itself an *apologia* for the truth they contain, albeit imperfectly.[7]

Returning to the Christian faith's own self-understanding, the Catholic tradition avows that the assent of faith indeed puts the believer in touch with truth, with reality. As St. Thomas Aquinas defines it, "Believing is an act of the intellect assenting to the divine truth at the command of the will moved by the grace of God."[8] Each part of Aquinas's definition is important, but for our present purpose we want to take note of his emphasis on belief as an act of the intellect that terminates in truth, indeed with God himself. Whereas for Nietzsche belief has merely a pragmatic value, for Aquinas belief's primary object is not praxis but truth. And, as we saw above, even imperfect belief can put one to a greater or lesser extent in touch with this truth.

Aquinas goes so far as to speak of the discipline of theology as a science (*scientia*) whose truth claims enjoy greater certitude than those of any other science.[9] What is the basis for such certitude? Faith is called a theological virtue, because it unites us to God (*theos*) and enables us to participate in God's own knowledge of himself. It is a vision we attain through receptivity to God's self-disclosure in Christ and, through his Church, a revelation testified to by her Scriptures and tradition.[10] For the Christian, faith does not merely consist

---

7. One of the themes in Ratzinger's writing is that it is the saints—those who truly live the Christian faith—who guarantee its truth to us through the beauty of their lives. At the same time, there is a fascinating line in one of Ratzinger's discussions of truth in relation to the saints in which he says, "In every age there have been, and still are, 'pagan saints.'" Ratzinger, *Truth and Tolerance* (San Francisco: Ignatius Press, 2004), 207. If the saints of Christendom are the greatest argument for its truth, then it can also be said that the saints of other religious traditions constitute the greatest proof that God's grace and truth operate outside the visible boundaries of the Christian faith, albeit in an imperfect and participatory way. See ibid., 226.

8. St. Thomas Aquinas, *Summa Theologiae*, trans. the Fathers of the English Dominican Province (Westminster, Md.: Christian Classics, 1981), II-II, q. 2, a. 9; *Catechism of the Catholic Church*, §155.

9. St. Thomas Aquinas, *Summa Theologiae*, I, q. 1, a. 5.

10. Benedict XVI and Francis, *Lumen Fidei*, §36. On the equal reverence due to Scripture

in accepting Jesus, but rather in seeing things with Jesus' very eyes—a participation in his way of seeing.[11] In the words of the contemporary magisterium echoing Aquinas, faith is a supernatural, infused virtue capable of illuminating every aspect of human existence.[12] So, against Nietzsche, the Christian faith definitely has an intellectual component by virtue of its definitive truth claims, yet as we will see below Benedict does not think that these assertions even begin to exhaust the reality of what it means to believe.

We would also do well to pause for a moment to consider faith from the vantage point of another great medieval theologian, St. Anselm of Canterbury. As the Magnificent Doctor taught, faith really does provide man with knowledge of God, but it is not even remotely close to complete in this life. Moreover, it cannot be had without the *experience* of faith, which Benedict describes as taking place when we incarnate God's word in our own daily lives through charity and contemplation. In his catechesis on Anselm, Benedict recalls this doctor's famous prayer that he thinks ought to guide all who wish to deepen their knowledge of the truths of faith: "I do not endeavor, O Lord, to penetrate your sublimity, for in no wise do I compare my understanding with that; but I long to understand in some degree your truth, which my heart believes and loves. For I do not seek to understand that I may believe, but I believe in order to understand. For this also I believe, that unless I believed, I should not understand."[13]

---

and sacred tradition, see Vatican Council II, *Dei Verbum*, §9. For an incisive statement on Christianity as the living Word of God in Christ which transcends Scripture and tradition, see *Catechism of the Catholic Church*, §108.

11. Benedict XVI and Francis, *Lumen Fidei*, §18.

12. Ibid., §§7, 4. For an excellent treatment of Aquinas on faith and the other virtues within a robust framework of the Christian moral life, see John Rziha, *The Christian Moral Life: Directions for the Journey to Happiness* (Notre Dame, Ind.: University of Notre Dame Press, 2017).

13. Anselm, *Proslogion*, chap. 1, quoted in Benedict XVI, "Saint Anselm," general audience (September 23, 2009).

Faith and Apophaticism

Although Aquinas holds that faith is a supremely luminous light that lends man a share in God's very own knowledge, he is also keenly aware of the objection many of us still harbor seven centuries later: if faith is eminently certain, then why is it so easy to doubt? The Angelic Doctor answers in this profound passage:

> It may well happen that what is in itself the more certain may seem to us the less certain on account of the weakness of our intelligence, "which is dazzled by the clearest objects of nature; as the owl is dazzled by the light of the sun." Hence the fact that some happen to doubt about articles of faith is not due to the uncertain nature of the truths, but to the weakness of human intelligence; yet the slenderest knowledge that may be obtained of the highest things is more desirable than the most certain knowledge obtained of lesser things.[14]

This in brief is how Aquinas accounts for the reality that the light of faith, though in itself the brightest of all lights available to us here below, appears "dark" in the eyes of so many. While sin surely plays a part in our inability to grasp divine truth, for Aquinas the very nature of our created intellect is inadequate to the task of piercing the depths of supernatural truth in this life. Thus not everyone who struggles with faith does so because they are living a life of habitual grave sin. In point of fact, the history of Catholic spirituality teaches us that many of the greatest saints—Mother Teresa, Thérèse of Lisieux, Faustina, to name just a few—struggled with spiritual darkness not despite their holiness but precisely because of it.

The Church has a venerable theological tradition of reflecting on this darkness that all believers experience in varying degrees over the course of our pilgrimage of faith. It is called "apophatic" or "negative" theology, depending on whether you privilege the Latin or Greek form of the word. In a nutshell, apophaticism emphasizes the un-

---

14. St. Thomas Aquinas, *Summa Theologiae*, I, q. 1, a. 5 ad 1, citing Aristotle, *Metaphysics*, II, lect. 1.

knowability of God's transcendent being and thus the radical limitations of every affirmation we seek to make in regard to the divine. As a representative illustration of this approach, Aquinas writes that "the highest modality of our knowing here below" and the "summit of our knowledge of God in this life" consists not in knowing what God is, but what he is not.[15] St. Thomas articulates elsewhere that in this life "we know God as unknown" and that we "do not know what he is, but we know nonetheless *that* he is."[16] Though negative theology has a firm foundation in Aquinas and a long pedigree in both the Eastern and Western Church, given our focus we will be dwelling below primarily on the apophaticism of Benedict XVI.

As we will see Benedict do in the case of the other theological virtues in subsequent chapters of this book, he takes an existential approach to apophaticism, writing with an eye to how it impacts our spiritual lives and what it requires of us by way of a response to the unfathomable reality of God. In his encyclical on faith *Lumen Fidei*, he writes accordingly, "Theology thus demands the humility to be 'touched' by God, admitting its own limitations before the mystery, while striving to investigate, with the discipline proper to reason, the inexhaustible riches of this mystery."[17] By no means does Benedict advocate that we stop striving to articulate rationally as much as we can about God, but he does wish to issue a stark reminder of our human limitations when it comes to talking about the ineffable divine nature. The prime virtue required for the pursuit of rational knowledge of God is therefore humility, which in its own turn entails not merely a willingness to admit our limitations but moreover an openness to being "touched" in a personal encounter with the Lord.

---

15. Aquinas, *De veritate*, q. 8, a. 1 ad 8; Aquinas, *Summa contra Gentiles*, III, 39, no. 2270, cited in Jean-Pierre Torrell, OP, *Saint Thomas Aquinas*, vol. 2, *Spiritual Master* (Washington, D.C.: The Catholic University of America Press, 2005), 30 and 37. For an outstanding discussion of apophaticism in Aquinas, see Torrell, *Spiritual Master*, 25–52.

16. Aquinas, *Super Boet. De Trin.*, q. 2, a. 2, ad 1, cited in Torrell, *Spiritual Master*, 42.

17. Benedict XVI and Francis, *Lumen Fidei*, §36.

In a moving response to the question of how he deals with darkness in his own faith life, Benedict again emphasizes the role that humility has played over the course of his earthly pilgrimage:

> I know if I do not understand something that doesn't mean that it is wrong, but that I am too small for it. With many things it has been like this: I gradually grew to see it this way. More and more it is a gift; you suddenly see something which was not perceptible before. You realize that you must be humble, you must wait when you can't enter into a passage of the Scriptures, until the Lord opens it up for you. And does He open it up? Not always. But the fact that such moments of realization happen signifies something great for me in itself.[18]

I find the above text especially powerful because it resonates deeply with my experience when it comes to having to wait to "enter into" a given passage of Scripture until the Lord himself "opens it up for you." Over the course of my academic career, I have been intrigued—and challenged—by countless problematic texts in the Bible. I myself have often wondered how such and such a passage can be true, how it can truly be God's word, and Benedict's words continue to be verified by my own experience. Sometimes, if we are patient, the Lord will clarify a problem we have been having or open up for us a heretofore troubling biblical text. On the other hand, at other times the Lord does not fulfill our expectations and calls us to loving perseverance anyway. All the while, our persistence in seeking answers from the Lord is not by any means necessarily a sign of weakness or pride. Often we ask God tough questions out of a sincere desire to know and to love him better.[19]

Those of us who have probed a burning question for years without receiving an answer from above have much to learn from Benedict's humble attitude. For Benedict teaches by example that if we do not

---

18. Benedict XVI and Peter Seewald, *Last Testament: In His Own Words* (London: Bloomsbury, 2016), 10.
19. Ratzinger, *Introduction to Christianity*, 79–80.

understand a mystery of the faith, our first inclination should be to suppose that the problem lies in us, not in God or in the Church—an attitude encapsulated well in his saying "I am too small for it" in the above text. This is not to say that the Church invariably does a stellar job of conveying the truths of the faith in practice, but often our inability to grasp a given reality is due to the limited grasp of our finite intellect in confrontation with the august mystery of God.

Moreover, the Catholic tradition reveals that at times God may even wish to withhold from us the gift of clarity for the sake of a greater spiritual good. Such is the rationale for the "dark night" often described by Catholic mystics such as St. John of the Cross. John recognized that, while all of God's creation is good and gives us a glimpse of its divine maker, nevertheless God cannot be known directly through created things. Even our good feelings and thoughts in God's regard ultimately fall short of him. In order to achieve the goal of uniting the soul perfectly with himself, the Lord may take away our good feelings toward him (spiritual desolation) or even take away the experience of certainty with respect to his existence or love for us (doubt).[20]

20. The Catholic spiritual tradition has not assigned a single unified meaning to the term "doubt." For instance, authors such as Aquinas understand doubt to consist in an intellectual state wherein one is inclined neither toward nor away from a proposition, while others speak of doubt more in relation to the psychological experience of mental unrest. Here I am referring to the latter, as when Pope Francis, in a way similar to Benedict, speaks of doubt even being a good thing. I do not think that the pope is suggesting that we should be indifferent to the Church's truth claims; rather, I believe that he is pointing to the experience of those of us who, while assenting wholeheartedly to the Church, still experience great difficulties with respect to some of her truth claims. For some interesting comments from the pontiff in this regard, see his first papal interview with Fr. Antonio Spadaro, SJ, titled "A Big Heart Open to God," *America* (September 30, 2013), https://www.americamagazine.org/faith/2013/09/30/big-heart-open-god-interview-pope-francis. For further discussion on the experience of the mental unrest that we call doubt as distinct from doubt as a decision of the will to not accept the Church's teaching, see John Henry Newman, *Apologia pro Vita Sua and Six Sermons* (New Haven, Conn.: Yale University Press, 2008), 321; and Josef Pieper, *Faith, Hope, Love* (San Francisco: Ignatius Press, 1997), 49–54. Basing his thought primarily on the work of Aquinas, Pieper's resonances with Benedict can be seen in lines such as these: "The curious existence of certainty and uncertainty ... not only describes but actually constitutes the psychological experience of the believer.... It is astonishing to see with what outspoken candor a theologian such as Thomas Aquinas describes this element of uncertainty in the act of belief." Ibid., 52, 54.

Dispositions of the Saints That We Need to Face Uncertainty

We can take inspiration for our own journey through this valley of the shadow of death in the lives of three saints whom Pope Benedict holds up as examples of imitation. In his catechesis on St. James the Greater, we are exhorted to learn from James "promptness in accepting the Lord's call even when he asks us to leave the 'boat' of our human securities, enthusiasm in following him on the paths that he indicates to us over and above any deceptive presumption of our own, readiness to witness to him with courage."[21] Like James, we must be ready to follow Christ to the point of giving our very lives for him. And even if our faith never requires blood martyrdom, we all must have the readiness and docility to leave the "boat" of our human securities and presumptions whenever the Lord should call us. As a good Jew of his day, surely James did not expect the Messiah to look quite like Jesus, a crucified king. And yet, despite his lack of full understanding, the apostle did not allow his preconceptions to stop him from following the truth that he had come to know and experience in the person of Christ.

Perhaps unexpectedly to many, Benedict also signals the life of "doubting" St. Thomas as a model for our faith life. Thomas is well known for his skepticism about the truth of Jesus' resurrection (Jn 20:25), exhibiting the sort of doubt to which I can closely relate in my own life. However, here Thomas's frank willingness to confront the Lord is actually put forward by Benedict as an example for us:

---

21. Benedict XVI, "James, the Greater," general audience (June 21, 2006). Of course, these are not the only three saints Benedict offers as examples for emulation. He spent years of Wednesday audience talks on the lives of the saints, always with an eye to suggesting how we might imitate and learn from each. In his encyclical on faith, Benedict not only quotes from the saints extensively but also mentions two in particular, Francis of Assisi and Teresa of Calcutta, whose focus on heaven did not cause them to forget the sufferings of this world but on the contrary deepened their engagement with it. Benedict XVI and Francis, *Lumen Fidei*, §57.

The Apostle Thomas's case is important to us for at least three reasons: first, because it comforts us in our insecurity; second, because it shows us that every doubt can lead to an outcome brighter than any uncertainty; and, lastly, because the words that Jesus addressed to him remind us of the true meaning of mature faith and encourage us to persevere, despite the difficulty, along our journey of adhesion to him.[22]

As we see here, for Benedict doubt is not something unequivocally negative but rather a reality that can lead to a great good if confronted with sincerity and humility. In this way, Thomas's persevering questioning becomes a model for us on the path to mature faith in Christ. Faith involves the humility to ask God the tough questions that matter to us most, confident that God will see through the good work he has begun in us, keeping us in his love no matter the answer he gives to our questions or whether he seems to answer them at all.

The third saint put forward by Benedict as an example of how to deal with uncertainty is, like Thomas, a model of how to ask tough questions of the Lord, but it is a woman whom we do not typically consider a "doubter." Indeed, the saint I am talking about here—the Mother of God—certainly was willing to accept the Lord's will, yet it is not as if she understood the divine plan perfectly from the very moment of the Annunciation: "How shall this be, since I have no husband?" (Lk 1:34). But Mary does not just ask a bold question. More importantly still, she exhibits a willingness to reciprocate with the Lord. Writes Benedict:

> Mary does not stop at a first superficial understanding of what is happening in her life, but can look in depth, she lets herself called into question by events, digests them, discerns them, and attains the understanding that only faith can provide. It is the profound humility of the obedient faith of Mary, who welcomes within her even what she does not understand in God's action, leaving it to God to open her mind and heart.[23]

22. Benedict XVI, "The Virgin Mary, Icon of Obedient Faith," general audience (December 19, 2012).
23. Ibid.

In Mary, therefore, we learn that our freedom to ask questions of our Lord does not imply that the Lord has an obligation to answer us, or at least not to answer in the way we expect. Indeed, his reply sometimes takes the form of another unsettling question.

In his final official interview book, Benedict casts further light on the reality that God is not an object capable of being circumscribed by our created intellects. In the course of answering the question of how he came to choose his episcopal motto "co-worker of the truth," the pontiff made this profound remark related to the Marian text that I discussed above. That God does not always answer our questions should tell us something about our religion in relation to possessing the truth. For Benedict, our faith is not so much about getting answers and grasping the truth as it is about letting the truth grasp *us*:

> Indeed, we cannot say "I have the truth," but the truth has us, it touches us. And we try to let ourselves be guided by this touch.... One can work with the truth, because the truth is person. One can let truth in, try to provide the truth with value. That seemed to me finally to be the very definition of the profession of a theologian; that he, when he has been touched by this truth, when truth has caught sight of him, is now ready to let it take him into service, to work on it.[24]

Here we find a theme that emerges throughout the career of Joseph Ratzinger all the way through his pontificate as Pope Benedict. Truth is a *person*, and Christianity is not merely a religion of the truth that can be found in a book but a religion of the living and incarnate Word who is Truth. As such, it is not so much that we are in pursuit of capturing this truth. On the contrary, it is first and foremost the Truth who pursues us, has us, guides us. At the end of the day, the deep questions that Benedict encourages us to ask in imitation of the Apostles and the Mother of God have as their end this dynamic relationship with truth and a consequent readiness to be taken into its service. In imitation of the Handmaid of the Lord, we may overcome a great

---

24. Benedict XVI and Seewald, *Last Testament*, 241.

many problems in life by learning to see ourselves not as masters of the faith but instead as servants of the truth who are willing to be continually renewed and mastered by faith in Jesus Christ.[25]

Divine Pedagogy: The Scriptures Themselves Teach Us How to Struggle through Life's Darkness

Not only do the lives of individual saints teach us how to live our faith in the face of uncertainty, the Bible itself as a whole enshrines this approach in the collective life of God's pilgrim people. One of the most illuminating dimensions of Benedict's thought lies in his insight that what we find in the history of the Chosen People's journey with God mirrors how the Lord works in our own lives. In one of his weekly catecheses on prayer, he thus writes, "Scripture is an ongoing dialogue between God and man, a progressive dialogue in which God shows himself ever closer, in which we can become ever better acquainted with his face, his voice, his being."[26]

In passages such as these, Benedict weaves seamlessly between speaking of God's people of ages past and his people today, the reason being that God revealed himself historically to the people of Israel progressively, just as he gradually reveals to us his full plan for our lives today. In the "school" of the divine pedagogue, God meets us pupils where we are. Taking into account all our weaknesses, he gradually leads us by the hand to the fullness of truth and life.

Benedict applies this same notion of divine revelation as an ongoing dialogue to our own situation in professing the Creed. Asking what it really means to say "I believe in God," the pontiff replies, "What Israel had to do in the early days of its history, and the Church had to do again at the beginning of her career, must be done afresh

---

25. Benedict XVI, "'The Church and the Scandal of Sexual Abuse" (April 10, 2019), https://www.catholicnewsagency.com/news/full-text-of-benedict-xvi-the-church-and-the-scandal-of-sexual-abuse-59639.

26. Benedict XVI, "The Liturgy, School of Prayer."

in every human life."[27] Like Israel, we do not completely understand the truths of the Catholic faith. Though the Church may possess the fullness of truth, this does not guarantee that each of us has grasped that truth fully. This is why Benedict says that each of us has to walk the same path that our Israelite ancestors forged for us.

Building on patristic thought, I therefore like to speak of there being a twofold "divine pedagogy" at work in Scripture. First, the whole of Scripture testifies to the gradual process by which our Lord led his chosen people over the millennia toward the fullness of truth in Christ. But this same pedagogy also takes place in our own lives as we re-live the struggle of Israel to know and love God over the course of our earthly pilgrimage. Like Israel, we will have our triumphs and our tragedies. We will have our Exodus highs and our exilic or Ecclesiastes lows. In all of this, the Lord is there for us as he was for ancient Israel, wooing us constantly back to himself.[28] And through all of this, we are called to relive Israel's exodus personally and as a Church. As Benedict writes in his encyclical *Deus Caritas Est* and we will discuss in our later treatment of charity, "Love is ... an ongoing exodus out of the closed inward-looking self towards its liberation through self-giving, and thus towards authentic self-discovery and indeed the discovery of God."[29]

In a catechesis from his series on the life of prayer, Benedict regards the patriarch Jacob's nocturnal struggle and encounter with God as emblematic of our own journey of faith.[30] While biblical exegetes give a variety of interpretations to this passage, when looked upon canonically in light of the biblical narrative as a whole, the text opens up to broader dimensions. Benedict's profound commentary merits to be cited at some length:

---

27. Ratzinger, *Introduction to Christianity*, 151.
28. For an extensive treatment of this twofold divine pedagogy, see my *Dark Passages of the Bible*, esp. chaps. 2–3.
29. Benedict XVI, *Deus Caritas Est* (2005), §6; Benedict XVI, "Desire for God," general audience (November 7, 2012).
30. Benedict XVI, "The Nocturnal Struggle and Encounter with God," general audience (May 25, 2011).

For the believer the episode of the struggle at the Jabbok thus becomes a paradigm in which the people of Israel speak of their own origins and outline the features of a particular relationship between God and humanity. Therefore, as is also affirmed in the *Catechism of the Catholic Church*, "From this account, the spiritual tradition of the Church has retained the symbol of prayer as a battle of faith and as the triumph of perseverance" (§2573). The Bible text speaks to us about a long night of seeking God, of the struggle to learn his name and see his face; it is the night of prayer that, with tenacity and perseverance, asks God for a blessing and a new name, a new reality that is the fruit of conversion and forgiveness.

For the believer Jacob's night at the ford of the Jabbok thus becomes a reference point for understanding the relationship with God that finds in prayer its greatest expression. Prayer requires trust, nearness, almost a hand-to-hand contact that is symbolic not of a God who is an enemy, an adversary, but a Lord of blessing who always remains mysterious, who seems beyond reach. Therefore the author of the sacred text uses the symbol of the struggle, which implies a strength of spirit, perseverance, tenacity in obtaining what is desired. And if the object of one's desire is a relationship with God, his blessing and love, then the struggle cannot fail but ends in that self-giving to God, in recognition of one's own weakness, which is overcome only by giving oneself over into God's merciful hands.[31]

I find the above text especially compelling because it echoes the theme of questioning discussed above and applies it to the most intimate dimension of our lives: our life of prayer, our ongoing inner dialogue with the Lord. Citing the *Catechism*, Benedict speaks of prayer as a "battle" that requires of us great perseverance and great nearness, to the point of "hand-to-hand combat" with the Lord. Like Jacob, we too have to pass through the long night of seeking God. But why does the Lord come to us in this and not some easier way? Benedict writes:

---

31. Ibid. For a great variation on the theme of Israel's centuries-long struggle to grasp hold of God—and of God "struggling" to make himself known to his people, see Ratzinger, *In the Beginning: A Catholic Understanding of the Story of Creation and the Fall* (Grand Rapids, Mich.: Eerdmans Publishing Co., 1995), 10–11.

Dear brothers and sisters, our entire lives are like this long night of struggle and prayer, spent in desiring and asking for God's blessing, which cannot be grabbed or won through our own strength but must be received with humility from him as a gratuitous gift that ultimately allows us to recognize the Lord's face. And when this happens, our entire reality changes; we receive a new name and God's blessing.[32]

Benedict here drives home the point that God's blessing is not something we can attain through our own power. Faith itself is a gift to be received with the virtues of humility, docility, and patience. Yet if we are willing to accompany the Lord on the long night of his Passion, we will be rewarded with a new name and God's blessing.

After a lifetime of tutelage and struggle under the divine pedagogue, we may expect to have gained some wisdom and found many answers to questions that troubled us in times past. Other questions may remain but just not bother us as greatly as they once did. And, although I do not think I am currently approaching the end of my earthly pilgrimage (though one never knows the day or the hour), I am quite certain that other questions will remain unanswered until the day I finally return to God. All this is to say that submitting to the will of the divine pedagogue is no guarantee that we will have all the answers for which we hope in our present life.[33]

To draw on another saintly example from Scripture, we may recall the end of Job's drama. Benedict looks to Job's desperate, even impious pleas to God as a model for how we are to relate to the divine mystery. Like Christ crying out from the cross, "My God, my God, why

---

32. Benedict XVI, "The Nocturnal Struggle and Encounter with God."
33. Here is a particularly beautiful quote in which Cardinal Ratzinger made the same point: "Doubt need not be immediately associated with a fall from faith. I can sincerely take up the questions that press upon me while holding fast to God, holding to the essential core of faith. On the one hand, I can try to find solutions for the seeming contradictions. On the other hand, I can also be confident that, though I can't find them all, there are solutions even when I can't find them. There are things that remain unsolved for the moment that should not be explained by forced interpretations." Ratzinger, *Salt of the Earth* (San Francisco: Ignatius Press, 1997), 31.

have you forsaken me?" (Mt 27:46), Job unabashedly lets God have it, to the point of expressing his regret at having been born (Jb 3:11–13; 10:18) and being seen by God as an enemy (Jb 13:24). After citing Augustine's classic phrase *Si comprehendis, non est Deus* ("If you understand, it is not God"), Benedict makes it clear that Job's protests against God are not meant to challenge his authority or accuse him of error. "Instead," Benedict writes, "our crying out is, as it was for Jesus on the Cross, the deepest and most radical way of affirming our faith in his sovereign power."[34] Immersed like the rest of us in the dramatic complexity of historical events, Job remains unshakably certain that God is his Father, even as his silence is utterly incomprehensible.

Far from issuing an explanation for his sufferings, God finally breaks his silence by thundering to Job from the whirlwind, "Where were you when I laid the foundation of the earth?" (Jb 38:4). This is simply a biblical illustration of what we saw above in the case of the saints: to walk the path of faith is not primarily about receiving answers from the Lord but more about letting the Lord pose the question to us of how we are going to live our life in the light of his love and law. As Benedict writes, "After all, God's answer to Job explains nothing; rather, it sets boundaries to our mania for judging everything and being able to say the final word on a subject, and it reminds us of our limitations. It admonishes us to trust the mystery of God in its incomprehensibility."[35] The eponymous protagonist of the Book of Job had all his fortunes restored at the end of his life, but we ourselves may not end up so lucky. This is why Benedict says in another place:

Faith is not a light which scatters all our darkness, but a lamp which guides our steps in the night and suffices for the journey. To those who suffer, God does not provide arguments which explain everything; rather, his response is that of an accompanying presence, a history of goodness which touches every story of suffering and opens up a ray of light. In Christ, God himself wishes to

---

34. Benedict XVI, *Deus Caritas Est*, §38.
35. Ratzinger, *Introduction to Christianity*, 26.

share this path with us and to offer us his gaze so that we might see the light within it. Christ is the one who, having endured suffering, is "the pioneer and perfecter of our faith" (Heb 12:2).[36]

Our Journey with Christ as Leap, Risk, and Gamble

In addition to speaking of our Christian journey as an existential struggle, Benedict deploys a number of other expressions that describes the life of faith more provocatively. In his *Introduction to Christianity*, we find it spoken of as a "leap" which is "risky":

Belief has always had something of an adventurous break or leap about it, because in every age it represents the risky enterprise of accepting what plainly cannot be seen as the truly real and fundamental. Belief was never simply the attitude automatically corresponding to the whole slant of human life; it has always been a decision calling on the depths of existence, a decision that in every age demanded a turnabout by man that can only be achieved by an effort of will.[37]

In keeping with his earlier understanding of faith as a "risky" exodus out of oneself, Benedict goes so far as to speak of believers' free acceptance of Christ as a "gamble": "Indeed, it involves them and uplifts them in a gamble for life [*scommessa di vita*] that is like an exodus, that is, a coming out of ourselves, from our own certainties, from our own mental framework, to entrust ourselves to the action of God who points out to us his way to achieve true freedom, our human identity, true joy of the heart, peace with everyone."[38]

Why does Benedict consider faith as a risky gamble, and how can he speak of it in this way if it is supposed to be supremely certain? In addition to what I said above about certitude, I think that another part

---

36. Benedict XVI and Francis, *Lumen Fidei*, §57.
37. Ratzinger, *Introduction to Christianity*, 51–52.
38. Benedict XVI, "What Is Faith?" general audience (October 24, 2012).

of the answer is that faith of its very essence involves putting our trust in another's judgment and *acting* in accordance with it. It involves the risk that the person we have trusted with everything is not right after all, and yet we nonetheless base our life's most important decisions on his wisdom. We ourselves, as finite creatures, cannot prove beyond the shadow of a doubt that a trusted authority is indeed in the truth; and yet we entrust ourselves anyway.

Developing the Holy Father's image of faith as a risk, we might say that our quest for union with the Lord demands that we lay all our life's chips on the table. We must also be willing to endure a long night of suffering for the sake of this enterprise. The risky exodus out of our creature comforts may entail a certain "loss," but it is of such a kind so as to be counted as nothing because of the surpassing worth of what we thereby gain: knowledge of Christ Jesus our Lord (Phil 3:7–8). Perhaps it is not surprising in this connection that Benedict wishes to draw our attention to Blaise Pascal's famous "wager." While he does not seem to endorse the notion without certain reservations, Benedict refers us to Pascal's suggestion offered to those who want to reach faith but do not know how. To these seekers Pascal says, "Take a lesson from those who were earlier racked by doubts like yourself.... Follow the way by which they began; by acting as if they believed, by taking holy water, by having Masses said, and so on. This will bring you quite naturally to believe and will stupefy you."[39] It is surely not the case that everyone who follows Pascal's recommendation will find their way to God and his Church. Nevertheless, the philosopher's advice resonates deeply with Benedict's insistence that faith demands an existential "risk," "gamble," or "experiment."

---

39. Blaise Pascal, *Pensées*, fragment 233, following the translation in Ratzinger, *Introduction to Christianity*, 176–77.

Faith as Understanding, Taking a Stand

At this point I would like to hone in on what I think constitutes the nature of the "risk" or "gamble" of faith that Benedict emphasizes so frequently and emphatically. What begins here I consider to be the heart of this chapter, and, by extension, the heart of this book, for it is here that Benedict ventures a definition (actually, a variety of definitions from different angles) of what the Christian faith is. In the attempt to arrive at a definition of what it fundamentally means to say *credo* ("I believe"), Benedict writes the following in the extensive treatment of the question we find in his *Introduction to Christianity*:

It means that man does not regard seeing, hearing, and touching as the totality of what concerns him, that he does not view the area of his world as marked off by what he can see and touch but seeks a second mode of access to reality, a mode he calls in fact belief, and in such a way that he finds in it the decisive enlargement of his whole view of the world. If this is so, then the little word credo contains *a basic option vis-à-vis reality* as such; it signifies, not the observation of this or that fact, but *a fundamental mode of behavior toward being,* toward existence, toward one's own sector of reality, and toward reality as a whole....

What is belief really? We can now reply like this: *It is a human way of taking up a stand in the totality of reality, a way that cannot be reduced to knowledge* and is incommensurable with knowledge; it is the bestowal of meaning without which the totality of man would remain homeless, on which man's calculations and actions are based, and without which in the last resort he could not calculate and act, because he can only do this in the context of a meaning that bears him up.[40]

Notice that, contrary to many Christians, Benedict does not think of belief primarily as something intellectual. For him it is rather a "basic option vis-à-vis reality," a "fundamental mode of behavior toward being," a "way of taking up a stand in the totality of reality." As he puts

---

40. Ratzinger, *Introduction to Christianity*, 50–51, 72–73 (emphasis added).

it in another place, when we proclaim "I believe in God," we are telling our Lord not just that we are convinced he exists, but moreover that we are "founding our entire life on him, letting his Word guide it every day, in practical decisions, without fear of losing some part of myself."[41]

In a few key places throughout his corpus, Benedict appeals to the Hebrew verb "to believe" (ʾāman) to drive home his point about the nature of belief. For instance, he makes much of the prophet Isaiah's warning to King Ahaz, "If you do not believe [taʾămînû], then you will not be established [têʾāmênû]" (Is 7:9 RSV). There is a delightful word play in this passage in the original Hebrew. The first instance of ʾāman occurs in the Hiphil stem, in which the verb means either 1) to stand firm, or 2) to believe or put trust. However, the second instance occurs in the Niphal stem, in which it has meanings including 1) to be carried by a nurse; 2) to be made firm, sure, lasting; 3) to be confirmed, established, sure; 4) to be verified, confirmed; 5) to be reliable, faithful, trusty.[42] Although Benedict himself does not comment on these finer points of the Hebrew verb ʾāman, he does take the opportunity to discuss its various shades of meaning. On a material level, he notes, it denotes firmness, firm ground, or a foothold. By extension, it denotes a person's steadfastness or faithfulness, his firmness in adherence to the Lord. It also denotes truth itself, that which holds firm always. Cast in covenantal terms, it refers to God's fidelity and to man's faith, which is to say their firm mutual commitment to upholding their covenantal bond.

---

41. Benedict XVI, "'I Believe in God,'" general audience (January 23, 2013).

42. Francis Brown, Samuel Rolles Driver, and Charles Augustus Briggs, *Enhanced Brown-Driver-Briggs Hebrew and English Lexicon* (Oxford: Clarendon Press, 1977), 53. Although not employed in this passage, ʾāman also occurs in the Qal stem, in which it can refer to a support person such as foster parent or a nurse, the supports or pillars of a door, or the action of supporting and nourishing. For further analysis of the Hebrew and Greek of this verb, with the indication that its occurrence in the plural results from being spoken to both King Ahaz and his advisors, see John D. W. Watts, *Isaiah 1–33*, rev. ed., Word Biblical Commentary 24 (Nashville: Thomas Nelson, 2005), 131–32.

In light of these and the other nuances of the word to which we could appeal, Benedict sharpens his preliminary definition of faith, now calling it the act of "holding on to God through which man gains a firm foothold for his life" and of "taking up a position, as taking a stand trustfully on the ground of the word of God."[43] Again, for Benedict the essence of faith is not something intellectual but rather relational and behavioral or experiential. Put in another way that echoes how he described it above, "Essentially, [belief] is entrusting oneself to that which has not been made by oneself and never could be made and which precisely in this way supports and makes possible all our making."[44] Of course, this is by no means to say that Benedict's approach to faith is anti-intellectual—he would be the last to allege against Aquinas that faith involves no concrete intellectual content, no "deposit" of truth. Indeed, in a catechesis dedicated to the question of what precisely faith is, Benedict sounds the following note that resonates with Aquinas's view: "Faith [is] a confident entrustment to a 'You,' who is God, who gives me a different certitude, but no less solid than that which comes from precise calculation or from science."[45]

Related to this point on certitude and Christian belief, Benedict does one more fascinating thing in his exegesis of Isaiah 7:9. He observes that the Septuagint renders this verse, "Unless you believe, you will not understand." While it might seem that the Greek translator's choice of the verb συνῆτε ("understand") has profoundly altered the sense of the original Hebrew *tê'āmênû* ("be established") discussed above, Benedict makes the case that the later version preserves the essential meaning of the original. Standing, he observes, certainly has something to do with under-standing: "We need knowledge, we need truth, because without these we cannot stand firm.... Faith without

---

43. Ratzinger, *Introduction to Christianity*, 69.
44. Ibid., 70. See also the very similar discussion of *'āman* in Benedict XVI and Francis, *Lumen Fidei*, §10.
45. Benedict XVI, "What Is Faith?" For a helpful treatment of the necessity of faith's intellectual dimension, see Pieper, *Faith, Hope, Love*.

truth does not save."⁴⁶ Contrary to Nietzsche's insinuation, Benedict holds that a false faith ultimately will not make one happy. Sure, a false faith may bring consolation and cheer for a time, yet the pope insists that such a faith "remains prey to the vagaries of our spirit and the changing seasons, incapable of sustaining a steady journey through life."⁴⁷

Faith's Truth Is Seen Only from the Inside "by Experimentation" with the Heart

A crucial tenet of Benedict's "existentialist" approach to Christianity, central to this book, follows from his above reflection on the relationship between belief and understanding in the Greek of Isaiah 7:9. As Benedict has contended for decades, the faith's truth cannot be seen from the outside, but—paradoxically to some—only in the context of lived belief. When he celebrated Mass at St. Patrick's Cathedral in New York in 2008, Benedict gave a fascinating homily in which he described the great building as an allegory of faith and the search for truth. Like any Gothic cathedral, from the outside, the church's windows appear dark and dreary. But once one enters the church, these same windows suddenly come alive with resplendent light passing through their stained glass. This, then, is the allegory he draws: "It is only from the inside, from the experience of faith and ecclesial life, that we see the Church as she truly is: flooded with grace, resplendent in beauty, adorned by the manifold gifts of the Spirit."⁴⁸ Here, Benedict teaches in poetic fashion a truth that he has reiterated in many different places and ways throughout his career. As we have already

---

46. Benedict XVI and Francis, *Lumen Fidei*, §§23–24; Ratzinger, *Introduction to Christianity*, 69–70. Is 7:9's verb συνῆτε, from συνίημι, is employed frequently in biblical wisdom literature to denote revealed insight, a faculty that not everyone possesses. For a helpful entry on this word, see *New International Dictionary of New Testament Theology and Exegesis*, ed. Moisés Silva (Grand Rapids, Mich.: Zondervan, 2014), s.v. συνίημι.

47. Benedict XVI and Francis, *Lumen Fidei*, §24.

48. Benedict XVI, homily for votive Mass for the universal Church (April 19, 2008).

been contending in earlier chapters, the truth of the Catholic Church ultimately can be seen only from the inside when we fast from our own preconceptions and desires with a willingness to embark upon what Benedict dubs the "experiment of faith." It is of this journey that he writes, "Only by entering does one experience; only by cooperating in the experiment does one ask at all; and only he who asks receives an answer."[49]

Benedict develops the notion of the faith as experiment that we have been drawing upon in his *Introduction to Christianity*, an exposition that we will do well to meditate upon here. As is frequently the case in his writings, he makes an appeal to the sciences for an analogy:

> We know today that in a physical experiment the observer himself enters into the experiment and only by doing so can arrive at a physical experience. This means that there is no such thing as pure objectivity even in physics—that even here the result of the experiment, nature's answer, depends on the question put to it. In the answer there is always a bit of the question and a bit of the questioner himself; it reflects not only nature in itself, in its pure objectivity, but also gives back something of man, of what is characteristically ours, a bit of the human subject. This too, *mutatis mutandis*, is true of the question of God. There is no such thing as a mere observer. There is no such thing as pure objectivity.[50]

Benedict's concern here is to clarify what one can and cannot expect from an apology for the truth of the faith. There is no such thing as a

---

49. Ratzinger, *Introduction to Christianity*, 175–76; Ratzinger, "Why I Am Still in the Church," 132–53.

50. Ratzinger, *Introduction to Christianity*, 175. Some may find it unacceptable to say that pure objectivity does not exist, while others simply may not see it as a problem because they have the utmost confidence in their faith (which is a beautiful thing). Unfortunately, the arguments of these individuals are typically not all that helpful to those of us who have undergone a similar experience to that of Benedict. For those of us who consider the pure objectivity issue as a problem, I think this line of Henri de Lubac rings true: "To one who has seen a problem, the most beautiful and true things, uttered by someone who has not seen it, are but words and yet more words." Henri de Lubac, *Paradoxes of Faith* (San Francisco: Ignatius Press, 1987), 54.

completely objective inquiry even in the field of natural science, let alone in the domain of faith. We cannot go around pretending that all rational people will inevitably draw the same conclusions that we do concerning the things of God. Indeed, God—whose pursuit is the highest inquiry possible—eludes circumscription even more than knowledge in the most demanding theoretical sciences.

Moreover, he who considers what little knowledge he does have concerning the things of God to be unemotional and objective is in reality only deceiving himself.[51] There is more to man's pursuit of God than what takes place at the theoretical level. This is true of any inquiry, but it is the case with God in particular since he is not an object but rather a person. Knowledge of God, therefore, also entails an affective dimension, or what today is often called a "personal relationship." Benedict makes much of St. Paul's teaching that one "believes with his heart" (Rom 10:10). Biblically speaking, the heart represents "the core of the human person, where all his or her different dimensions intersect: body and spirit, interiority and openness to the world and to others, intellect, will, and affectivity."[52] As Benedict puts it concisely in his commentary on the Beatitudes, "the organ for seeing God is the heart—the intellect alone is not enough."[53] Accordingly, what distinguishes a true intellectual assent of faith is that it is expressed through *love*. This love is open to deep transformation and yearns to live in conformity with the demands of the truth.[54]

In its turn, this very love brings its own form of enlightenment, transforming us inwardly and enabling us to see reality with new eyes.

---

51. Ratzinger, *Introduction to Christianity*, 175–76.

52. Benedict XVI and Francis, *Lumen Fidei*, §26.

53. Benedict XVI, *From the Baptism in the Jordan to the Transfiguration*, 92. See also Joseph Ratzinger, "The Dignity of the Human Person" [commentary on *Gaudium et Spes*], in *Commentary on the Documents of Vatican II*, vol. 5, ed. Herbert Vorgrimler (New York: Herder and Herder, 1969), 155.

54. While Benedict does not cite him explicitly on this point, Newman's distinction between "notional" and "real" assent offers a valuable parallel to the pontiff's understanding of what constitutes belief. See Newman, *An Essay in Aid of a Grammar of Assent*, 49–92.

"One who loves," writes Benedict, "realizes that love is an experience of truth, that it opens our eyes to see reality in a new way, in union with the beloved."[55] Citing St. Gregory the Great, the pontiff thus writes that *amor ipse notitia est*—love is itself a source of knowledge possessed of its own logic.[56] Yet we are not talking sentimentality here. In the end, truth needs love, and love needs truth. Love untethered from truth may produce good feelings for a time, but it is only in concert with the truth that it can transcend the passing moment:

> If love is not tied to truth, it falls prey to fickle emotions and cannot stand the test of time. True love, on the other hand, unifies all the elements of our person and becomes a new light pointing the way to a great and fulfilled life. Without truth, love is incapable of establishing a firm bond; it cannot liberate our isolated ego or redeem it from the fleeting moment.[57]

Like the false faith discussed above in response to Nietzsche, here too we find that love without truth is incapable of making one truly happy, unable to stand the test of time. Indeed, Benedict's comments deeply resonate with the great mystics of the Church who reject the notion that our relationship with God consists above all in knowing or above all in loving but rather in an all-embracing knowing-loving or loving-knowing.[58]

Faith or Charity Alone?

Benedict's conviction that the Christian faith is, at bottom, a love affair can be seen especially clearly in his writings on the theology of St. Paul. This point was rendered beautifully in the pontiff's homily

---

55. Benedict XVI and Francis, *Lumen Fidei*, §27.
56. Ibid., §28.
57. Ibid., §27.
58. For an outstanding treatment of this dynamic of knowing-loving or loving-knowing in saints such as John of the Cross and Teresa of Avila, see Jordan Aumann, OP, *Spiritual Theology* (Westminster, Md.: Christian Classics, 1987), esp. chap. 8 ("Progressive Purgation") and chap. 12 ("Grades of Prayer").

inaugurating the Pauline Year in 2008. Commenting on Galatians 2:20 ("I live by faith in the Son of God who loved me and gave himself for me"), Benedict writes:

> All Paul's actions begin from this center. His faith is the experience of being loved by Jesus Christ in a very personal way. It is awareness of the fact that Christ did not face death for something anonymous but rather for love of him—of Paul—and that, as the Risen One, he still loves him.... Paul's faith is being struck by the love of Jesus Christ, a love that overwhelms him to his depths and transforms him. His faith is not a theory, an opinion about God and the world. His faith is the impact of God's love in his heart. Thus, this same faith was love for Jesus Christ.[59]

For St. Paul and Benedict who takes him as his guide, the experience of being loved by Christ forms the basis of a friendship that is not merely theoretical but transformative, imbuing all areas of one's life with the virtue of charity. For this reason, in his Pauline Year catecheses, Benedict writes that it is essential to grasp that Christian moral living is "not born from a system of commandments but is a consequence of our friendship with Christ."[60]

Benedict's words here resonate remarkably well with Fr. Servais Pinckaers's now classical statement that "Catholic moral teaching is not a mere code of prescriptions and prohibitions.... Catholic morality is a response to the aspirations of the human heart for truth and goodness."[61] As we discussed in our earlier chapter on the nature of human freedom, Pinckaers distinguishes those who hold a "morality

---

59. Benedict XVI, homily for the opening of the Pauline Year (June 28, 2008). For a more thorough overview of how Benedict employs the thought of St. Paul in his own writings, see Matthew Ramage, "The Reception of St. Paul in the Works of Joseph Ratzinger/Benedict XVI," *Letter and Spirit* 11 (2016): 147–71.

60. Benedict XVI, "The Doctrine of Justification: The Apostle's Teaching on Faith and Works," general audience (November 26, 2008). In addition to being found on the Vatican's website, Benedict's Pauline Year catecheses are also contained in Benedict XVI, *St. Paul* (San Francisco: Ignatius Press, 2009).

61. Pinckaers, *Morality: The Catholic View*, 1.

of obligation" from those who hold a "morality of happiness."[62] The former view moral codes primarily as constraints upon human freedom, while the latter understand ethical norms in general, and the Church's doctrines in particular, as aids toward human happiness. A morality of happiness does not dispense one from the requirement of fulfilling obligations. Quite the contrary, as a vision of morality that stems above all from living faith in Christ, it finds the obedience of faith and responsibility of love to be a yoke that is easy, a burden that is light. For this reason, Benedict observes that St. Paul "does not use expressed commands very often (1 Thes 4:10), although he is aware that he has the authority to do so."[63]

Benedict's view on the interplay of faith and love perhaps comes across best in a catechesis specifically concerned with the doctrine of justification. Recalling that Martin Luther translated St. Paul's teaching on justification in Romans 3:28 as occurring by faith "alone" (*allein*), it may be surprising for some to discover that Benedict thinks a Catholic can affirm Luther's teaching if it is understood in a precise way:

> Luther's phrase: "faith alone" is true, if it is not opposed to faith in charity, in love. Faith is looking at Christ, entrusting oneself to Christ, being united to Christ, conformed to Christ, to his life. And the form, the life of Christ, is love; hence to believe is to conform to Christ and to enter into his love. So it is that in the Letter to the Galatians in which he primarily developed his teaching on justification St. Paul speaks of faith that works through love (Gal 5:14).[64]

For Benedict as for St. Paul, the theological virtues are inseparable from one another. Thus true belief—embarking on a friendship with

---

62. For a discussion of these contrasting moral approaches, see Pinckaers, *Sources of Christian Ethics*, 17–22.

63. Joseph Ratzinger, Heinz Schürmann, and Hans Urs von Balthasar, *Principles of Christian Morality* (San Francisco: Ignatius Press, 1986), 67; 2 Cor 8:8.

64. Benedict XVI, "The Doctrine of Justification: From Works to Faith," general audience (November 19, 2008).

Christ—is not merely an intellectual affair but necessarily already entails love of him who has called us to new life. Accordingly, the expression "faith alone" can also be flipped on its head. Concerning the gospel reading for the Solemnity of Christ the King (Mt 25:31–46), Benedict therefore observes:

> It is the Gospel of the judge whose sole criterion is love. What he asks is only this: Did you visit me when I was sick? When I was in prison? Did you give me food to eat when I was hungry, did you clothe me when I was naked? And thus justice is decided in charity. Thus, at the end of this Gospel we can almost say: love alone, charity alone. But there is no contradiction between this Gospel and St. Paul. It is the same vision, according to which communion with Christ, faith in Christ, creates charity. And charity is the fulfilment of communion with Christ. Thus, we are just by being united with him and in no other way.[65]

Benedict's provocative articulation of this dynamic relationship between faith and love in turn helps overcome the common misconception that St. Paul's doctrine is incompatible with that of St. James.[66]

---

65. Ibid.

66. The following comments on Paul in relation to James are especially important: "Often there is seen an unfounded opposition between St. Paul's theology and that of St. James, who writes in his Letter: 'as the body apart from the spirit is dead, so faith apart from works is dead' (Jas 2:26). In reality, while Paul is primarily concerned to show that faith in Christ is necessary and sufficient, James accentuates the consequential relations between faith and works (Jas 2:24). Therefore, for both Paul and James, faith that is active in love testifies to the freely given gift of justification in Christ." Benedict XVI, "The Doctrine of Justification: The Apostle's Teaching on Faith and Works." As Benedict does well to observe in another catechesis, the compatibility of St. Paul and St. James ultimately can be seen only in light of a proper understanding of what "works of the law" signified for Jews at the time of Christ. For St. Paul it was specific Jewish "works" such as circumcision and dietary laws—not good deeds in general—from which the Christian has been liberated and which are not salvific. Benedict XVI, "The Doctrine of Justification: From Works to Faith."

Conclusion

We have covered a lot of ground in this first of two chapters surveying Benedict XVI's theology of the virtue of faith. Beginning by engaging Nietzsche on the question of whether or not faith yields true knowledge, we proceeded to explore the issue of how much certitude faith enjoys and the related approach of apophatic theology, the experience of mystical darkness, and Benedict's description of faith as a leap, risk, and gamble. Finally, we delved into an exploration of Isaiah 7:9 and saw how Benedict exegetes this verse to depict the life of faith as an "experiment" performed with the heart, a journey in which we can only arrive at understanding if we first believe and take a loving stand in the totality of reality. In the next chapter, we will continue our exploration by investigating other themes in Benedict's vision of the Christian of faith which build upon and complete the ones we have discussed here.

5

FAITH (II)

*Obedience to What Precedes Us and What Being
a Christian Really Means*

To Have Faith Is to Live an Ecclesial Existence

We began our previous chapter by putting Benedict XVI into dialogue with Nietzsche on the question of whether the virtue of faith yields real knowledge, or whether it is rather just a coping mechanism that helps to dull our senses to the reality of a bleak and meaningless world. By way of addressing Nietzsche's criticisms, we explored the issue of how much certitude faith enjoys, we laid out the broad outlines of apophatic theology, we delved into the experience of mystical darkness, and we outlined Benedict's description of faith as a leap, risk, and gamble. Finally, we meditated on Isaiah 7:9 and saw how Benedict exegetes this verse to depict the life of faith as an "experiment" performed with the heart, a journey in which we can only arrive at understanding if we first believe and take a loving stand in the totality of reality.

In this chapter, we now continue our exploration by investigating other themes in Benedict's vision of the Christian of faith which build upon and complete the ones we have just discussed. In particular, we will be focusing upon faith as obedience to that which precedes us, true reality that cannot be seen. We will find that, for Benedict, the Church is the precisely this entity that precedes us and saves us from a "self-made" faith. Wrapping up the chapter, we will revisit the apophatic approach to theology and see how viewing the doctrine of the Trinity from the standpoint of negative theology helps us to truly grasp what being a Christian really means. Finally, we will conclude with some practical ideas for how to run the "experiment of faith" in our own lives.

Faith as Obedience to That Which Precedes Us, True Reality That Cannot Be Seen

Building to the relationship of faith and love articulated in the above sections, we can now do more to specify the precise meaning that Benedict has in mind when speaking of the truth that is demanded by faith and of the sort of behavior that constitutes the heart of faith:

It means affirming that the meaning we do not make but can only receive is already granted to us, so that we have only to take it and entrust ourselves to it.... Christian belief—as we have already said—means opting for the view that what cannot be seen is more real than what can be seen. It is an avowal of the primacy of the invisible as the truly real, which upholds us and hence enables us to face the visible with calm composure—knowing that we are responsible before the invisible as the true ground of all things.[1]

We arrive here at a theme that undergirds Benedict's thinking on virtually every topic related to the virtue of faith, in particular when it comes to divine revelation and the liturgy: the truth is not something we can make for ourselves but rather something that must be received.[2] Even the wisest of human beings eventually run up against

---

1. Ratzinger, *Introduction to Christianity*, 73–74 (emphasis added).
2. For a thought-provoking treatment of authentic worship as something received as op-

intellectual roadblocks in their area of specialization. So much more is this the case when it comes to the faith. We may study theology for decades and still face insoluble problems, contradictions that we just cannot seem to reconcile. For those of us who have ever had this experience, Benedict wisely points out that *"No one can pull himself up out of the bog of uncertainty.... Meaning that is self-made is in the last analysis no meaning. Meaning, that is, the ground on which our existence as a totality can stand and live, cannot be made but only received."*[3]

Framing this whole point in light of what we saw above on the biblical meaning of belief, Benedict summarizes what he thinks it means to say, "I believe":

"Amen" simply says once again in its own way what belief means: the trustful placing of myself on a ground that upholds me, not because I have made it and checked it by my own calculations but, rather, precisely because I have not made it and cannot check it. It expresses the abandonment of oneself to what we can neither make nor need to make, to the ground of the world as meaning, which first of all discloses to me the freedom to make.[4]

Of course, to say that we cannot "check" the faith is not to say that we should not try to verify its truth inasmuch as we are able or that we should blindly accept what we know to be false. To repeat what we discovered above, faith needs truth. For Benedict, true faith is not a blind surrender to the irrational but rather a movement toward the *logos*, toward the truth itself which alone is the ground that enables one to stand firmly over the entire course of life's pilgrimage. All the same, Benedict's words provide a salutary corrective for those of us who tend to think we have figured out more about God and about life than we really have.

---

posed to invented by us, see Ratzinger, *Spirit of the Liturgy*, 1–23. On divine revelation preceding us and even preceding Scripture, see Ramage, *Jesus, Interpreted*, 75–76, along with the Ratzinger sources cited in its footnotes.

3. Ratzinger, *Introduction to Christianity*, 72–73 (emphasis added).
4. Ibid., 75.

The Church, the Community That Precedes Us and Saves Us from a "Self-Made" Faith

We have already seen how Benedict's encyclical on faith sets out to meet the challenge of responding to Nietzsche's criticism that faith is for the weak who cannot handle the cold truth of life without God. Another figure critical of the Church whom Benedict engages is Jean-Jacques Rousseau. The specific complaint lodged by Rousseau that concerns us here comes from a speech by one of the characters in his *Émile*: "So many men between God and me!"[5] Why does the Catholic Church so stubbornly insist on mediating the faith to her faithful? Why not simply let each believer engage God directly? Is God not capable of reaching us without the help of finite human beings? Is not our belief less warranted when we have to receive it through fallible human hands?

It turns out that Rousseau's fault-finding in the Church in reality reveals some of the Christian faith's deepest wisdom, and it is connected with our characterization of faith in the text above as a response to that which precedes us. Reflecting on St. Paul's Letter to the Ephesians, Benedict has this to say to those who, along the lines of Rousseau, think that a mediated faith is an immature faith:

The words "adult faith" in recent decades have formed a widespread slogan. It is often meant in the sense of the attitude of those who no longer listen to the Church and her pastors but autonomously choose what they want to believe and not to believe hence a do-it-yourself faith. And it is presented as a "courageous" form of self-expression against the Magisterium of the Church. In fact, however, no courage is needed for this because one may always be certain of public applause. Rather, courage is needed to adhere to the Church's

---

5. Jean-Jacques Rousseau, *Émile: or, On Education* (New York : Basic Books, 1979), 296; Benedict XVI and Francis, *Lumen Fidei*, §14; The encyclical's translation differs only slightly from that of Bloom that I have reproduced here for the sake of English readers who might wish to follow up with a good translation of this source.

faith, even if this contradicts the "logic" of the contemporary world. This is the non-conformism of faith which Paul calls an "adult faith."[6]

As Benedict says here and elsewhere, a "do-it-yourself faith" wherein one chooses to forego the mediation of the Church and decide for oneself what to believe and not to believe is in reality not that courageous. Indeed, it is not faith at all but rather merely the confirmation of one's prior views and decisions. Nowhere is this stated more succinctly than in an essay penned by Ratzinger on the question of why he is still Catholic despite all the problems he encounters as a believer: "A faith of one's own devising ... a self-made faith would only vouch for, and be able to say, what I already am and know anyway."[7]

These ruminations stayed with Benedict over the course of his career and can even be seen in *Lumen Fidei* where he bluntly asks: how can we be certain, after all these centuries, that our faith puts us in touch with the "real Jesus"? His response follows along the precise lines we have just witnessed, adding, "Were we merely isolated individuals, were our starting point simply our own individual ego seeking in itself the basis of absolutely sure knowledge, a certainty of this sort would be impossible."[8] As an individual, I cannot possibly verify all the truths of the faith for myself. Yet Benedict reminds us that this is not the only way we attain knowledge. Membership in the community of the Church saves us from the superhuman task of personally verifying every last proposition we would accept. Accepting that which precedes us in the form of Holy Mother Church's magisterial authority is an eminently liberating act.

To be sure, faith does not make all of our problems go away, and

---

6. Benedict XVI, First Vespers homily for the closing of the Pauline Year (June 28, 2009). Much of this section has been adapted from my article "Reception of St. Paul," 147–71.

7. Ratzinger, "Why I Am Still in the Church," 147. For a similar formulation which speaks of how "the redeemed ego finds itself again in a greater new ego" and "faith is necessarily what may be called churchly faith," see Joseph Ratzinger, *The Yes of Jesus Christ* (New York: Crossroad Publishing Company, 2005), 36–37.

8. Benedict XVI and Francis, *Lumen Fidei*, §38.

it is no excuse for intellectual laziness. Yet entering into this "ecclesial existence" reveals a beautiful way of life which itself is a testimony to its truth. Like the beauty of the Gothic cathedral's stained-glass windows discussed above, this is the sort of thing that one can only see from the inside.[9] Of course, this is not to say that everything is rosy for the person who pursues the path of faith through integration into the ecclesial "we" of the Church. Benedict enjoins us not to forget that the exodus from our own ego and incorporation into a greater one is a challenging affair. Indeed, entry into the Mystical Body requires something much more radical than the revision of a few opinions and attitudes. It is nothing less than a "death event ... an exchange of the old subject for another" in which our ego "is fitted into a new subject," receiving itself anew in and together with a greater "I."[10]

Like any number of other religions, the Catholic community of faith boasts a global and diverse body of adherents, but there is something peculiar in the "that which precedes us" of the Catholic tradition: the magisterial teaching authority comprised by her pope and bishops. It is precisely this divinely instituted teaching authority—not a majority vote of those who affiliate with the name Catholic—that safeguards the integrity of the faith handed on over the centuries. Says Benedict: "Because it draws its life from faith, theology cannot consider the magisterium of the pope and the bishops in communion with him as something extrinsic, a limitation of its freedom, but rather as one of its internal, constitutive dimensions, for the magisterium ensures our contact with the primordial source and thus provides the certainty of attaining to the word of Christ in all its integrity."[11] A brief case in point reveals the vital importance of the magisterium as asserted by Benedict here. The books that Christians universally rec-

---

9. On the expression "ecclesial existence" and the related "ecclesial form of faith," see ibid., §§22, 36.

10. Joseph Ratzinger, *Nature and Mission of Theology* (San Francisco: Ignatius Press, 1995), 51.

11. Benedict XVI and Francis, *Lumen Fidei*, §36.

ognize as "biblical" are by no means self-evidently so. None of them is stamped "inspired by God." Without the magisterium, Christians would never have had any way of knowing with certitude which books belonged in the Bible or not. Without the magisterium of the Catholic Church, we would never have had the Bible in the first place. This very authority that gave us the Bible centuries ago is the same one which continues to ensure its proper interpretation even today.

Benedict draws a crucial implication of the magisterium's role in reflecting on the meaning of St. Leo the Great's saying, "If faith is not one, then it is not faith":[12] "Since faith is one, it must be professed in all its purity and integrity. Precisely because all the articles of faith are interconnected, to deny one of them, even of those that seem least important, is tantamount to distorting the whole.... To subtract something from the faith is to subtract something from the veracity of communion."[13] As Benedict indicates, people today find it hard to conceive of a unity in truth under the umbrella of the magisterium. As I mentioned in our earlier chapter on freedom, we tend to fear that assent and obedience to the Church will lead to the destruction of our freedom. In reality, however, it turns out that this is precisely the Church's genius, part of the gospel's paradoxical path to freedom. Ironically, if we choose not to follow the path of total obedience to the magisterium, we end up locked within the boundary of our own ego with no faith at all. In other words, what we call "faith" is really just a ratification at every turn of what we had already thought to be true beforehand through the light of our own reason.[14]

---

12. St. Leo the Great, *In Nativitate Domini Sermo*, 4, 6, quoted in Benedict XVI and Francis, *Lumen Fidei*, §47.

13. Benedict XVI and Francis, *Lumen Fidei*, §48. For an interesting critique of this paragraph, see Rausch, *Faith, Hope, and Charity*, 96, wherein the author observes that Benedict and Francis might have nuanced their statement by attending to the hierarchy of truths taught in the Second Vatican Council's *Unitatis Redintegratio* (1964), §11, http://www.vatican.va/archive/hist_councils/ii_vatican_council/documents/vat-ii_decree_19641121_unitatis-redintegratio_en.html.

14. Ratzinger, "Why I Am Still in the Church," 133–53. For a more in-depth discussion

In his *Introduction to Christianity*, Benedict advances this same point by developing his thought that adult Christian faith comes from God in contrast with philosophy which comes from man. Reflecting again on the Pauline dictum that "faith comes from what is heard" (Rom 10:17), Benedict writes: "Faith [in contrast with philosophy] comes to man from outside, and this very fact is fundamental to it. It is—let me repeat—not something thought up by myself; it is something said to me, which hits me as something that has not been thought out and could not be thought out and lays an obligation on me.... Faith cannot and should not be a mere product of reflection."[15] By no means is Benedict here pitting faith against reason or claiming that philosophy is a bankrupt discipline. To the contrary, for Benedict faith heals reason and liberates it from the danger of remaining imprisoned within our own ego, inventing our own version of reality. The task of reason, then, is to ensure a responsible reception of the faith—to assist in the process of making what is received more and more our own by handing ourselves over to the truth.[16]

According to Benedict, the following is the upshot of understanding faith as the reception of that which precedes us: "Because of this, because faith is not something thought up by me but something that comes to me from outside, its word cannot be treated and exchanged as I please; it is always foreordained, always ahead of my thinking. The positivity of what comes toward me from outside myself, opening up to me what I cannot give myself, typifies the process of belief or faith."[17] Here we have a similar point to that which Benedict made above concerning the danger of construing our own self-made faith. It

---

of this reality, including a contribution to the discussion based on John Henry Newman's theology of assent, see my article "Benedict XVI on Freedom in Obedience to the Truth: A Key for the New Evangelization," *Homiletic and Pastoral Review* (May 12, 2014), https://www.hprweb.com/2014/05/benedict-xvi-on-freedom-in-obedience-to-the-truth-a-key-for-the-new-evangelization/.

15. Ratzinger, *Introduction to Christianity*, 92.
16. Ibid.
17. Ibid.

is the attitude of humbly receiving truths that precede us—not that of being the arbiter of whether or not the Church is right or wrong on a given issue—that makes for "adult faith."

Apophaticism, Revisited: The Doctrine of the Trinity as Negative Theology

If there is one area in which the importance of the Catholic Church having a magisterium has been most evident over the ages, it surely has to do with the theology of the Trinity. Father, Son, and Holy Spirit: are these not three gods (tritheism)? Or are the persons not simply ciphers for different aspects of the one God (modalism)? Against these and other such views, the defined doctrine of the Trinity professes that the eternal God is three persons in one nature—"Trinity" thus neither refers to three gods, nor to three aspects of God. If there are infallible, irreversible teachings in Christianity, the doctrine of the Trinity surely numbers among them. And we owe the preservation of this perennial teaching to the same magisterium of the Catholic Church described as so important in the above section. But what does the doctrine of the Trinity actually mean? In this section, operating on the Christian premise that our faith in the Trinity is true, we will be considering the limitations of the doctrine and other such magisterial teachings. In what might be seen as a great paradox, we will find that Benedict acknowledges that the doctrine has its limitations and remains necessary and normative anyway.

A selection from Ratzinger's preface to the second edition of his *Introduction to Christianity* concisely captures what he considers to be the sort of attitude we ought to have in our theologizing about the Trinity. Ratzinger maintains that sincere engagement with the mystical concept of God in Asian religions poses a challenge to Christians, for it forces us to accept that, "The fact that we now acknowledge him to be *triune* does not mean that we have meanwhile learned everything about him. On the contrary, he is only showing us how little we know about him."[18] It is not that Benedict thinks the terms "person" and "nature" are unhelpful or that Asiatic conceptions of the divine are equally truthful to the ways we point to God in the Christian tradition. On the contrary, after considering various other approaches to the nature of God (modalism, monarchism, etc.), Benedict concludes that the Trinity is a consequence of the futility of these very approaches:

> If one surveys the whole question it is possible to observe that *the ecclesiastical doctrine of the Trinity can be justified first and foremost on the negative side, as a demonstration of the hopelessness of all other approaches.* Indeed, perhaps this is all we can really accomplish here. The doctrine of the Trinity would in that case be essentially negative—the only remaining way to reject all attempts to fathom the subject, a sort of cipher for the insolubility of the mystery of God.[19]

The Trinity makes perfect sense to no human on this side of the veil of eternity. It is reasonable, but it also exceeds the capacities of reason. Indeed, the doctrine is a constant reminder that any human attempt to reduce God to the scope of our own comprehension is absurd. In Benedict's own words, "We can only speak rightly about him if we renounce the attempt to comprehend and let him be the uncomprehended."[20] Far from abject resignation, this position is one of deep humility and reverence for the mystery. It is actually a form of divine praise, of admitting that God cannot be confined to the pigeonholes of human knowledge.

Some of Benedict's most illuminating thoughts on the Trinity arise over the course of his survey of the doctrine's gradual and embattled development in the first few centuries of the Church. Describing the history of the dogma of the Trinity as a "graveyard of heresies," he writes: "This character of allusion, in which the concept becomes

---

18. Ibid., 25.
19. Ibid., 171 (emphasis added).
20. Ibid.

a mere hint, and comprehension a mere reaching out toward the incomprehensible, could be accurately mapped by the ecclesiastical formulas themselves and their early history. Every one of the main basic concepts in the doctrine of the Trinity was condemned at one time or another; they were all adopted only after the frustration of a condemnation."[21] Examples of what Benedict is talking about here include the concepts of *prosopon* (person) and *homoousios* (consubstantial with the Father), both of which had been condemned in the third century before being affirmed definitively in the fourth. Benedict is not ashamed of this historical reality. On the contrary, he goes so far as to aver, "The doctrine of the Trinity is only possible as a piece of baffled theology, so to speak."[22] Indeed, Benedict follows Newman in taking a distinctly positive approach to the role of heresy over the ages. Shifting his metaphor dramatically from the graveyard to the cathedral, he explains:

> Every heresy is at the same time the cipher for an abiding truth, a cipher we must now preserve with other simultaneously valid statements, separated from which it produces a false impression. In other words, all these statements are not so much gravestones as the bricks of a cathedral, which are, of course, only useful when they do not remain alone but are inserted into something bigger, just as even the positively accepted formulas are valid only if they are at the same time aware of their own inadequacy.[23]

Returning to his thoughts on the impossibility of complete objectivity outlined above, Benedict points us again to an analogy from the sciences as a way of pointing to the limits of our Trinitarian theology. As the physicist is aware of the tensions in describing light as both particle and wave, all the more so in Trinitarian theology we must learn to hold two realities together (God is three, God is one) while admitting that what we have before us is not a comprehensive explanation but

---

21. Ibid., 171–72.
22. Ibid., 172.
23. Ibid., 172–73.

rather a "a provisional assessment of the whole, which is not accessible to us as a unified whole because of the restrictions implicit in our point of view."[24]

As his ensuing comments make clear, Benedict is not opposed to the prospect of pursuing additional linguistic avenues to signify the mystery of the Trinity. Indeed, on the subject of the dogmatic formula "one being—three persons," he states quite frankly: "In face of this discovery one is not entitled to go too far in the direction of taking these words as the only possible ones and deducing that the matter can be stated only in this way and in no other. That would mean a failure to recognize the negative character of the language of theology, the purely tentative fashion in which it speaks."[25] According to Benedict, that the early Church used these particular Greek words to define the Trinity was providential and yet in a certain sense accidental. It was necessary for the Church to put the mystery of the Trinity into words, not leaving its meaning to individual whim. Even so, the dogmatic formula itself refracts a human element, that is, the categories of late antique philosophy.[26] From a purely intellectual point of view, it must be acknowledged that the arrangement of words "could have been quite different yet, precisely as a form of words, has its own significance—that of uniting people in the community of the confessing word."[27]

While he certainly does not countenance the position of those who reject the received understanding of the Trinity while simultaneously claiming to represent the Catholic tradition, Benedict's theology here does have affinities with some of those who have sought to cast the Trinity in different modes of expression for the purpose of evangelizing non-Western peoples, or with figures such as John Paul II who compared the *Logos* to the Tao. Indeed, it seems that Benedict's words invite such complementary approaches to the mystery: "Only

24. Ibid., 173.
25. Ibid., 181.
26. Ibid., 177.
27. Ibid., 97.

by circling round, by looking and describing from different, apparently contrary angles can we succeed in alluding to the truth, which is never visible to us in its totality."[28]

All that said, Benedict would be the last to conclude from all this that the dogma of the Trinity needs to change or be radically reinterpreted. What is needed is not a reversal of the doctrine but rather a renewal of its understanding drawing on the best of ancient and modern thought within the heart of the Catholic tradition. We need, in other words, to deepen our appreciation of the paradox that the dogma of the Trinity is a normative yet not exhaustive signpost to the inscrutable reality of God.[29] We are not suggesting a pivot toward Taoist epistemology here. In Taoism, "Those who know don't say, and those who say don't know." But in Christianity, we must say, for God has spoken to man and revealed the good news. All the same, we must be willing to bow down in the presence of the unfathomable divine mystery and acknowledge the limits inherent in what we are indeed able to say.

On The Trinity and What Being a Christian Really Means

While Benedict's theology of the Trinity is deeply rooted in the ancient Catholic dogmatic tradition, one of the new things he brings to the theological table is what I call in this book an existential or experiential component. For Benedict, Christianity is not an idea but life, not a system of knowledge but above all a *way*.[30] Like the path of Christianity considered as a whole, the doctrine of the Trinity itself is existential in nature: the Trinity is an affirmation that the highest unity, the primordial heart of reality, lies not in the solitary atom but

---

28. Ibid., 173–74.

29. For an insightful contemporary approach to this paradox, see Myron Bradley Penner, *The End of Apologetics: Christian Witness in a Postmodern Context* (Grand Rapids, Mich.: Baker Academic, 2013), 121–23.

30. Ratzinger, *Introduction to Christianity*, 99–100. On the early Church's self-understanding as "the Way," see Acts 9:2; 19:9–23.

rather in the relation of love. Benedict believes that this truth ought to serve as a reference point for all theology and as an anchor for all Christian thought.[31]

Concretely, to profess the Trinity as an affirmation of love at the heart of reality is to commit oneself to "going beyond oneself freeing the self precisely through being taken into service by something not made or thought out by oneself, the liberation of being taken into service for the whole."[32] It consists in acknowledging that I am not my own, that my I is that of another. In other words, this is the basic content of Christianity, its essence: "Being a Christian means essentially changing over from being for oneself to being for one another."[33] Benedict thus suggests that the phrase "I believe" could be translated "I hand myself over to."[34] To profess faith in Christ, then, "means simply to make love the content of faith" and "to recognize the man who needs me as the Christ in the form in which he comes to meet me here and now."[35] This is no mere trite moralism; it is not a platitudi-

---

31. Ratzinger, *Introduction to Christianity*, 184, 187–88.
32. Ibid., 188.
33. Ibid., 190, 243–44, 252.
34. Ibid., 88.
35. Ibid., 208–9. While his religious convictions may be difficult to pin down, Jordan Peterson's off-the-cuff definition of belief has many resonances with Benedict's conviction that faith is above all a total way of life in which we make love and self-gift the core of all that we do. Describing Catholics as "as sane as people can get," the psychologist writes, "To be able to accept the structure of existence, the suffering that goes along with it and the disappointment and the betrayal, and to nonetheless act properly; to aim at the good with all your heart; to dispense with the malevolence and your desire for destruction and revenge and all of that; and to face things courageously and to tell the truth to speak the truth and to act it out, that's what it means to believe—that's what it means—it doesn't mean to state it, it means to act it out. And, unless you act it out you should be very careful about claiming it. And so, I've never been comfortable saying anything other than I try to act as if God exists because God only knows what you'd be if you truly believed." Jordan Peterson, interview with Dennis Prager at the Prager University summit, May 3–4, 2019, https://www.youtube.com/watch?v=L470-Jxwp6yg. Though also in many ways unconventional, I deeply admire Mark Johnston's way of envisioning sacrifice or self-emptying kenosis as structuring the heart of reality itself, as he emphasizes that we do not need extraordinary gifts or rewards in order to find God since we are already on "holy ground" in the ordinary circumstances of acting out love in daily life

nous suggestion that we behave as nice people. On the contrary, the Christian Creed so understood signifies an all-encompassing movement of human existence out of ourselves and into the other who remains distinct yet inseparable from us. And this movement to which we are called in faith is grounded in the ultimate reality of God himself. As in the Trinity there is an identity of self-gift and being, so we too only find ourselves through a sincere gift of self.[36]

Finally, I would like to emphasize the intimate connection of Benedict's theology of the Trinity discussed in this last section with the rest of his thought laid out in these chapters on faith. We have investigated Benedict's apophaticism, his insistence that faith gives the believer access to reality and not just good feelings. We have also witnessed how he views the faith as a "risk" and "gamble" wherein we hand over our entire being to the unseen God who precedes us. Along the way, we have seen Benedict summon us to the "experiment" of faith, cognizant that the beauty and truth of the Christian faith can only be seen from the inside, in concert with the fullness of the tradition in its community and practices. To sum this point up, we may say with Benedict that the truth of any doctrine we profess can be glimpsed only in the context of a Christian faith fully lived.

Conclusion: Are We Running the "Experiment"?

Returning to the challenge of Nietzsche's critique with which this essay opened, the well-formed Christian is aware that his faith is no guarantee that life will be a picnic. Accordingly, Nietzsche's opposition of truth seeking and happiness simply does not reflect the picture of Christian faith developed by Benedict in these chapters, wherein true faith is understood to require a steadfast commitment to truth

---

even now. For more on this topic, see Johnston, *Saving God: Religion after Idolatry* (Princeton: Princeton University Press, 2009), 174–87.

36. The language in this last point is derived from ibid., 227; and Vatican Council II, *Gaudium et Spes*, §24.

seeking and to living in accord with the demands of the truth no matter the cost. As Henri de Lubac aptly put it in a classic text that had a great impact on Ratzinger's thinking, the real and compelling answer to Nietzsche will come only through living our Christian faith with courageous charity "in face of the world and perhaps against one's own self."[37]

Accordingly, when someone comes to me struggling with their faith—or when I find myself doing so—I ask these questions: Are you striving to live the Christian commitment with all it entails? Are you "living the experiment"? Are you praying? Are you frequenting the sacraments? Are you engaged in the life of the Christian community and of humble service to those in need? Are you actually trying to live the Church's moral teachings in your marriage and family life? If you are suffering, have you attempted to offer up your trials for the good of souls? Ultimately, one can make no guarantee that running the experiment will result in faith—for faith is also a gift—yet refraining from taking the great Christian "gamble" is a reliable strategy if one wishes not to have faith.

37. De Lubac, *Drama of Atheistic Humanism*, 128–29.

6

HOPE (I)

The Church's Vision of Cosmic Transubstantiation and Redemptive Suffering

Secular "Hope" or Theological Virtue?

In the preceding chapters, we have devoted a considerable amount of time probing the question of what it means to live the "experiment" of the virtue of faith in our secular age. But faith, of course, is not the only theological virtue essential to the Christian experience. The virtues of hope and love are inextricably bound up with faith, and it is to consideration of these that we now turn our attention. Later we will treat of charity, while here in the next two chapters we will reflect with Benedict XVI on hope, beginning in this chapter with a discussion of how hope has undergone a transformation in our contemporary secular world and followed by an articulation of what the nature and implications of the authentic theological virtue of hope are—why Christian hope is such a great good. As he did in the case of the virtues of faith and charity, Benedict devoted an entire wide-ranging encyclical to the theme of hope. In combination with his commentary on the Creed in *Introduction to Christianity*, this document will provide us with an apt outline from which to proceed in the present two chapters.

The Relationship of Faith and Hope

The title of the encyclical *Spe Salvi* is drawn from Romans 8:24: "For in this hope we were saved." A beautiful biblical text, this line from St. Paul nevertheless demands that we pose some important questions: What sort of hope—and what level of certainty—are involved here? As Paul says in the second half of the aforementioned verse, "Now hope that is seen is not hope. For who hopes for what he sees?" Accordingly, hope is not the same as knowledge. It is not tantamount to vision, nor does it yield infallible certitude. Indeed, according to Benedict, faith and hope seem to be interchangeable with one another. So what precisely is hope, and how is it to be distinguished from faith?

In the Catholic tradition, the theological virtues of faith, hope, and charity are understood to be inextricably united while nonetheless remaining distinct from one another. The virtue of faith that we have been examining is said to perfect the intellect by enabling us to participate in God's own knowledge of himself, seeing all things through Jesus' eyes. Moreover, Benedict and the other contemporary authors we have surveyed emphasize that faith is not primarily an intellectual matter but rather a holistic way of life best described as trust, faithfulness, or allegiance. As in the case of faith, the object of the theological virtue of hope is *theos*: God himself. However, whereas faith perfects our intellect to know and trust God in this life, the virtue of hope perfects our will to trust in God's promise of eternal life, a promise that we have confidence in being fulfilled not because of our own strength but on account of the unfathomable mercy and grace of God. As are all virtues, hope is a sort of mean between two vicious extremes. While one who truly has a virtue cannot have "too much" of it, there are two very different sins that oppose every virtue, an excess and a defect. In this case, the sin of despair militates against hope on one extreme (as a defect of trust in God's mercy), while the sin of presumption does so on the other (when we excessively trust in our own power, not thinking we need God's mercy).¹

In light of what we just said regarding the distinction between the virtues of faith and hope in the Catholic tradition, it is interesting that the first major heading of Benedict's encyclical reads "Faith Is Hope." The basis for this statement is Hebrews 11:1, which reads in the RSV, "Faith is the assurance [ὑπόστασις] of things hoped for; the conviction of things not seen." Benedict takes issue with modern translators who render the word *hypostasis* here as "assurance." Instead, he thinks that the Vulgate gets it right when it translates the verse *Est autem fides sperandarum substantia rerum, argumentum non apparentium*. The Latin text understands faith to be the "substance" (*substantia*) of things hoped for, the "proof" (*argumentum*) of things not seen. *Substantia*, insists Benedict, does a better job of rendering the Greek ὑπόστασις than does the English "assurance" or the German *feststehen* ("standing firm"). That faith is the *substantia* of things hoped for implies the presence of a profound relationship—or, as Benedict has it, even identity—between faith and hope. That said, I do not think that the pontiff is rejecting the traditional distinction between the two, just describing it from another angle. His precise understanding of their relationship is as follows: "Through faith, in a tentative way, or as we might say 'in embryo'—and thus according to the 'substance'—there are already present in us the things that are hoped for: the whole, true life."² Benedict is saying that the believer enjoys even now a share in the fullness of divine truth and life for which he hopes, a reality that nevertheless will be manifest fully only on the other side of this vale of tears after the "embryo" of our faith has grown to maturity. As he proceeds to add, "Faith is not merely a personal reaching out towards things to come.... It gives us even now something of the reality we are waiting for, and this present reality constitutes for us a 'proof' of the things that are still unseen."³

---

1. This definition of hope is drawn largely from *Catechism of the Catholic Church*, §1817.
2. Benedict XVI, *Spe Salvi*, §7.
3. Ibid. For further discussion of Heb 11:1 in the thought of Benedict XVI and Thomas Aquinas, see Ramage, *Dark Passages of the Bible*, 97–100.

Hope's Fulfillment: Eternal Life as Divine Union and Cosmic Transubstantiation

If faith gives believers even now a participation in the reality that they hope to possess in eternity, the next logical question to ask concerns what the nature of this life really is. Since we tend to appreciate a thing better by way of contrast with its rivals, it will be helpful to consider briefly the alternative versions of hope offered by our culture—to make clear what the object of our hope is *not*. For the Christian, it goes without saying that it is not something that can be achieved in this present world, but Benedict sees two major ways in which our society strives to accomplish this impossible task. First, many people often think that scientific advancements will cure all our ills. This "faith in progress," says Benedict, is a core aspect of a desacralized worldview—whose roots he traces back to Francis Bacon—which seeks the kingdom on earth, a kingdom not of God but of man. Important as science is and notwithstanding the innumerable contributions it has made to the betterment of life on earth, still Benedict takes great pains to emphasize that science is never going to be able to usher in a kingdom of peace and perfection on this side of the vale of tears. Science is not capable of redeeming man—only love is.[4]

Second, people today often attempt to make up for the lack of

---

4. Benedict XVI, *Spe Salvi*, §§16–19, 26. As I am following the main lines of Benedict's thought on hope, I do not have an extensive treatment of the "kingdom of God" in this chapter. However, there are places in Benedict's corpus worth consulting on this topic. See for example his *From the Baptism in the Jordan to the Transfiguration*, 46–63; and *Holy Week*, 24–52. For another helpful, contemporary, scholarly discussion of the kingdom, see Matthew Bates, *Salvation by Allegiance Alone: Rethinking Faith, Works, and the Gospel of Jesus the King* (Grand Rapids, Mich.: Baker Academic, 2017), 47–76; and Dale Allison, *Night Comes: Death, Imagination, and the Last Things* (Grand Rapids, Mich.: Eerdmans, 2016), 126. Against what he calls N. T. Wright's "geocentric" kingdom eschatology, Allison asks the important question of why some Christians feel compelled to share the Bible's presuppositions that the kingdom of God will be on this earth and that heaven is over our heads when its authors had no idea of the size and scope of the universe. For a thoughtful critique of *Spe Salvi* and explanation of why it lacks a robust theology of the kingdom—a critique that draws on N. T. Wright's own issues with Benedict's approach—see Rausch, *Faith, Hope, and Charity*, 74, 121–24, 128.

true hope that only God can provide by substituting politics for religion. According to Benedict, the central historical figure who brought about this transformation was Karl Marx. The pope links together the projects of Bacon and Marx, describing the latter's as a "scientifically conceived politics that recognizes the structure of history and society and thus points out the road towards revolution, towards all-encompassing change."[5] The common denominator between these two wrongheaded approaches to hope is that they both limit their horizon to this world. It is not that science and politics are irrelevant or that we ought not to be actively striving to improve the present human condition. As is frequently the case in heresies, the problem here is not so much in what is affirmed as in what is denied. Marx's central error was his materialism—the delusion that man can live by bread alone. Good social structures indeed help, but Benedict says that they are not enough, arguing that true progress cannot occur absent moral growth. And if the human reason that brings about this progress is to become fully human, it needs the healing and transformation that can only come when integrated with the saving power of faith. In his characteristically forthright manner, Benedict writes, "Let us put it very simply: man needs God, otherwise he remains without hope."[6]

If our hope cannot be fulfilled on this side of eternity, then it is also important to disabuse ourselves of one last would-be candidate for Christian hope. Eternal life is not, as some cultures of the past and some people today still conceive of it, merely a greatly prolonged continuation of our present mode of existence on the other side of the veil of time. The human person has an innate desire for the infinite. We want not just longer life but life itself. Or, as St. Augustine has it, "Our hearts are restless until they rest in You."[7] At the same time, we do not

---

5. Benedict XVI, *Spe Salvi*, §20.
6. Ibid., §§21–23; Benedict XVI, *Deus Caritas Est*, §28. On the need for reason to be integrated with the saving forces of faith, see Benedict XVI, "Faith, Reason, and the University: Memories and Reflections," speech to the representatives of science at Aula Magna of the University of Regensburg (September 12, 2006).
7. Augustine, *Confessions*, trans. J. G. Pilkington, ed. Philip Schaff, Nicene and Post-Nicene

quite know the thing toward which our hope drives us. According to Benedict, the words "eternal life" are intended to give a name to this "known unknown."[8] Inevitably, he admits that the expression is "inadequate" and "creates confusion," yet by no means does this lead Benedict to reject its usage. We have no choice but to give the object of our hope some linguistic referent, even if it comes with the risk of being misconstrued as an unending succession of days on the calendar.

Shifting our conception away from the temporal, Benedict suggests that we think instead of eternal life as "the supreme moment of satisfaction, in which totality embraces us and we embrace totality." Adopting language reminiscent of some of the greatest mystics of Church history, the pontiff makes this comparison:

It would be like plunging into the ocean of infinite love, a moment in which time—the before and after—no longer exists. We can only attempt to grasp the idea that such a moment is life in the full sense, a plunging ever anew into the vastness of being, in which we are simply overwhelmed with joy.... We must think along these lines if we want to understand the object of Christian hope, to understand what it is that our faith, our being with Christ, leads us to expect.[9]

The Christian spiritual tradition is replete with similar images of eternal life. For instance, we may consider Francis de Sales's classic *Treatise on the Love of God*. In this text, the saint speaks of the soul's goal of being "liquefied" in God, transformed beyond the limits of its natural form of existence as it becomes wholly mingled with, absorbed, and engulfed in God.[10] Or, to take a more recent example, C. S. Lewis's masterpiece essay "The Weight of Glory" casts our heavenly union

---

Fathers, 1st ser., 1 (Buffalo, N.Y.: Christian Literature Publishing Co., 1887), bk. 1, chap. 1, §1, http://www.newadvent.org/fathers/110101.htm.

8. Benedict XVI, *Spe Salvi*, §12.
9. Ibid.
10. Francis de Sales, *Treatise on the Love of God* (New York: Benziger Brothers, 1884), 273–75.

in spousal terms: "We do not want merely to *see* beauty.... We want something else which can hardly be put into words—to be united with the beauty we see, to pass into it, to receive it into ourselves, to bathe in it, to become part of it."[11] As for his part, Benedict himself speaks of believers' Eucharistic union with Christ in this life in spousal terms: "In the sacrament, which is an act of love, two subjects are fused in such a way as to overcome their separation and to be made one.... This means that Christ and the Church are one body in the sense in which man and woman are one flesh."[12]

An important feature of this mystical divine union is that it is not just between us and God: it is the glorious union and transformation *of all creation* in God. St. Paul tells us that the whole creation is "groaning in travail" with us as we await our adoption as sons and daughters (Rom 8:19–23). Cast in slightly different terms, St. John envisions "a new heaven and a new earth" to be revealed in the fullness of time (Rv 21:1). With their exalted expectations for the future of the created world, these sacred authors share with one another the profound conviction that the world we live in is fundamentally good and destined to share with us in glory. Appropriating Karl's Rahner's expression, Ratzinger speaks of this future state as a "pan-cosmic existence" which death alone opens up, leading to "universal exchange and openness, and so to the overcoming of all alienation." Making his own the words of St. Paul, Ratzinger then adds, "Only where creation achieves such unity can it be true that God is 'all in all.'"[13]

---

11. C. S. Lewis, "The Weight of Glory," in *The Weight of Glory and Other Addresses* (San Francisco: HarperSanFrancisco, 2001), 42.

12. Ratzinger, *Called to Communion*, 39.

13. Ratzinger, *Eschatology: Death and Eternal Life* (Washington, DC: The Catholic University of America Press, 1988), 192; Eph 1:23; Col 1:20. For the background to this text, see Karl Rahner, *On the Theology of Death* (New York: Herder and Herder, 1961); and Karl Rahner, *Nature and Grace* (New York: Sheed and Ward, 1964), 41. For Rahner, as for Ratzinger, this process of cosmic divinization and insertion into the life of the Trinity is not something that will happen automatically. In contrast with earlier stages of evolution, this final movement can only occur through the free and complete offering of ourselves and of all creation as a gift to God.

In one of his rare published writings as emeritus pontiff, Benedict described this unity as taking place when all of creation is subsumed into God's master narrative of love: "If we really wanted to summarize very briefly the content of the Faith as laid down in the Bible, we might do so by saying that the Lord has initiated a narrative of love with us and wants to *subsume all creation* in it. The counterforce against evil, which threatens us and the whole world, can ultimately only consist in our entering into this love."[14] Benedict has gone so far as to speak of this transformative dynamic as one of *transubstantiation*. In yet another post-retirement work, this time a brief address given on the sixty-fifth anniversary of his priestly ordination, the emeritus pontiff spoke these words:

> The cross, suffering, all that is wrong with the world: he transformed all this into "thanks" and therefore into a "blessing." Hence he fundamentally transubstantiated life and the world [*fondamentalmente ha transustanziato la vita e il mondo*].... Finally, we wish to insert ourselves into the "thanks" of the Lord, and thus truly receive the newness of life and contribute to the "transubstantiation" of the world [*transustanziazione del mondo*] so that it might not be a place of death, but of life: a world in which love has conquered death.[15]

In this short paragraph, Benedict speaks of the transubstantiation of the world as a reality that has already begun and yet which continues to grow by means of our own contribution as we insert ourselves into Christ's saving work as co-redeemers.

Given the overt sacramental language deployed by Benedict to describe the transformation of our world into Christological fullness, we might expect the pope to explicitly discuss the Eucharist somehow in

---

14. Benedict XVI, "The Church and the Scandal of Sexual Abuse," Catholic News Agency, April 10, 2019 (emphasis added), https://www.catholicnewsagency.com/news/full-text-of-benedict-xvi-the-church-and-the-scandal-of-sexual-abuse-59639.

15. Benedict XVI, address at the commemoration of the 65th anniversary of the priestly ordination of Pope Emeritus Benedict XVI (June 28, 2016), https://w2.vatican.va/content/francesco/en/speeches/2016/june/documents/papa-francesco_20160628_65-ordinazione-sacerdotale-benedetto-xvi.html.

this connection. Indeed, this is precisely what he does on multiple occasions. Indebted to Fr. Pierre Teilhard de Chardin whom he frequently references, for Benedict "the very goal of worship and of creation as a whole are one and the same—divinization."[16] As God draws his creation ever closer to himself through a series of ontological or evolutionary "leaps," Benedict writes that the transubstantiated host becomes "the anticipation of the transformation and divinization of matter in the Christological fullness" which in turn "provides the movement of the cosmos with its direction; it anticipates its goal and at the same time urges it on."[17] Again, he has written that man's divinization through Eucharistic communion is part of his plan for "the *resubstantiation* of the whole of earthly reality."[18] As a final illustration of this point, consider this homily which Benedict gave on the feast of Corpus Christi:

> This little piece of white Host, this bread of the poor, appears to us as a synthesis of creation. In this way we begin to understand why the Lord chooses this piece of bread to represent him. Creation, with all of its gifts, aspires above and beyond itself to something even greater. Over and above the synthesis of its own forces, above and beyond the synthesis also of nature and of spirit that, *in some way, we detect in the piece of bread, creation is projected towards divinization*, toward the holy wedding feast, toward unification with the Creator himself.[19]

---

16. Ratzinger, *Spirit of the Liturgy*, 28. There is an abundance of biblical, patristic, and liturgical backing for Ratzinger's theology of divinization. To name just a handful of germane biblical texts, see 2 Pt 1:3–4; 1 Jn 3:1–3; Eph 3:19; 1 Cor 15:28. My favorite primary source for the patristic view can be found in St. Maximus the Confessor, *On the Cosmic Mystery of Jesus Christ* (Crestwood, NY: St. Vladimir's Seminary Press, 2003), 45–75. For an outstanding work summarizing St. Augustine's theology of divinization, see David Meconi, SJ, *The One Christ: St. Augustine's Theology of Deification* (Washington, D.C.: The Catholic University of America Press, 2013). To mention just one (though perhaps the most evocative) liturgical illustration of divinization, one would do well to consider the words of the offertory rite, uttered *sotto voce* while the priest pours water into the chalice: "By the mystery of this water and wine may we come to share in the divinity of Christ who humbled himself to share in our humanity."

17. Ratzinger, *Spirit of the Liturgy*. 29.

18. Joseph Ratzinger, *Pilgrim Fellowship of Faith* (San Francisco: Ignatius Press, 2005), 78; see also 118.

19. Benedict XVI, homily for the Mass of Corpus Christi (June 15, 2006), emphasis add-

In passages such as these, we detect a common trope not only in the thought of Joseph Ratzinger/Benedict XVI, but also in his successor. For Pope Francis, caring for the earth does not mean leaving it alone and never touching it. On the contrary, Francis teaches us that developing the created world in a prudent way is the best way of caring for it. In so doing, we become instruments in the hands of God to bring out the Christological potential which he himself has inscribed in all things. In particular, we are called to work for the health and salvation of our weakest brothers and sisters, becoming with them a "universal subject" on the path to union with God.[20] We will return to this concept more in the next chapter when we treat of charity and its implications for our relationship with the environment.

Redemptive Suffering as the Path to Divinization

Christianity's cosmic vision of divinization that we have just sketched is nevertheless liable to a serious misconception. When people start to ponder what it means to become divine, it is tempting to think of this as something that occurs in the clouds, as it were, a dynamic that involves mystical visions, locutions, overwhelmingly positive emotions, and supreme certitude. While these things are not intrinsically bad, the truth is that they are not what divinization is about. If humanity is called to be mingled with divinity, then it is worth observing that Benedict considers the true measure of man's humanity-divinity to consist in our relationship with suffering and the

---

ed. For some other beautiful examples of the pontiff's appropriation of Teilhard de Chardin's cosmic liturgy wherein the whole of creation becomes a living host, see Benedict XVI, Homily (July 24, 2009); Benedict XVI, homily for the Easter Vigil (April 15, 2006); Ratzinger, *Introduction to Christianity*, 234–45; and Ratzinger, *Eschatology* (1988), 93. Notably, Pope Francis cites this very text as part of his ecological vision in *Laudato Si'* (2015), §236, http://w2.vatican.va/content/francesco/en/encyclicals/documents/papa-francesco_20150524_enciclica-laudato-si.html.

20. Francis, *Laudato Si'*, §124; Benedict XVI, *Spe Salvi*, §14.

sufferer.[21] That is to say, we are more human—and therefore more divine—to the extent that we enter into the suffering of this world, take it upon ourselves, and suffuse it with grace. Our response to this call is expressed beautifully in the virtuous deeds of *con-solation* (being with others in their solitude so that it ceases to be solitude) and *com-passion* (suffering with the other, making their needs your own). I think these are the sort of actions that the Second Vatican Council had in mind when it taught that the laity, in offering the Lord's body along with their own spiritual sacrifices, "consecrate the world itself to God."[22]

Benedict suggests a very practical way that all of us can implement the practice of spiritual sacrifice in our daily lives. On a rather melancholic note, he recalls that "there used to be a form of devotion—perhaps less practiced today but quite widespread not long ago—that included the idea of 'offering up' the minor daily hardships that continually strike at us like irritating 'jabs,' thereby giving them a meaning." While acknowledging that the practice of self-mortification has at times been carried out in unhelpfully exaggerated ways, the devotion nonetheless remains essential to the spiritual life. Benedict suggests that Christians who wish to navigate faith in our secularized world need to recover the habit of inserting our small sufferings into Christ's great sacrifice "so that they somehow became part of the treasury of compassion so greatly needed by the human race."[23]

The practice of self-mortification, an important part of the Church's profound spirituality of redemptive suffering, has deep biblical roots. As we discussed earlier in this book, human beings are called

---

21. Benedict XVI, *Spe Salvi*, §§38–39. Benedict's words closely echo those of his predecessor: "A society will be judged on the basis of how it treats its weakest members; and among the most vulnerable are surely the unborn and the dying." John Paul II, address to the ambassador of New Zealand to the Holy See (May 25, 2000), http://w2.vatican.va/content/john-paul-ii/en/speeches/2000/apr-jun/documents/hf_jp-ii_spe_20000525_ambassador-new-zealand.html.

22. Vatican Council II, *Lumen Gentium*, §34; 1 Pet 2:5.

23. Benedict XVI, *Spe Salvi*, §40.

to be made God (divinized or deified), but we can only do so to the extent that we imitate the God who became man in his life and in his death. Speaking of his own impending passion and also of our own spiritual lives, Jesus said, "Truly, truly, I say to you, unless a grain of wheat falls into the earth and dies, it remains alone; but if it dies, it bears much fruit" (Jn 12:24). Building on this same agricultural analogy, St. Paul says that our present, weak, perishable, physical bodies must undergo transformation through death so as to become powerful, glorious, imperishable, spiritual bodies (1 Cor 15:35–50). But this can only happen, Paul insists, if we are willing to suffer with Christ, humbling ourselves and becoming obedient unto death, even death on a cross (Rom 6:4–11; Phil 2:5–11).

At various points throughout history, Christians have been—and still are being called even today—to shed their blood as Christ did. Most of the time, though, the contemporary Christian's crucifixion takes a more mundane form. It consists in persevering virtuously day by day, repenting of our many failures and repeatedly getting back up again with God's grace. To adopt a slightly different agricultural metaphor, our daily redemptive suffering is a sort of spiritual pruning. As Jesus himself teaches in John's gospel, he is the vine, we the branches. If we bear fruit, he prunes us in order that we may bear even more in the future (Jn 15:2). Seen from this perspective, suffering is not a curse but rather one of God's greatest gifts. It is not a punishment for sin, but a means for greater union with Christ. Even more, suffering ennobles our nature by making us co-redeemers with Christ. In one of my favorite verses of the Bible, Paul writes, "I rejoice in my sufferings for your sake, and in my flesh I complete what is lacking in Christ's afflictions for the sake of his body, that is, the Church" (Col 1:24). Though Paul is aware that God does not *need* us absolutely speaking, he insists that God has nonetheless *chosen* to use us as his instruments to bring about his salvation for others. I can think of nothing that more greatly extols and ennobles our human nature than the Church's teaching that we are co-redeemers with God in the flesh precisely through our sufferings. I find that very grandeur of this claim and its resonance with my deepest aspirations make it a veritable *apologia* for the proposition upon which it is predicated, that is, the resurrection. However, as I insist throughout this book, the truth of the claim can only been seen in its doing—by cultivating the practice of redemptive suffering and embracing the crosses bestowed upon us.

Holy Saturday: Christ's Descent into Hell

In the first part of this chapter, we have considered hope as a theological virtue: its relationship with faith, contemporary worldviews that seek falsely to mimic it, its fulfillment through divine union and cosmic transubstantiation, and redemptive suffering as the privileged path to this end. In the next, meanwhile, we will concentrate on what it is that makes hope possible for the Christian: the saving mysteries of Christ's life, particularly the articles of the Creed dealing with his resurrection, ascension, and return in glory to judge the living and the dead. First, however, we will round out this chapter by exploring Benedict's understanding of Christ's descent into hell, an article of the Creed that is deeply connected with the theme of suffering that we have just been discussing.

Joseph Ratzinger indulged in a sustained commentary on the enigma of Holy Saturday on a number of occasions. In a way that dovetails perfectly with the running theme of this book, he begins each of his two lengthier treatments of it on a Nietzschean note, calling the somber moment of Holy Saturday "the day of the hiddenness of God" and even "the day of the death of God."[24] Together with the profession of Jesus' birth from the Virgin Mary, Ratzinger says of Jesus' descent into hell on Holy Saturday that "possibly no article of the Creed is so far from present-day attitudes of mind as this one." Of all the events of Christ's life, continues Ratzinger, this one seems to call most of all

---

24. Joseph Ratzinger, *The Sabbath of History* (Washington DC: William G. Congdon Foundation, 2000), 38; Ratzinger, *Introduction to Christianity*, 293.

for demythologization, an operation that "looks devoid of danger and unlikely to provoke opposition."[25]

Even so, our great thinker is not content simply with discarding the venerable belief that Christ preached to the spirits in the prison of Hades on Holy Saturday (1 Pt 3:18–20). As he typically does, Ratzinger instead turns our attention to the question of what—amidst the plethora of mythological elements that surround this event—constitutes its essence that withstands the test of all time. In this regard, I think that Ratzinger's theology of the last things aligns closely with that of Dale Allison. Allison does not think that we can divine much about the nature of the afterlife, but he does not thereby consider eschatology to be rendered pointless. The question, says Allison, is whether or not we think that the mythological imagination is an apt vehicle for conveying truth. I hold with Allison and Ratzinger that it is indeed. In our present day culture, many atheists and Christians alike equate "myth" with "falsehood," whereas the literary greats Lewis, Tolkien, and Chesterton see myth as a real though unfocused glimpse at divine truth, the endeavor to reach God by means of the symbolic imagination.[26]

So what is the content of the "myth" of Christ's descent into hell? Reflecting on Hans Urs von Balthasar's famous assertion that Christ participated in the solitude of hell "in the deepest sense of the word" on Holy Saturday, Ratzinger replies that he cannot endorse his friend's position wholeheartedly, and yet he does think that Balthasar is onto

---

25. Ratzinger, *Introduction to Christianity*, 293.
26. Allison, *Night Comes*, 81–84. Allison's discussion of myth spans the breadth of this book. In addition to the pages I have mentioned, also worth considering is his discussion of myth in relation to Michelangelo's *Last Judgment* in ibid., 61. His point is not to reject myth as such, but rather to find "a helpful as opposed to an unhelpful myth." On the mythology of the Bible, see C. S. Lewis, *Miracles, a Preliminary Study* (New York: Macmillan, 1978), 146; Lewis, "Is Theology Poetry?" in *The Weight of Glory*, 129; J. R. R. Tolkien, Verlyn Flieger, and Douglas A. Anderson, *Tolkien on Fairy-Stories* (London: HarperCollins, 2014); and G. K. Chesterton's chapter "Man and Mythologies" in *The Everlasting Man*, which can be found, among other places, in *The Collected Works of G. K. Chesterton*, vol. 2 (San Francisco: Ignatius Press, 1986), 233–47.

something profound that merits being salvaged. The solution that occurred to Ratzinger, capturing the "essential point of Balthasar's thesis," is penned in one place as follows:

> Jesus died. He "descended" into the mysterious depths death leads to. He went to the ultimate solitude where no one can accompany us, for "being dead" is above all loss of communication. It is isolation where love does not penetrate. And in this sense Christ descended "into hell" whose essence is precisely the loss of love, being cut off from God and man. But, however, wherever he goes, "hell" ceases to be hell, because he himself was life and love, because he is the bridge which connects man and God and thereby also connects men among themselves. And thus the descent is at the same time also transformation. The final solitude no longer exists—except for the one who wants it, who rejects love from within and from its foundation, because he seeks only himself, wants to be from and for himself.[27]

Clearly, the "descent" Ratzinger has in mind here is not of the physical variety. Instead, it is a metaphorical way of describing a real event: Christ's complete identification with us mortals in our death and abandonment. According to Ratzinger, hell does not denote a place but rather the experience of the complete loss of love. But when Christ himself passes through the utter darkness of this experience, he transforms it in love. Wherever he goes, hell thus ceases to be hell: it cannot be hell because love himself is there in person.

Ratzinger writes similarly in his other treatment of the descent into hell, this time beginning with his own existentialist definition of what "hell" means:

> We can now define exactly what this word means: it denotes a loneliness that the word love can no longer penetrate and that therefore indicates the exposed nature of existence in itself.... In truth—one thing is certain: there exists a night into whose solitude no voice reaches; there is a door through which we can only walk alone—the door of death. In the last analysis all the fear in the

---

27. Ratzinger, *Sabbath of History*, 21. For Hans Urs von Balthasar's position, see his *Mysterium Paschale* (San Francisco: Ignatius Press, 2012).

world is fear of this loneliness. From this point of view, it is possible to understand why the Old Testament has only one word for hell and death, the word *Sheol*; it regards them as ultimately identical. Death is absolute loneliness. But the loneliness into which love can no longer advance is—hell.

This brings us back to our starting point, the article of the Creed that speaks of the descent into hell. This article thus asserts that Christ strode through the gate of our final loneliness, that in his Passion he went down into the abyss of our abandonment. Where no voice can reach us any longer, there is he. Hell is thereby overcome, or, to be more accurate, death, which was previously hell, is hell no longer. Neither is the same any longer because there is life in the midst of death, because love dwells in it. Now only deliberate self-enclosure is hell or, as the Bible calls it, the second death (Rv 20:14, for example). But death is no longer the path into icy solitude; the gates of *Sheol* have been opened. From this angle, I think, one can understand the images—which at first sight look so mythological—of the Fathers, who speak of fetching up the dead, of the opening of the gates.[28]

As in the previous selection, hell is the state of loneliness, the complete loss of love. But since love himself descends into our loneliness and dwells in it, he empties it of its grip upon us—or, to use the old expression, he "harrows" it. This is an incredibly profound and moving statement of hope that has provided me with untold consolation in my own life: the Lord of love himself has completely identified with my own loneliness, my own suffering and abandonment. In so doing, he has transformed it from an experience of desolation and loss into the greatest of goods—a foretaste in eternal life, an anticipatory "resurrection" that is made possible only by first bearing a cross in union with him who carried it before us.

---

28. Ratzinger, *Introduction to Christianity*, 300–301. Also worth pondering in this regard are Ratzinger's thoughts on the bizarre passage (only) in Matthew's gospel where at the death of Jesus tombs opened and the bodies of the saints were raised (Mt 27: 52): "The apparently mythical passage in St. Matthew's Gospel becomes comprehensible, too.... The door of death stands open since life—love—has dwelt in death." Ibid. For further commentary on this text, see Ramage, *Jesus, Interpreted*, 171–72. On *Sheol* and development of doctrine on the afterlife in Judaism, see Ramage, *Dark Passages of the Bible*, 196–273.

Reflecting on this mystery during his pontificate, Benedict continued to describe descent into Hell in existential terms, this time tightly connecting Christ's descent into hell with his entering into the sin of others. Unlike Dante, however, Jesus does not enter the inferno as a spectator. On the contrary, the emeritus pontiff continues, "he goes down in the role of one whose suffering—with—others is a transforming suffering that turns the underworld around, knocking down and flinging open the gates of the abyss." He then connects this mystery with Jesus' baptism and with our own baptism which is "the gift of participation in Jesus' world-transforming struggle in the conversion of life that took place in his descent and ascent."[29]

As we witness in all of the above treatments of Holy Saturday, it is characteristic of Ratzinger's biblical exegesis that he is simply not afraid to admit that our tradition has grown immensely over the ages in its penetration of the truth of divine revelation. The descent into hell offers a particularly stunning illustration of exactly this dynamic. Ratzinger sees no reason to continue maintaining the ancient mythological belief that hell (Hebrew *Sheol*, Greek *Hades*) was geographically underground. Since a physical descent of Christ into the underworld contradicts what we know in light of science, he reasons correctly that the question of where Christ's body was on Holy Saturday cannot be the essential point of the ancient tradition. Its principal affirmation, its inspired message, must therefore lie somewhere else. A thinker whose approach is deeply existentialist, Ratzinger looks not to the physical but rather the experiential level for the core of this event.

What is more, Ratzinger's career-long exegetical enterprise demonstrates that he is not concerned merely with the experience of the first Christians or even with human experience in general. He always has an eye to how the events of the gospel might be relevant *for us*, how they might be playing out *today*. It is in this very spirit that he transposes the mystery of Holy Saturday into our present cultural

---

29. Benedict XVI, *From the Baptism in the Jordan to the Transfiguration*, 20.

situation with a pointed rhetorical question: "Holy Saturday, the day of the burial of God—is that not in an uncanny way our day? Does our century not begin to become one large Holy Saturday, a day of God's absence, a day an icy emptiness grows even in the hearts of the disciples ... so that they sink into hopelessness, failing to notice that the one thought to be dead is in their midst?"[30] As we have said throughout this book, our present cultural context can be described as a "postmodern" or "secular" age. We live in a time when age-old truths once considered self-evident are no longer taken for granted. Ours is a time when Christianity stands as merely one among many disparate lifestyle choices, with no immediately obvious warrant for being considered superior to its competitors. Moreover, even in the hearts of the disciples—our hearts—we often find an icy emptiness and hopelessness. This observation once again prompts Ratzinger to recall Nietzsche's famous words and direct them to our current state:

> Holy Saturday is the day of the "death of God," the day that expresses the unparalleled experience of our age, anticipating the fact that God is simply absent, that the grave hides him, that he no longer awakes, no longer speaks, so that one no longer needs to gainsay him but can simply overlook him. "God is dead and we have killed him." This saying of Nietzsche's ... expresses the content of Holy Saturday, "descended into hell."[31]

In the same vein but with a slightly different emphasis, Ratzinger again describes our present context with Nietzsche's famous words:

> God is dead and we have killed him.... We killed him enclosing him in the shell of antiquated modes of thinking, by banishing him to a piety void of reality, which becomes more and more a devotional slogan or archaeological curiosity. We killed him through the ambiguity of our lives that obscured him. After all, what could make God more questionable in this world than the questionability of the faith and love of his faithful?[32]

---

30. Ratzinger, *Sabbath of History*, 38.
31. Ratzinger, *Introduction to Christianity*, 294.
32. Ratzinger, *Sabbath of History*, 39.

If the greatest *apologia* for the Church is the beauty and saints she has produced, then the harrowing corollary of this truth is that the strongest argument against the Church is the absence of the theological virtues, for which outsiders look in vain to find among believers— among us. This, for Benedict, is ultimately what it means for Nietzsche to say that God is dead, and that *we* have killed him.

Tragic as the death of God was two thousand years ago, and tragic as his continued death is in our own age, we have to remember that the grief of Holy Saturday was only a penultimate reality. For, the Christian faith tells us that Holy Saturday's descent into hell is followed by Easter Sunday, the day of resurrection and first day of a new and definitive creation. Here we come to the heart of the Christian faith, the great paradox at the heart of reality that is disclosed fully only through the death and resurrection of Jesus. Benedict puts it in this way:

> The darkest mystery of faith is simultaneously the brightest sign of a hope that is without limits. And one thing further: only through the failure of Good Friday, only through the deathly stillness of Holy Saturday could the disciples be led to grasp who Jesus really was and what his mission truly meant.... Their image that they had formed of God, into which they tried to force him, had to be destroyed so that they could see heaven above the rubble of the destroyed house. We needed the darkness of God, the silence of God, in order to experience the chasm of his greatness and the abyss of our nothingness.[33]

---

33. Ibid., 39–40. For his connection of Holy Saturday with Nietzsche's diagnosis of the death of God in our modern age, Ratzinger is indebted again to Henri de Lubac. As one who frequently finds himself moved to religious conviction by means of art, Ratzinger especially appreciates de Lubac's association of a shattering aesthetic experience had by Dostoevsky with Nietzsche's philosophy of the death of God. Referred to by Benedict/Ratzinger on at least two separate occasions, the event in question involved Dostoevsky breaking down before Hans Holbein's painting of the deceased Christ lying in the tomb, a historical moment later enshrined in narrative by the author with the haunting observation, "Looking at that painting might cause one to lose his faith." Ratzinger refers to this at the outset of his *Sabbath of History*, 20; and, as pontiff, in his co-authored encyclical *Lumen Fidei*, §16. For de Lubac's treatment of the episode, see his *Drama of Atheist Humanism*, 287–89.

Far from a disaster, Christianity professes that the tragic death of God on Good Friday and his absence on Holy Saturday were essential for man's salvation. That Christ had to suffer in order to ransom us from our sins is something Christians have always held (as we are told already in Lk 24:26, for example), but Ratzinger's emphasis here is new. While not denying traditional explanations of why God died for man's sins, Ratzinger's perspective on the mystery is phenomenological, that is to say, rooted in how we as human beings experience God and how we come to know him. Seen in this light, the darkness of Holy Saturday was not a necessary experience on God's side. Rather, it was necessary *for us*: to destroy the idol we had made of God by trying to force him into our own categories of thinking. This it did for the disciples two millennia ago, and it still does for Christians today—perhaps especially today. Christian belief in our secular age requires a real crucifixion of the self with its instinctual desires, secularist assumptions, and cultural realities pulling us in a thousand different directions. The reality of God and truth of the Church are far from self-evident in our day. Often it seems that God is dead, but if we are willing to accompany Christ all the way through the darkness of Holy Saturday, then—and only then—we will come to know that God's silence is not the end of the story. In the lived experience of these saving mysteries, we come to know that on the other side of the Cross's catastrophe lies what, following Tolkien's neologism, we may call the "eucatastrophe" of resurrection.

Conclusion

The goal of this chapter has been the same as previous chapters: to offer a rival story to that of the secularist, to paint a picture of the authentic teachings and experience of the Christian faith that enable the believer to navigate life intelligently in our secularized world. In particular, so far we have discussed how hope has undergone a transformation in our contemporary secular world and followed up with an articulation of what the nature and implications of the authentic theological virtue of hope are—why Christian hope is such a great good. Along the way, one of the most important themes we meditated upon was the connection of hope with redemptive suffering, especially understood in light of Christ's descent into hell. Having reflected on this first article of the Creed, we now turn to the other articles of the Creed that concern hope: Jesus' resurrection, ascension, and return in glory to judge the living and the dead.

7

HOPE (II)

The Mysteries That Make Hope Possible and Their Implications for Our Lives

If Christ Is Not Raised, Your Faith Is Vain

In the last chapter, we discussed the virtue of hope in itself: how hope has undergone a transformation in our contemporary secular world, followed by an articulation of what the implications of the authentic theological virtue of hope are—in short, why Christian hope is such a great good. Along the way, one of the most important themes we meditated upon was the connection of hope with redemptive suffering, especially understood in light of Christ's descent into hell. Having reflected on this article of the Creed, in the present chapter we will now be surveying the other articles of the Creed that concern hope: Christ's resurrection, ascension, and return in glory to judge the living and the dead. For the Christian, nothing that has ever happened in the universe is more important than these mysteries; for, as St. Paul says, "If Christ has not been raised, your faith is futile and you are still in your sins" (1 Cor 15:17). After exploring the meaning of this and the rest of the mysteries that make hope possible, we will round out our chapters on hope with Benedict's reflection on how all of us today, subject to Faust's despair, can overcome it only by "entering the experiment" of Christian hope. In line with the aim of this book as a whole, my goal here is to paint a portrait of Christian hope as a great good that is uniquely available to those who have faith, a good that gives our life meaning but which is not available apart from living the experiment of faith.

The Resurrection

Given how creatively Ratzinger treats Holy Saturday, we naturally expect him to continue with his existentialist approach in the matter of the resurrection—and so he does. Posing the question of what resurrection itself means, he replies that it can only be grasped aright in light of the emptiness we experience on Holy Saturday: "Only from this angle can one understand what 'resurrection' means. It is the greater strength of love in the face of death."[1] This description of love fits seamlessly with Ratzinger's understanding of Christ's descent into hell as his entering completely into the abyss of man's abandonment, experiencing as totally as possible the isolation from love that is death. Expounding further on the meaning of the resurrection, Ratzinger goes so far as to pinpoint what he takes its implications to be for the meaning of Christian faith as such: "The Christian message is basically nothing else than the transmission of the testimony that love has managed to break through death here and thus has transformed fundamentally the situation of all of us."[2]

The reality that Christ's love has burst through the gates of hell does not thereby mean that we all automatically get to join him in Paradise. If we wish to be with Love himself eternally, our actions must transcend the here and now as we let ourselves be totally transformed by love. In a fascinating passage that speaks to how he considers it possible for Christ's love to lead us into eternal life, Ratzinger thus writes:

1. Ratzinger, *Introduction to Christianity*, 302.
2. Ibid., 307.

Only where someone values love more highly than life, that is, only where someone is ready to put life second to love, for the sake of love, can love be stronger and more than death. If it is to be more than death, it must first be more than mere life. But if it could be this, not just in intention but in reality, then that would mean at the same time that the power of love had risen superior to the power of the merely biological and taken it into its service.[3]

After crossing the boundary of death, the person thus transformed by love will have transcended the limits of space and time. His existence will no longer be limited to this finite world, precisely because all the seemingly mundane facets of his natural life (*bios*) have been "encompassed by and incorporated in the power of love," which itself is not bound to the material world but lives on perpetually. Accordingly, after leaving behind the present temporal "realm of biological evolutions and mutations," the saved person will be able to undergo that "last stage of evolution," a "leap" to a quite different plane: not merely natural, but "definitive" life (*zoe*). In this final state, the body will no longer be subject to decay but instead entirely subject to the Spirit, being transformed into what St. Paul calls a "spiritual body" (1 Cor 15:44).[4]

In close connection with the texts I have just cited, Ratzinger pauses to comment on the type of biblical hermeneutic that is necessary to get the resurrection right. Raising the point that all talk of the resurrection seems to contradict what we know about the nature of matter and thus appears "hopelessly mythological," Ratzinger responds by remarking that "exegesis itself quite often produces its own philosophy" while unjustifiably posing as "a supremely refined distillation of the biblical evidence," Ratzinger emphasizes that a hermeneutic truly open to the full breadth of what reason has to offer cannot easily dismiss the reality of the resurrection.[5] In order to grasp the true meaning of the biblical resurrection narratives, it is imperative

3. Ibid., 304.
4. Ibid., 269–70.
5. Ibid., 307.

that we inquire carefully into the "real intentions of the biblical testimony" while considering anew the relation between the biblical text and the Hellenistic world in which the New Testament took shape.⁶ What follows is a classic piece of Ratzingerian exegesis in which he does precisely this. He sets it up in this way:

> The awakening of the dead (not of bodies!) of which Scripture speaks is thus *concerned with* the salvation of the one, undivided man, not just with the fate of one (perhaps secondary) half of man. It now also becomes clear that *the real heart of the faith* in resurrection does not consist at all in the idea of the restoration of bodies, to which we have reduced it in our thinking; such is the case even though this is the pictorial image used throughout the Bible. What, then, is *the real content of the hope symbolically proclaimed* in the Bible in the shape of the resurrection of the dead? I think that this can best be worked out by means of a comparison with the dualistic conception of ancient philosophy.⁷

I have italicized a few expressions in the above citation, because they are classic expressions throughout Ratzinger's writings in places where he is trying to implement the Second Vatican Council's exhortation to search out the inspired and inerrant intentions of Scripture's sacred authors. Ratzinger has a keen sense for what is and is not essential in the Bible, and he is always vigilant to distinguish the truths that the Bible is teaching from elements of its cultural milieu or worldview that require adaptation in our modern context.⁸

That said by way of preface, what is it about the biblical view of resurrection that Ratzinger deems in need of refinement? His very firm answer: "The idea of the *anima separata* (the 'separated soul' of Scholastic theology) has in the last analysis become obsolete."⁹

---

6. Ibid., 269.
7. Ibid., 349–50 (emphasis added).
8. Vatican Council II, *Dei Verbum*, §§11–12. For more on this enterprise of ascertaining the biblical intention according to Benedict XVI, see Ramage, *Jesus, Interpreted*, 77–85.
9. Ratzinger, *Introduction to Christianity*, 351. Again, Benedict's approach to the issue of a separated soul mirrors that of Elizabeth Anscombe, who writes, "I believe that something

Though by no means a fan of "de-Hellenization" or stripping away all the Greek elements in Christianity, Ratzinger nevertheless finds the Greek dualism of body and soul to be rather alien to the Bible's more holistic, unified view of man. According to Ratzinger, the idea of resurrection in the Bible refers to the immortality not of the soul but of the *person*.[10] When people think of the human soul, unfortunately they sometimes picture it as a separate substance that dwells in our bodies. Ratzinger does not weigh in here on the Aristotelian, Thomistic ontology of the soul as the form of the body. Instead, he proceeds in his typically existential, personalist fashion and refocuses our understanding of the soul in terms of relationality:

> The distinguishing mark of man, seen from above, is his being addressed by God, the fact that he is God's partner in a dialogue.... "Having a spiritual soul" means precisely being willed, known, and loved by God in a special way; it means being a creature called by God to an eternal dialogue and therefore capable for its own part of knowing God and of replying to him. What we call in substantialist language "having a soul" we will describe in a more historical, actual language as "being God's partner in a dialogue." This does not mean that talk of the soul is false (as is sometimes asserted today by a one-sided and uncritical biblical approach); in one respect it is, indeed, even

---

does show the spirituality of the soul, but that nothing shows its immaterial substantiality: in fact, that the latter conception—the conception of an *immaterial substance* at all—is a delusive one." Anscombe, "The Immortality of the Soul," in *Faith in a Hard Ground: Essays on Religion, Philosophy and Ethics* (Luton: Andrews UK Ltd., 2011), 71. Aquinas himself, while certainly holding to the idea of the separated soul, acknowledges the problems entailed with it in his *Super ad 1 Cor.* 15, 2, no. 924, stating that it is difficult (but not impossible) to sustain the soul's immortality if the resurrection of the body is denied.

10. Ratzinger, *Introduction to Christianity*, 350. Also critiquing the dualism of the New Testament as "naïve," Dale Allison makes the insightful observation, "Whether we should be monists or dualists or pluralists or idealists or whatever cannot be resolved by appeal to chapter and verse." Allison, *Night Comes*, 35. When it comes to the precise relationship of the nature of reality, I am sympathetic with Allison when he admits, "All I can do is insist upon this: not being a materialist doesn't entail being philosophically or scientifically illiterate.... Although I am dubious about materialism, I've nothing to offer in its place." Ibid., 36. As far as my own journey is concerned, I have found what Benedict XVI/Joseph Ratzinger articulates here to be the most illuminating attempt of anyone I have read to negotiate this immense mystery.

necessary in order to describe the whole of what is involved here. But, on the other hand, it also needs to be complemented if we are not to fall back into a dualistic conception that cannot do justice to the dialogic and personalistic view of the Bible.[11]

As Benedict would write more concisely after becoming pope in his foreword to the latest edition of *Eschatology*, "Soul is nothing other than man's capacity for relatedness with truth, with love eternal.... Beginning with our baptism, we belong to the body of the resurrected one and are in this sense already attached to our future. Never again are we totally disembodied."[12]

So if the distinguishing mark of man is his soul—his being in relationship with God—what does this mean for the traditional image of resurrection as a restoration of body-soul unity?

The foregoing reflections may have clarified to some extent what is involved in the biblical pronouncements about the resurrection: their essential content is not the conception of a restoration of bodies to souls after a long inter-

---

11. Ratzinger, *Introduction to Christianity*, 354–55. For an entry point to the Thomistic conception of the soul's relation with the body, see St. Thomas Aquinas, *Summa Theologiae*, I, q. 76. Relationality (and its brokenness) is also the lens through which Ratzinger views the creation of man and original sin. See Ratzinger, *In the Beginning*, 71–74; Ratzinger, "Belief in Creation and the Theory of Evolution," in *Dogma and Preaching* (San Francisco: Ignatius Press, 2011), 141–42; Benedict XVI, general audience (February 6, 2013). Elsewhere Ratzinger adds that the essence of mind or spirit is "being-in-relation." Ratzinger, "On the Understanding of 'Person' in Theology," in *Dogma and Preaching*, 192–94. For an insightful contemporary introduction to the philosophy of mind that addresses the issue of dualism raised by Ratzinger here, see James Madden, *Mind, Matter, and Nature: A Thomistic Proposal for the Philosophy of Mind* (Washington, D.C.: The Catholic University of America Press, 2013).

12. Ratzinger, *Eschatology: Death and Eternal Life*, 2nd ed. (Washington, D.C.: The Catholic University of America Press, 2007), xxi; cf. ibid., 259. For further discussion of the soul as man's capacity for relatedness to truth, see Rausch, *Faith, Hope, and Charity*, 110–11. Rausch observes that Ratzinger's conception of the human person is not rooted primarily in Aristotelian philosophy, according to which relations are accidents, but rather in Christianity, wherein relation takes its place alongside substance as the key constituent of being. Benedict's approach finds a friend in the philosophy of Elizabeth Anscombe, who writes of the soul's spirituality, "I put forward that the spirituality of the human soul is its capacity to get a conception of the eternal and to be concerned with the eternal as an objective, and perhaps also as something that can be leant on and feared." Anscombe, "Immortality of the Soul," 74.

val; their aim is to tell men that they, they themselves, live on; not by virtue of their own power, but because they are known and loved by God in such a way that they can no longer perish. In contrast to the dualistic conception of immortality expressed in the Greek body-soul schema, the biblical formula of immortality through awakening means to convey a collective and dialogic conception of immortality: the essential part of man, the person, remains; that which has ripened in the course of this earthly existence of corporeal spirituality and spiritualized corporeality goes on existing in a different fashion. It goes on existing because it lives in God's memory. And because it is the man himself who will live, not an isolated soul, the element of human fellowship is also part of the future; for this reason the future of the individual man will only then be full when the future of humanity is fulfilled.[13]

Again, notice Ratzinger's characteristic language at work above: "the essential content" of the resurrection does not lie in the common dualistic way that we have envisioned it. Rather, the "aim" of the doctrine of resurrection is the assertion that human persons cannot ultimately perish because we are known and loved by God. All love wants eternity—and God's love, says Benedict, "not only wants it but effects it and is it"[14] In other words, it is a love so strong that it keeps alive "not

---

13. Ratzinger, *Introduction to Christianity*, 353. Ratzinger also has an extended discussion of this topic in his *Eschatology* (2007), 157–61. Here he makes the above point very concisely: "Immortality cannot be accounted for in terms of the isolated individual existent.... Relation makes immortal: openness, not closure, is the end in which we find our beginning." Ibid., 158. On living on in God's memory, see also ibid., xx; Ratzinger, "What Comes after Death?" in *Dogma and Preaching*, 255–59. Responding to the question of how man can remain in existence after our composite bodies disintegrate, Ratzinger states, "This can be the case, however, only if God remembers man: Only *he* remains; only *his* thought is reality. And this is precisely the hopeful certainty the biblical faith intends to offer: the Eternal One remembers man; man lives in God's remembering and thus truly lives in himself, for God's remembrance is not a shadow but reality.... Immorality, according to the Christian faith, fundamentally has to do with love. The only eternal thing is love. God is eternity. And *his* love, in turn, is man's eternity; in being loved by eternal Love, he is lifted up imperishably.... The hope of man and of mankind is love—that is the answer of the Christian faith, which is thereby entirely realistic—oriented toward the sober praxis of everyday life." Ibid., 258–59.

14. Ratzinger, *Introduction to Christianity*, 350. It appears that Ratzinger is incorporating and responding here to the thought of Karl Barth. According to Barth, all creation is eternally present to God, and thus we will continue to exist eternally even if we do not do so as

just his memory, the shadow of his 'I,' but that person himself."[15] This for Benedict is what it means to live on in God's memory. And, what is more, it is not just a matter of us as individuals continuing to be held in existence by God. Our future as individuals in God is only fulfilled in fellowship with all of humanity—and indeed, in light of our earlier discussion, in union with all of God's renewed creation.

Benedict's relational approach to the question of eternal life finds support in the biblical testimony in some places which at first glance might appear to contradict his thesis. Especially relevant are Jesus' saying "It is the spirit that gives life, the flesh is of no avail" (Jn 6:63) and St. Paul's extensive discussion of the resurrection in 1 Corinthians 15. For example, Paul issues this message: "I tell you this, brethren: flesh and blood cannot inherit the kingdom of God, nor does the perishable inherit the imperishable" (1 Cor 15:50). In both passages, we see a sharp distinction between the bodily and spiritual, perishable and imperishable. However, says Ratzinger, it is not that the Bible is trying to denigrate our embodied reality:

> In Paul's language "body" and "spirit" are not opposites; the opposites are called "physical body" and "spiritual body." ... One thing at any rate may be fairly clear: both John [6:63] and Paul [1 Cor 15:50] state with all possible emphasis that the "resurrection of the flesh," the "resurrection of the body," is not a "resurrection of physical bodies." Thus, from the point of view of modern thought, the Pauline sketch is far less naïve than later theological erudition with its subtle ways of construing how there can be eternal physical bodies. To recapitulate, Paul teaches, not the resurrection of physical bodies, but the resurrection of persons, and this not in the return of the "fleshly body," that is, the biological structure, an idea he expressly describes as impossible ("the

---

individuals. For Benedict, on the other hand, we will continue to exist in God—*and* still as individuals—because of God's love for us. God's love is efficacious: he who is love wants to love us for eternity, and thereby makes it so. See Karl Barth, *Church Dogmatics*, vol. 3, pt. 2, *The Doctrine of Creation, Part 2* (Edinburg: T. & T. Clark, 1986), 538–40. I am grateful to my colleague Andrew Salzmann for pointing out this connection to Barth and apologize to him for the infelicities in my attempt to articulate it here.

15. Ratzinger, *Introduction to Christianity*, 304–305.

perishable cannot become imperishable"), but in the different form of the life of the resurrection, as shown in the risen Lord.[16]

At a certain point, we all have to acknowledge the limitations of our ability to pronounce definitively on much of anything when it comes to the nature of our existence in eternal life. Notwithstanding the provisional nature of our conclusions, Ratzinger is adamant about one key point: the resurrection will not be of our present physical bodies through a reconstitution of their biological structure. In keeping with the holistic view of man that we have just articulated, for Ratzinger the resurrection is not of bodies but of *persons*.

The Ascension and Life in Heaven

After considering Christ's descent into hell and resurrection, we are now in a position to say a few related words concerning the mystery of the ascension (narrated in Lk 24:51 and Acts 1:9). As in his discussion of the resurrection, Ratzinger is on the lookout to distinguish the essential from the accidental in the biblical narrative. Naturally enough, Luke describes Christ's ascension into heaven with the language available in his own day, as he has Jesus literally moving upwards out of the disciples' sight in a cloud. Benedict admits that Luke's cosmology is antiquated by today's standards, that the thought of Jesus' body being taken up to a physical place above us makes no more sense than the notion that his body traveled to the center of the earth on Holy Saturday. All the same, our greater scientific knowledge does not warrant our writing off the biblical account as mere fiction: "No one today will seriously contest these discoveries. There is no lon-

---

16. Ratzinger, *Introduction to Christianity*, 357–58. For a similar position to Ratzinger's from an outstanding contemporary biblical scholar's reflection on the last things, see Dale Allison, *Night Comes*, 29. Allison reports that even N. T. Wright, the great modern apologist for the resurrection, shared with him a similar view on the subject over the course of a conversation. In fact, Wright allegedly remarked that Origen long ago solved most of the issues related to the material continuity (or lack thereof) of the resurrected body without our present one.

ger such a thing as a world arranged literally in three stories. But was such a conception ever really intended in the articles of faith about the Lord's descent into hell and Ascension to heaven? It certainly provided the imagery for them, but it was just as certainly not the decisive factual element in them."[17] As above, notice the key terms used here. The ancient biblical cosmology was not being "intended in the articles of faith." While it "certainly provided the imagery for them," it was "just as certainly not the decisive factual element in them." What Benedict says here reminds me of a powerful statement by C. S. Lewis on this topic: "Even if it can be shown, then, that the early Christians accepted their imagery literally, this would not mean that we are justified in relegating their doctrines as a whole to the lumber-room."[18]

But if we ought to keep professing belief in Christ's ascension into heaven, it is not enough to say what the mystery does *not* essentially mean. Here is Ratzinger's attempt at a positive answer to the question of what the Christian means by the ascension and life in heaven:

> Hell is wanting only to be oneself; what happens when man barricades himself up in himself. Conversely, it is the nature of that upper end of the scale which we have called heaven that it can only be received, just as one can only give hell to oneself. "Heaven" is by nature what one has not made oneself and cannot make oneself.... As fulfilled love, heaven can always only be granted to man; but hell is the loneliness of the man who will not accept it, who declines the status of beggar and withdraws into himself.
>
> Only from this standpoint does it become clear now what is really meant in the Christian view by heaven. It is not to be understood as an everlasting place above the world or simply as an eternal metaphysical region.... Heaven is to be defined as the contact of the being "man" with the being "God"; this confluence of God and man took place once and for all in Christ when he went beyond *bios* through death to new life. Heaven is accordingly that future of man and of mankind which the latter cannot give to itself, which is therefore closed to it so long as it waits for itself, and which was first and

---

17. Ratzinger, *Introduction to Christianity*, 311.
18. C. S. Lewis, *Miracles*, 119.

fundamentally opened up in the man whose field of existence was God and through whom God entered into the creature "man."[19]

Heaven is described here with the very language we saw Ratzinger use to speak of faith, that is, as the acceptance of that which one has not and cannot himself make. This means that the life of faith on earth is an anticipation of our life in heaven, that, as Benedict says, we enjoy even now the substance of our hope through a life of faith. And if receiving from God what we cannot give to ourselves is heaven, then that which we can give to ourselves can only be hell. Hell is not a place God "sends us to," but rather the loneliness of the man who by his own decision will not accept God's invitation to the eternal wedding feast. Again, I am reminded of some haunting sayings of C. S. Lewis: that "the gates of hell are locked on the inside" and that "there are only two kinds of people in the end: those who say to God, 'Thy will be done,' and those to whom God says, in the end, 'Thy will be done.'"[20]

In a short meditation on the liturgical feast of the Ascension, Ratzinger continues his endeavor to ascertain the inner logic of Christ's return to the Father. As we just saw above, so too here he urges us away from thinking of the mystery along the lines of the spacetime horizon and instead in light of its existential import:

Christ's Ascension is therefore not a spectacle for the disciples but an event in which they themselves are included. It is a *sursum corda*, a movement the above into which we are all called. It tells us that man can live toward the above, that he is capable of attaining heights. More: the altitude that alone is suited to the dimension of being human is the altitude of God himself.[21]

---

19. Ratzinger, *Introduction to Christianity*, 313–14. Allison shares Ratzinger's view of heaven as that which we cannot give to ourselves: as in our beginning, so in our end. Allison, *Night Comes*, 44. On hell as the loneliness and isolation that we give ourselves, Lewis's depiction of hell as the "grey town" spreading out indefinitely is particularly apt. Lewis, *The Great Divorce* (San Francisco: HarperSanFrancisco, 1973), 12–13.

20. C. S. Lewis, *The Problem of Pain* (New York: Macmillan, 1962), 127; C. S. Lewis, *Great Divorce*, 75. On hell as a self-imposed punishment, see also John Paul II, General Audience (July 28, 1999).

21. Ratzinger, *Images of Hope*, 58. It is instructive to compare and contrast how Ratzinger

Strange as it may seem, for Ratzinger the ascension of the Lord is not even primarily about Jesus. This is not to say that he would deny the Word's divinity and coequality with God the Father. Nevertheless, if I am understanding Ratzinger aright, he is deliberately bracketing the question of what would have been recorded on a video camera and locating the essential focus of the mystery in its relevance for our lives.

"Christ's Ascension," Ratzinger says, "is the rehabilitation of man.... The image of man has been raised up."[22] We do not read here that Jesus' ascension has implications for man—rather, we are told that its meaning *is* the rehabilitation of man. Ratzinger proceeds to explain what precisely he intends by this:

> Only from this height is his essence really illuminated.... Only from there can we really learn to love the human condition [*Menschsein*] in ourselves and in the other.... The most effective counterforce to the corruption of man lies in the memory of his greatness, not in the memory of his defilement. Christ's Ascension impresses upon us the memory of greatness. It immunizes us against the false moralism of the disparagement of man. It teaches us to respect and gives us back the joy of being human. If all this is taken into consideration, the claim that Christ's Ascension is the canonization of a superseded cosmology disposes of itself. The issue is the measure of being human, not how many floors the universe has. The issue is God and man, the true height of being human, not the position of the stars.[23]

This is another piece of classic Ratzingerian exegesis, as he stakes a claim as to what is (the true height of being human) and is not (how

---

describes the ascension of Jesus and assumption of Mary into heaven. In both cases, Ratzinger places the emphasis on the theological significance of each event, but clearly he considers the resurrection of Jesus to be more of a historical event (while admitting that it doubtlessly also transcends the historical). According to Ratzinger, the tradition "clearly defines the content of this article of faith [Mary's assumption] as a theological, not historical, affirmation," entirely oriented toward the veneration of the Mother of God who is alive even now in God. Ratzinger, *Daughter Zion: Meditations on the Church's Marian Belief* (San Francisco: Ignatius Press, 1983), 72–82.

22. Ratzinger, *Images of Hope*, 58.
23. Ibid., 59–60. 126.

many floors the universe has) "at issue" in the biblical account of the ascension. The biblical picture speaks of Christ, to be sure, but its central concern actually lies in its message about the greatness of the human person. Again, when I read Benedict on eschatological matters of this sort, it feels as if I am reading C. S. Lewis. Indeed, I think that Lewis is making this very point with his famous essay on the weight of glory. In Lewis's view, it is hardly possible to think too often or deeply about the greatness of our neighbor. Each and every human person is called to the heights of divine perfection, to become God by grace. How would our lives, and our world as a whole, change if lived day by day with awareness of our neighbor's future glory? "It is a serious thing," says Lewis, "to live in a society of possible gods and goddesses.... There are no *ordinary* people. You have never talked to a mere mortal.... Next to the Blessed Sacrament itself, your neighbor is the holiest object presented to your senses."[24]

As a final word on the subject of the greatness of man shown in Jesus' ascension, it is fitting that we pause to recall how man is to achieve this greatness. As we saw above, divinization is not something that happens in nebulous mystical experiences but rather above all in the life of charity and redemptive suffering. Ratzinger thinks that this same lesson can be learned from meditation on what he calls the "naïve" paintings that show only the feet of Jesus in the clouds at his ascension: "It occurs to me that precisely in the apparent naiveté of this representation something very deep comes into view. All we see of Christ in the time of history are his feet and the cloud."[25] In

---

24. Lewis, "Weight of Glory," 45–46.
25. Ratzinger, *Images of Hope*, 61. Acknowledging the naiveté of the Ascension image (and the related images of the resurrection of bodies and the descent into hell), Dale Allison makes this helpful remark that also demonstrates great respect for the theological content of these images: "If we cast aside literalism, resurrection language must be a way of suggesting an eschatological future that transcends prosaic description, a future that can only be intimated through sacred metaphor and sanctified imagination. In other words, resurrection, like the parables of Jesus, characterizes God's future for us via an analogy, in recognition of the fact that we can't do any better. We see dimly." Allison, *Night Comes*, 40.

other words, the ascension not only reminds us of man's greatness, but also of just how much God towers over earthly proportions. The cloud thus conceals and reveals God at the same time. We cannot see God face to face in this life, but we can at least touch his feet when we bow down in worship. Ironically, this is precisely how we ascend to God: by bowing down in worship—and in humbly bowing before our neighbor in the gesture of washing his feet.[26]

Christ's Return as Judge and the Question of an Intermediate State

We now conclude our portrait of the virtue of hope as outlined in the Creed with an exposition of its final article dealing with Christ: his return in glory as judge of the living and the dead. Benedict's most developed thought on this mystery is found in his encyclical *Spe Salvi*, which contains a fascinating section subtitled "Judgment as a Setting for Learning and Practicing Hope." Many of us picture the final judgment as a horrific and tragic moment, but Benedict sees it otherwise. Indeed, he thinks that the eclipse of hope in the modern era is intimately bound up with the decline of faith in this event. In reality, he says, "faith in the Last Judgement is first and foremost hope."[27]

How can this be? Should we not be afraid of Christ's judgment, the day when all our sins will be made manifest and Christ will call us to account for them? While Benedict by no means denies the importance of a proper filial fear of the Lord, as usual his emphasis is different from the way the mystery is often construed. As Benedict teaches, there can be no ultimate justice apart from the resurrection of the dead and final judgment of all human beings. But the justice with

---

26. Ratzinger, *Images of Hope*, 61.
27. Benedict XVI, *Spe Salvi*, §43. On the question of Christ's return in time and the meaning of Jesus' eschatological discourse, an issue not discussed here, see Ratzinger, *Eschatology* (1988), 35–45; and Ramage, *Jesus, Interpreted*, 194–231. On a note related to the waning of belief in the last judgment, Dale Allison observes that "as hell has sunk, it has dragged allied expectations, including resurrection, down with it." Allison, *Night Comes*, 32.

which the pontiff is concerned is not primarily in regard to our guilt so much as it is with the innocent sufferer whose life finds no real resolution in this vale of tears. With the resurrection and judgment, the suffering person's tragic existence is at last set right, his past pain undone by the overwhelming gift of divine glory now bestowed. So convicted is Benedict on this point that he puts forward this bold statement:

> I am convinced that the question of justice constitutes the essential argument, or in any case the strongest argument, in favor of faith in eternal life. The purely individual need for a fulfillment that is denied to us in this life, for an everlasting love that we await, is certainly an important motive for believing that man was made for eternity; but only in connection with the impossibility that the injustice of history should be the final word does the necessity for Christ's return and for new life become fully convincing.[28]

Benedict's position here reads along the lines of C. S. Lewis's argument from desire, itself an application of Aristotle's dictum that nature does nothing in vain. Just as the pan-human desire for food would make no sense in a world where no food existed, this argument holds that the universal human desire for perfect happiness—which is denied to all of us while on earth—is incomprehensible unless there actually exists the possibility of attaining the object of this desire. Aquinas himself even makes this same sort of argument in his commentary on 1 Corinthians when he writes, "Moreover, since man naturally de-

---

28. Benedict XVI, *Spe Salvi*, §43. In keeping with his evolutionary analogy for the gradual divinization of creation, Ratzinger elsewhere describes Christ's return in judgment as the final moment in the "complexification" of all things as they move toward "unification in the personal." Borrowing the language of Teilhard de Chardin, Ratzinger affirms that the omega point of creation is not a thing, much less an annihilation: it is a "you," a person. This is a significant reason to think of the last judgment, which brings about this state of affairs, as hope. Ratzinger, *Introduction to Christianity*, 322. The personalism of Teilhard's evolutionary Christology is discussed at length in Henri de Lubac, *The Religion of Teilhard de Chardin* (New York: Desclee Co. 1967), a text which Ratzinger surely read given the immense influence de Lubac had on his thought as a whole. Another germane book that could well have influenced Ratzinger is de Lubac's *Teilhard de Chardin: The Man and His Meaning* (New York: Hawthorn Books, 1965).

sires salvation of the body as well [in addition to the soul], a natural desire would be frustrated."[29]

I find Benedict's words profoundly moving and helpful, though I think a clarification or tweak may be necessary. The reason I say this is that I believe the argument from desire actually compels us to take one of two positions. On the one hand, Benedict could be right: human nature does not make sense unless there is such a thing as perfect fulfillment in eternal life, and thus such a reward is indeed in store for us. On the other hand, the nihilist could be right that our desire for eternal life is ultimately futile because the universe we live in itself is futile. In other words, the Christian living in a secular age has to acknowledge that a Nietzschean interpretation of our experience is also possible. As we have established earlier in this book, one cannot disprove the nihilist's outlook as an uninterested third-party observer. Sure, we must admit, it could be that our natural desire for justice will finally end up being in vain. After all, could it not be that our desire for eternity is simply evolution's way of giving us a reason to keep living so that the species might endure? Obviously, I do not think that this is the full story, or else I would not be a Christian. My point is to drive home the reality that Benedict (by his own admission) has not definitely proven that there is such a thing as eternal life. At the end of the day, faith in eternal life is just that: faith. Yet I think that Benedict provides us with compelling reasons to believe, a reasoned account that ought to bolster our confidence in the truth of Christ and impart fresh vibrancy to our life.[30]

---

29. Aquinas, *Super ad 1 Cor.* 15, 2, no. 924 (translation mine). In addition to its affinities with the thought of Lewis and Aristotle, a similar argument for immortality (and, in turn, for God's existence as its cause) is made by Immanuel Kant, who notes that all human beings experience an unconditional obligation to follow the moral law while aware that by so doing we will never be fully happy in this life. If human nature is not to be absurd, Kant reasons, then the existence of an afterlife must be postulated as the locus wherein man's natural desire for happiness will be fulfilled. See his *Critique of Practical Reason* (New York: Prometheus Books, 1996), 147–58.

30. For this assessment of what Benedict's argument does and does not achieve in light of

Although it does not constitute one of our faith's so-called last things, the above discussion of justice provides the ideal connection to treat of our final issue related to the virtue of hope: the question of whether there is such a thing as an intermediate state between death and resurrection. The Catholic Church calls this state Purgatory. Throughout the tradition, Christians have sometimes spoken of Purgatory as having a discrete duration, with the associated notion that prayers for the dead can "take off" a certain number of days of their loved one's purgation. Benedict himself commends the traditional practice of praying for the dead, which is a constant tradition of the Church throughout the ages and rooted in Scripture (cf. 2 Mc 12:39–45). However, it is another thing to conceptualize what precisely takes place in Purgatory, especially when it comes to the issue of time. We do know that with death our life-choice becomes definitive—Purgatory is not a "second chance" or "additional time" to change our minds about God after we die. Indeed, Benedict countenances the fairly recent theological suggestion that the "fire" of Purgatory which burns and saves is an image of Christ himself.[31]

According to Benedict, one key feature of Purgatory is that it enables Christians to make sense of the relationship between justice and mercy. Catholicism's belief in Purgatory is thus a magnificent demonstration of the truth that God's grace does not cancel out justice. Described with the metaphor of purification by fire (cf. 1 Cor 3:12–15), Purgatory is painful justice, yet it is very different from the sort of pain with which Jesus associates the fires of hell (cf. Mt 13:42, for example). Here is how Benedict describes it:

---

postmodern man's realization of the looming possibility of a nihilistic world, I am indebted to observations of my colleague Andrew Jaeger.

31. Benedict XVI, *Spe Salvi*, §47. For a more extended treatment of the intermediate state, see Ratzinger, *Eschatology* (1988), 119–29. For the image of the fire and the duration (or lack thereof) in Purgatory, see ibid., 228–31. In a similar sort of move to that made by Benedict here in suggesting that Purgatory's "fire" be seen as Christ, Allison offers an interesting alternate possibility for understanding the final accuser or "judge" as our conscience. Allison, *Night Comes*, 54.

His gaze, the touch of his heart heals us through an undeniably painful transformation "as through fire." But it is a blessed pain, in which the holy power of his love sears through us like a flame, enabling us to become totally ourselves and thus totally of God. In this way the inter-relation between justice and grace also becomes clear: the way we live our lives is not immaterial, but our defilement does not stain us forever if we have at least continued to reach out towards Christ, towards truth and towards love.[32]

This paragraph reminds me of how Dante differently depicts the suffering of souls in *Purgatorio* and the souls in his *Inferno*. (Actually, in Dante's world Purgatory is fire, while the nethermost region of hell is an ice sheet (symbolizing the damned souls' eternal immobility). Dante and Benedict share the conviction that Purgatory's suffering is blessed. Dante achieves this by having his souls in Purgatory sing through their suffering, even remaining in their suffering voluntarily when given the chance to leave a circle of purification early.[33] The reason for their decision has everything to do with what Benedict is talking about here. These souls do not want to receive God's mercy at the expense of his justice—which in God are one and the same. Purgatory is an amazing development of Christian belief, for it allows us human beings to "pay" a certain price for our sins, to undergo a process of purification that involves a real effort that brings about the genuine cultivation of our entire person. Yet it is not as if we mortals could ever render to God complete justice for what we have done—we cannot perfect ourselves. Purgatory is therefore not only an enterprise of justice, but also an immense gift of divine mercy.

The following comment is indicative of just how immense Benedict considers God's mercy to be, the extent to which Purgatory is able to transform even the worst of sinners: "For the great majority of people—we may suppose—there remains in the depths of their being

---

32. Benedict XVI, *Spe Salvi*, §47.

33. The singing of souls can be found throughout the *Purgatorio*; for the point about not desiring to leave their purgation early, wishing that justice be served, see Dante Alighieri, *Purgatory*, trans. Anthony M. Esolen (New York: Modern Library, 2003), *Purgatorio* 21:61–66.

an ultimate interior openness to truth, to love, to God."³⁴ As evidence of its conviction regarding the immense magnitude of God's mercy, Benedict notes that the Church has a universal tradition that the souls of the departed are able to receive solace and refreshment through the Eucharist, prayer, and almsgiving.³⁵ The pontiff has in mind here the comfort of those who are suffering in the intermediate state, but the Christian tradition even contains instances of the belief that the souls of the damned receive a periodic respite from their suffering on the Church's great feast days.³⁶

That said, it is neither my aim nor Benedict's to weigh in on the question of whether or not the souls in hell ever find refreshment, much less the question of whether hell is fully occupied or empty or what it means to have "hope" for the salvation of all.³⁷ Given our limited ability to know what God's freedom entails, I think that we have to have great epistemological modesty here. Nevertheless, I do think we have certitude about this: that Christians ought to be praying and working for the salvation of all. Otherwise, what are we praying when we say, "Save us from the fires of hell. Lead all souls to heaven, especially those most in need of thy mercy"? Furthermore, regardless of how many souls reside in hell eternally, the Christian cannot lightly

---

34. Benedict XVI, *Spe Salvi*, §46. Benedict urges us not to be too hasty even when it comes to the salvation of history's greatest traitor, Judas: "It darkens the mystery around his eternal fate, knowing that Judas 'repented and brought back the thirty pieces of silver to the chief priests and the elders' (Mt 27: 3–4).... Even though he went to hang himself (cf. Mt 27: 5), it is not up to us to judge his gesture, substituting ourselves for the infinitely merciful and just God." Benedict XVI, "Judas Iscariot and Matthias," general audience (October 18, 2006).

35. Benedict XVI, *Spe Salvi*, §48.

36. For more on this subject, see Allison, *Night Comes*, 97–98, 118. C. S. Lewis's imagined story about a journey through hell also witnesses well to this tradition. Lewis, *Great Divorce*, 67–68.

37. As many readers will be well aware, this is an age-old debate that found renewed vigor with the publication of Hans Urs von Balthasar's *Dare We Hope "That All Men Be Saved"?* (San Francisco: Ignatius Press, 1986). For a critique of Balthasar's position, see Ralph Martin, *Will Many Be Saved? What Vatican II Actually Teaches and Its Implications for the New Evangelization* (Grand Rapids, Mich.: Eerdmans Publishing Co., 2012), 129–90. For a summary and analysis of this volume, see my review in *Nova et Vetera* 12, no. 4 (2014): 1313–17.

dismiss the possibility of his own eternal damnation. In this regard, I find myself largely agreeing with Dale Allison's assertion that the purpose of hell is ultimately exhortative. It is the starkest of reminders that whether or not we obey the commandments really matters. It is a warning alarm to rouse us out of our complacency and turn us back toward the Lord. Indeed, this is something we ought to be doing whether hell lies before us or not.[38]

Conclusion: On the Need to "Enter the Experiment" of Hope

I would like to conclude this chapter on hope with the help of an Easter homily of Ratzinger on Goethe's *Faust*. Widely considered the greatest work of Ratzinger's native German tongue, *Faust* places before its audience a man who, despairing over the poverty of the human condition and vanity of man's quest for the divine, ponders abolishing his own existence. Faust ends up encountering the devil, Mephistopheles, with whom he strikes an agreement: Mephistopheles promises to give Faust everything he wants on earth in exchange for the protagonist eventually serving him in hell. It turns out, though, that even these great pleasures granted to Faust at his own behest do not make him happy and indeed only augment his despair. It is for this reason that Ratzinger writes, "Faust stands for modern man, who at first experiences himself at the dawn of the new age as having the same rank as God and believes he can take creation in hand in a new and better way, only then to fall into the despair of one who in fact is only a worm who writhes in the dust."[39] One hears echoes of this line in Benedict's

---

38. Allison, *Night Comes*, 113–14. Allison's focus on hell as exhortation is not precisely Benedict's view, but it does have deep resonances with Benedict's existential approach that we have detailed above. Moreover, it is very reminiscent of the way that Benedict deals with the issue of the Second Coming of Christ, locating the core of the New Testament's expectation that Jesus would return soon not in the New Testament writers' assumptions about its timing but rather in their exhortation to spiritual watchfulness. For a more extensive treatment of this question, see Ramage, *Jesus, Interpreted*, 218–23.

39. Ratzinger, *Images of Hope*, 37.

comments on the transformation of hope in the modern era, wherein our culture tries to substitute the hope of eternal life with scientific and political progress here and now. While science and politics are important, man is made for more than just this earth.

Whether we like or not, Benedict says that we are all Faust nowadays. Earlier in this book, we borrowed Charles Taylor's expression and described our present day as "a secular age." In Ratzinger's language, ours is a world in which everything is possible, and yet nothing really certain and dependable. Given this reality, he poses the question that we all should be asking, the question which is the central concern of this book: how are we to live as Christians in this secular age? Or, as Ratzinger puts it, how should we celebrate Easter today? One thing is for sure: skepticism is not a stable foundation for life. One does not gamble away one's own fate with the dice of a hypothesis: "The doubting [*Zweifel*] of all certainties—nothing any longer can be held to be impossible, nor can anything be held to be definitively certain—does not lead us out of Faust's despair [*Verzweiflung*]."[40]

So how do we break free from Faust's despair? The answer of the ancient Church, says Ratzinger, was that one finds freedom only by walking the path of discipleship with Christ: "One must immerse oneself in it in order through the experiment of life to come to the experience of reality."[41] This is precisely the path that we have seen Benedict suggest earlier in our treatment of the virtue of faith. If one wishes to see the truth of the Christian faith, one has to commit to the "experiment" of living it fully, from the inside. As Ratzinger describes this dynamic here in relation to hope, the truth of the Christian experience is indeed verifiable, "not in the attitude of the spectator, but only in entering into the experiment of life with God."[42] And again, it will come as no surprise to the reader at this point that the precise nature of the

---

40. Ibid., 38–39.
41. Ibid., 41–42. For the early Christian understanding of the faith as "the Way," see Acts 9:2; 19:9–23.
42. Ratzinger, *Images of Hope*, 42.

experiment or path in question is the experiment of *the cross*, when we bow down in service and self-gift for our brothers and sisters. When we live this kind of existence, it opens up doors of perception that are otherwise unavailable to man: "Some things are discerned, not through domination, but only through service, and these are the higher ways of perception. For what we are able to dominate is beneath us. A thinking that persists in dissecting and putting together is in its essence materialistic and reaches only to a certain threshold."[43] According to Ratzinger, we ultimately cannot perceive the reality of God by trying to dissect or dominate him, for the simple reason that he is above, not below us. An additional pool of evidence for the living God is available if only we are willing to pursue him along the way of the cross. Paradoxically, the knowledge of Christ's face is found when we follow behind him along his path to death.[44] Does this amount to a refutation of Nietzsche's allegations against Christianity? I do not think so, but I do think that the person who has undergone "the experiment" of the faith can at least say this much: it would be odd if the whole edifice of Christian life so beautifully corroborated our experience while its core aspirations were mere delusions.

At least this is how things look from where I currently stand. And, though I have been at the job for fewer decades than he, my current state of being is much like Allison's when it comes to the last things: "I remain full of questions. At the same time, I've drawn a few conclusions with which I'm almost comfortable. In the end, my study has been, I'm happy to report, like that of Boethius: it has brought consolation."[45]

---

43. Ibid., 40.
44. Ibid., 41–42.
45. Allison, *Night Comes*, 13.

8

CHARITY (1)

God's Love and Our Response in Truth

Love Is Not an Ideal, But an Encounter

"God is love, and he who abides in love abides in God, and God abides in him" (1 Jn 4:16). These are the words with which Benedict XVI opens his powerful encyclical on the nature of love and its practice in today's world. From the very outset of his pontificate, the pontiff was concerned to get the nature of love right, convinced as he is that living as a Christian in our secular age cannot be a mere matter of following ethical rules or aspiring to lofty ideals, but must involve an "encounter with an event, a person, which gives life a new horizon and a decisive direction."[1] At a time when love has been relegated to the domain of emotion by many, and used as an excuse for hatred and violence by others, Benedict's message is both timely and significant.[2]

---

1. Benedict XVI, *Deus Caritas Est*, §1.
2. It is hard to see how Benedict's observation about the association of love with a duty of vengeance could have any other principal target than the radical jihadism of which he spoke in his famous (and in some circles infamous) Address at the University of Regensburg, September 12, 2006. On Benedict's conviction articulated therein that violence is contrary to charity and therefore to the nature of God, see my article "Violence Is Incompatible with the Nature of God: Benedict, Aquinas, and Method C Exegesis of the 'Dark' Passages of the Bible," *Nova et Vetera* 13, no. 1 (2015): 273–95.

Although we are treating the virtue of love, *caritas*, last in this central section of our book, it was actually the topic of the pontiff's very first encyclical (Benedict had a habit of writing things out of the order we might expect—for example, the third and final installment of his *Jesus of Nazareth* series covered the infancy of Jesus!). Over the course of this volume, we have already glimpsed many of Benedict's insights on charity, particularly with regard to its relationship with faith. In this chapter, we will focus especially on this pope's two encyclicals devoted to love or charity, *Deus Caritas Est* (God Is Love) and *Caritas in Veritate* (Charity in Truth).[3] Following Benedict's own ordering, the first part of our treatment will cover the nature of love itself, addressing what it means to say that God is love and what implications this has for man as the image of God. As we have been doing periodically throughout the book, in this section we will be discussing an important objection to the Christian virtue of charity raised by Nietzsche and examining how Benedict responds to it. In the second part, we will explore how Catholic social teaching calls us to respond to God's love—how we can live "the experiment of faith" in relation to this virtue in our world today.

Part 1: God Is Love

A "Speculation" on the Nature and Semantic Range of the Word "Love"

To begin this chapter, we will walk with Pope Benedict as he contemplates the nature of love itself in the encyclical *Deus Caritas Est*. As he says in the document's introduction, the first part of this encyclical is "speculative" (*speculativa*) in nature. While in the English language, "speculative" tends to be understood as "conjectural," this is not the sense intended by Benedict here. Rather, in line with ancient tradition

---

3. As is evidenced by the different ways Benedict's encyclicals are named in English, sometimes the virtue *caritas* is translated "love" and other times "charity." We will discuss the nuances of these words further below.

and with the etymology of the term itself, I think that Benedict here intends his "speculation" on love to be a profound perception of spiritual truth, a most certain and firm gazing at divine realities.[4] In other words, he is trying to achieve what we have been attempting over the course of this book: to paint a picture of the virtue, to give us a sense of what the lived experience of Christian love is, in order that we might thereby take the "risk" of embarking upon the "experiment" of love in our own lives.

So what is love? Today, people tend to think of love as an emotion, a feeling of closeness to or affection for someone or something. We thus rightly speak of love of country, love of our profession, love between friends, love between parents and children, love between family members, love of neighbor, love of God, and love between man and woman. This last sort of love, observes Benedict, "would seem to be the very epitome of love; all other kinds of love immediately seem to fade in comparison."[5] We need to ask, then, whether all these forms of love are just so many expressions of our deep-seated emotions, or whether we are using the same word "love" in all these instances to designate what are in fact distinct realities.

In step with a long tradition of thought that antedates the Christian faith itself, Benedict has a much more nuanced appreciation of the word's semantic range than is common today. He holds that love is fundamentally a single reality with different dimensions.[6] These contours or manifestations of love can be glimpsed especially well when we attend to the various words employed in the ancient Greek language which in English we tend to render "love": *philia*, *eros*, and *agape*.[7] Though it does occupy an important place in the Catholic

---

4. Benedict XVI, *Deus Caritas Est*, §1. For a thorough exploration of the nature of "speculative" science according to St. Thomas Aquinas, see Servais Pinckaers, OP, "Recherche de la signification véritable du terme 'spéculatif,'" *Nouvelle Revue Théologique* 81, no. 7 (1959): 673–95.

5. Benedict XVI, *Deus Caritas Est*, §2.

6. Ibid., §8.

7. Ibid., §3. For a more extended discussion of the Greek words for love, see C. S. Lewis,

spiritual tradition, the love of friendship (*philia*) is not central to Benedict's concern here.[8] Instead, he focuses on the reciprocity of *eros* and *agape*, which are intimately related but can be thought of as "ascending" and "descending" love, respectively.

As English words derived from it suggest, *eros* is "at first mainly covetous and ascending, a fascination for the great promise of happiness, in drawing near to the other."[9] Ascending is the right adjective with which to describe *eros* because it is the love that causes you to seek union with the beloved who is "higher." (We could probably come up with a dozen pop songs that express this idea, such as the one when I was a senior in high school which went "She's so high, high above me, she's so lovely.") *Eros* is also "ecstatic," for it causes you to "stand outside" of yourself and gravitate toward the beloved by whose arrow you have been wounded. In this way, our love of *eros* for someone, while inherently interested in the lover's own good, is also an immense compliment toward the beloved. As I like to tell my college students, it would *not* be a compliment to tell your potential mate that you love them purely with *agape*: that would mean that you were only a giver in the relationship and received nothing from your beloved!

Eros may therefore be self-seeking, yet this does not cause the Church to look down upon it, much less condemn it. Human beings cannot always be giving—our *eros* keeps us constantly aware that we

---

The Four Loves (New York: Harcourt Brace, 1960). In addition to the three treated by Benedict here, Lewis also dedicates a portion of his book to *storge*, the natural love of affection that parents experience for their children or the fondness we experience for others because of our familiarity with them). For a critique of the four loves as conceived by Lewis, see Alexander R. Pruss, *One Body: An Essay in Christian Sexual Ethics* (Notre Dame, Ind.: University of Notre Dame Press, 2013), 12–13. Says Pruss: "Although we know from experience that there are different forms of love, biblical Greek does not use *agape* to indicate a particular form of love. In reality, the various loves (romantic, filial, friendly, sacrificial) are all forms of *agape*, which is not a form of love but love itself."

8. For an outstanding representative of this tradition, see St. Aelred of Rievaulx, *Spiritual Friendship* (Kalamazoo, Mich.: Cistercian Publications, 1974). See also St. Francis de Sales, *Introduction to the Devout Life*, pt. 3, chaps. 17–21.

9. Benedict XVI, *Deus Caritas Est*, §7.

also need to receive love. As Benedict puts it, "Anyone who wishes to give love must also receive love as a gift."[10] Indeed, the need of *eros* to receive love is very important at the outset of a relationship, for it is what fosters the desire for union between two persons that will eventually lead them to become one flesh for life in holy matrimony. As one of my friends once put it, drawing on Plato, *eros* is the "divine madness" that leads two people to do that crazy deed of getting married that they would never do if they were thinking completely rationally. Over time, says Benedict, a healthy *eros* enshrined in marriage becomes less and less concerned with itself, and increasingly intent on the happiness of the beloved. Reflecting on its Hebrew equivalent, *dodim*, Benedict speaks of *eros* as "a love that is still insecure, indeterminate, and searching" which with time and maturity leads to *ahabà*, the Hebrew form of the similar-sounding Greek *agape*.[11]

If *eros* is ascending love, then *agape* is descending love, the quintessentially biblical expression of love which in Latin goes by the name of *caritas* (whence the English *charity*). By contrast with the "searching" love of *eros*, charity expresses the real discovery of the other, embracing the whole of the beloved's existence as we move beyond the selfish character that prevailed before we fell in love. Charitable love is no longer just an intoxicating quest for personal satisfaction, but concern and care for the other. Love now seeks the good of the beloved through renunciation and sacrifice, rising to higher and higher levels through inward purification. Benedict says that the love of charity or *agape* within the context of romantic relationships is distinguished from *eros* in that charity wishes to be definitive or faithful, in a twofold sense: both in the sense of *exclusivity* (I will love you alone in

---

10. Ibid.
11. Ibid, §§6–7. For the image of being "wounded" by the arrow of beauty, see Ratzinger's speech "The Feeling of Things, the Contemplation of Beauty" (August 24, 2002), http://www.vatican.va/roman_curia/congregations/cfaith/documents/rc_con_cfaith_doc_20020824_ratzinger-cl-rimini_en.html. The Hebrew *dodim* in its related forms occurs in various places in the Old Testament, but especially throughout the Song of Songs (for example, 1:13–16; 2:3–17).

this way) and in the sense of *perpetuity* (I will love you forever). In evocative biblical language, Benedict describes *agape* as "a journey, an ongoing exodus out of the closed inward-looking self towards its liberation through self-giving, and thus towards authentic self-discovery and indeed the discovery of God."[12]

Clearly, the biblical concept of charity I have just sketched is packed with a lot more meaning than our typical English use of it conveys. In our everyday language, charity tends to be equated with what was traditionally called almsgiving. There is nothing wrong with almsgiving; in fact, it is an important part of the Christian life of charity. Almsgiving, though, is merely one expression of the virtue of charity which is much deeper and broader ranging than the act of giving to the needy.[13] Charity is the most excellent of the virtues, and of the three theological virtues it alone remains in Heaven.[14] The Catholic tradition speaks of charity as the virtue that perfects our will to love God for his own sake, and in turn all things in God. Accordingly, it has implications for every facet of our life, every domain in which we would seek to exercise virtue. In fact, charity is called "the form of the virtues," for charity gives to all the cardinal virtues (justice, prudence, temperance, and fortitude, and the various sub-virtues associated with each) their form, that is, it is what makes them to be their true selves by ordering them not merely to good human ends but moreover to God himself.[15]

If our standard English usage of the word "charity" fails to capture its depth, then considering charity from the perspective of another language may be of some help. For instance, the Italian language has a beautiful way of expressing the distinction between *eros* and *agape*

---

12. Benedict XVI, *Deus Caritas Est*, §6.

13. St. Thomas Aquinas helpfully defines almsgiving as "an act of charity through the medium of mercy." Aquinas, *Summa Theologiae*, II-II, q. 32, a. 1. As Aquinas observes in this text, almsgiving's nature as an act of mercy "appears in its very name, for in Greek *eleemosyne* it is derived from having mercy *eleein* even as the Latin *miseratio* is."

14. 1 Cor 13:13; Aquinas, *Summa Theologiae*, II-II, q. 32, a. 6.

15. On charity as the form of the virtues, see Aquinas, *Summa Theologiae*, II-II, q. 32, a. 8.

at which Benedict is driving here. In Italian, one way to tell someone that you love them is to say *Ti voglio bene*, meaning "I want your good." This is a very common expression and is not always intended to convey the fullness of biblical *agape*, but it is the closest expression to it that I have found in the languages I know. Meanwhile, the Italian language reserves *Ti amo* ("I love you") for romantic situations. The verb *amo* used in these contexts is derived from *amor*, the Latin equivalent to *eros*. In America, we do not have the luxury of this cultural and linguistic-practice distinction between the two ways of saying "I love you," and as a result many people (myself included) do not like to tell others outside their immediate family that they love them. A case in point: on my first stint of living in Italy many years ago, I was weirded out by my Christian brothers and sisters telling me that they "loved me" (*Ti voglio bene*). What I did not initially grasp was that this love had nothing to do with romantic feelings—it simply meant that they wanted the good for me, that they wanted me to be well.

Nietzsche's Critique: Christianity Has Poisoned Eros

Notwithstanding the fact that Benedict has an overall positive approach to *eros*, in the popular mind Christianity is seen as a moralistic system opposed to personal pleasures. Once again citing Nietzsche at a key point in his theological discourse, Benedict acknowledges the widely held view that Christianity has "poisoned" *eros* with all her commandments and prohibitions.[16] The Church's norms governing human sexuality, vastly different from the practices of our current culture, lead many to the impression that the Christian God does not want us to be happy. But is this the case? Has Christianity really destroyed *eros*?

In a typical balanced response, Benedict says that, yes, Christianity

---

16. Benedict XVI, *Deus Caritas Est*, §3. For the claim that Christianity "gave Eros poison to drink," see Nietzsche, *Beyond Good and Evil* (Buffalo, N.Y.: Prometheus Books, 1989), IV, no. 168.

did in fact wage war on *eros*—not on the love itself, but on "a warped and destructive form of it, because this counterfeit divinization of *eros* actually strips it of its dignity and dehumanizes it."[17] Actually, the "war" on *eros* that Benedict has in mind here is not even specifically Christian. He is thinking of the Old Testament's constant invectives against the fertility cults of the Ancient Near East, of which the practice of temple prostitution comprised an important part. Temple prostitutes had the allegedly "sacred" job of bestowing divine intoxication upon their visitors, yet, as Benedict observes, "they were not treated as human beings and persons, but simply used as a means of arousing 'divine madness': far from being goddesses, they were human persons being exploited."[18] Seen in this light, the Bible's criticisms of unbridled *eros* are not constitutive of a war on love itself, but rather an unmasking of the use and objectification of our brothers and sisters done in the name of religion.

Ironically, Christianity is often criticized as being opposed to the body, yet the Bible's critiques of *eros* in reality serve to uphold the dignity of the body in a culture that is not up to the task. Biblical faith teaches us that persons are not commodities to be bought and sold for our use or pleasure. Sexual exploitation in our day—whether in the form of prostitution, pornography, having one-night stands merely for the pleasure of it, no-fault divorce, or whatever other forms it takes—is hardly an affirmation of the human body's goodness. When pausing to consider how many people's lives have been ruined by such things in the name of sexual freedom, you have to ask: are we really happier in a society that prizes free sex and the ability to use anyone to reach our pleasurable ends as its highest value? Who really poisoned *eros* after all?

Contrary to our society's insistence that we ought to be able to do whatever we want, whenever we want, and with whomever we want regardless of whether it involves using other people, St. John Paul II

---

17. Benedict XVI, *Deus Caritas Est*, §4.
18. Ibid. On the creation narrative in Genesis as a response to these fertility cults, see Ratzinger, *In the Beginning*, 66.

famously taught that the opposite of love is not hate but rather the *use* of other persons as mere means to our own ends.[19] In Benedict's words, all this is to say that *eros*, while fundamentally good, "needs to be disciplined and purified if it is to provide not just fleeting pleasure, but a certain foretaste of the pinnacle of our existence, of that beatitude for which our whole being yearns."[20] Accordingly, far from rejecting or "poisoning" *eros* as Nietzsche alleged, the Church's moral disciplines heal our love of *eros* and restore its true grandeur.

God's Eros and Agape for Man as Revealed in Scripture

So far we have been discussing the Bible's "war" on warped forms of *eros*, but it is equally important for us to consider the positive side of the Bible's message on this form of love. According to Benedict, the newness of the Bible's faith is seen above all in its image of God. Christianity makes the unique claim that God himself is Triune, an eternal communion of three persons exchanging life and love. Reflective of his own inner nature, God loves his creatures with a personal love which Benedict describes both in terms of *agape* and *eros*. As *agape*, God's love for us is completely self-gift. God stands to gain nothing from loving us, yet he does it anyway. At the same time, says Benedict, the Bible depicts God as "a lover with all the passion of a true love ... describ[ing] God's passion for his people using boldly erotic images."[21] God is thus often portrayed as "jealous" for our love, and angry and heartbroken when we reject him. Indeed, the Bible's preferred image of God's love for us is that of marriage—while its preferred image for our idolatry is adultery (see, for example, Hos 1–2; Ezek 16; Is 62; and the Song of Songs). Again, God does not need anything from us

---

19. For John Paul II's understanding of love as the opposite of use, see his *Love and Responsibility* (San Francisco: Ignatius Press, 1993), esp. 28–31. (This was written before he became pope.)

20. Benedict XVI, *Deus Caritas Est*, §4.

21. Ibid., §§9–10.

that he does not already have, yet it is remarkable that Christianity understands God to be desirous of our love. The image of God's *eros* for man in truth serves to reinforce just how gracious and selfless his *agape* toward us is. He wants our good so much that he can be described as having *eros* for it.

According to Benedict, the second novelty of the Bible's faith is closely connected with its image of God's love for us: its image of the human person. Reflecting on Genesis 2:24's teaching that a man and woman become "one flesh" in marriage, the pontiff writes that monogamous marriage corresponds to the Bible's image of the Triune God: "Marriage based on exclusive and definitive love becomes the icon of the relationship between God and his people and vice versa. God's way of loving becomes the measure of human love. This close connection between *eros* and marriage in the Bible has practically no equivalent in extra-biblical literature."[22] Benedict's understanding of human marriage as an "icon" of God's love echoes his predecessor John Paul II's theology of the body which in turn has been further developed by his successor, Pope Francis. In brief, the insight of these popes is that God's Trinitarian love is "mirrored" in the life of a man and woman when they give themselves totally to one another. The married becomes a family in begetting new life, thereby making visible on earth the divine "family": the eternal exchange of love wherein the Father and Son spirate a third divine person, the Holy Spirit. As the pontiffs note, this Trinitarian dimension of human love is also expressed in St. Paul's teaching that man and woman becoming "one flesh" in Christian marriage is a great "mystery" (*sacramentum*) of the union of Christ and his Church (Eph 5:21–33).[23]

---

22. Ibid., §11. While the Trinitarian nature of God has no equivalent outside of the Bible, it is nonetheless interesting to note that there exist extra-biblical parallels for the original unity of man and woman. In this connection, Benedict himself recalls the myth mentioned by Plato, according to which man was originally spherical, complete in himself and self-sufficient. As a punishment for pride, man was split in two by Zeus, and henceforth he pines for his other half. See Plato, *Symposium* (Indianapolis: Hackett, 1989), XIV–XV, 189c–192d.

23. For the late pontiff's catecheses on marriage, see John Paul II, *Man and Woman*

Having said that the newness of biblical faith as a whole consists in its image of God and image of man (who as a communion of persons in the family is the image of God), Benedict adds that the real novelty of the New Testament in particular "lies not so much in new ideas as in the figure of Jesus himself, who gives flesh and blood to those concepts—an unprecedented realism."[24] It is one thing to say that God is love, but it is another to *see* and *experience* God's love enacted in Christ. God's death on the cross is love in its most radical form, says Benedict, insisting that we define love on the basis of this complete divine gift of self. Indeed, Jesus himself says as much when he commanded his disciples during the Last Supper, "Love one another as I have loved you," an exhortation immediately followed by a description of what Jesus himself was about to do: "Greater love has no man than this, that a man lay down his life for his friends" (Jn 15:12–13).

In John's gospel cited immediately above, Jesus connects his love for us with his willingness to die and give himself as our food and drink. God's self-emptying *agape* and yearning of *eros* for us thus find their fullness of expression for all time in the sacrament of the Eucharist. Just as he did at the Last Supper, the Lord draws us into his own act of self-oblation when we receive his body and blood in the liturgy even today. In the Eucharist, we do not just statically receive God—we enter into the very dynamic of his self-giving. In this way, says Benedict:

> The imagery of marriage between God and Israel is now realized in a way previously inconceivable: it had meant standing in God's presence, but now it becomes union with God through sharing in Jesus' self-gift, sharing in his body and blood. The sacramental "mysticism," grounded in God's conde-

---

He Created Them: A Theology of the Body, trans. Michael Waldstein (Boston, Mass.: Pauline Books & Media, 2006). For the development of these same themes in light of Benedict and John Paul II, see Francis, *Amoris Laetitia* (2016), §§11, 30, 70, 121, http://w2.vatican.va/content/francesco/en/apost_exhortations/documents/papa-francesco_esortazione-ap_20160319_amoris-laetitia.html.

24. Benedict XVI, *Deus Caritas Est*, §12. This understanding of the New Testament's novelty is echoed in Benedict XVI, *From the Baptism in the Jordan to the Transfiguration*, 44, 116.

scension towards us, operates at a radically different level and lifts us to far greater heights than anything that any human mystical elevation could ever accomplish.[25]

What, precisely, are these previously inconceivable "heights" to which Eucharistic mysticism lifts Christians? The paradox of Christian mysticism is that we are "elevated" to God in the measure to which we empty ourselves and bow down in service of our brothers and sisters. Moreover, Benedict points out that Christian spirituality universalizes the command to love our neighbor as ourselves (Lv 19:18). By his words and by his sacrifice, Christ teaches us that our love is to extend not only to friends and neighbors, but also to our enemies. And Jesus himself incarnates this teaching by dying for everyone, including his enemies. Every time we receive the Eucharist, we are conformed a little more to this mystery and given the grace to live it out in our own lives. As we have seen earlier in this book, the goal of Eucharistic spirituality is divinization—that in us and in all of creation God becomes "all in all" (1 Cor 15:28). When we unite our own sufferings with the passion of Christ, his will becomes our own and we become more and more his. As a result, "God's will is no longer for me an alien will, something imposed on me from without by the commandments, but it is now my own will, based on the realization that God is in fact more deeply present to me than I am to myself."[26] As our union with the cross and self-abandonment to God increases, God himself increasingly becomes our joy.

---

25. Benedict XVI, *Deus Caritas Est*, §13.
26. Ibid., §§17–18.

Part 2: The Practice of Love as a Response to God's Love

Charity, Received and Given

Having contemplated the nature of love itself—what it means to say that God is love and what it means for man to be the image of a God who is love—we are now in a position to explore what Benedict thinks a response to God's love looks like in society today. As we read in the introduction to his encyclical *Caritas in Veritate*, Benedict describes charity as love that is at once both a received and given reality. We saw above that human beings are the objects of God's unfathomable love, which can be understood both as *eros* and *agape*. But in the latter half of *Deus Caritas Est* and in this second encyclical devoted to love, the pontiff turns our attention to how men and women can become subjects of charity, vessels to pour forth God's own love into our world.[27]

Charity in Truth, Truth in Charity

When it comes to the question of how we are to live the virtue of charity out in the world, the first point Benedict wishes to emphasize is that our charitable efforts must be grounded in *truth*. He sees Catholic social teaching as one particular dimension of the Church's overall mission of truth, an enterprise that consists in seeking the truth tirelessly wherever it may be found and proclaiming it everywhere it is not. In our current cultural context that tends to relativize truth, this mission is more significant than ever. To begin with, proclaiming that there even exists such a thing as truth is in many ways a countercultural statement. Moreover, the Church's openness to the full breadth of human reason stands as a prophetic witness in an age when—despite the fact that information has never been more widely available to all—fewer and fewer people are willing to truly listen to those who

---

27. Benedict XVI, *Caritas in Veritate*, §5.

hold views that differ from their own. The Catholic Church ought to be a beacon of light in today's world, professing boldly that we are not afraid of the truth, and that all truth—no matter its source—is of the Holy Spirit.

As Benedict describes it, Catholic social teaching simply is *caritas in veritate*—charity in truth—the proclamation of the truth of Christ's love in society. Truth is not much emphasized in contemporary discussions about how to go about the endeavor of creating social justice, yet Benedict insists that it is precisely truth that enables charity to set man free and bring him happiness: "Fidelity to man requires fidelity to the truth, which alone is the guarantee of freedom (cf. Jn 8:32) and of the possibility of integral human development."[28] Illumined by the best of what both reason and faith have to offer, Christian charity understands the human person in a way that transcends mere justice. It knows that man does not live by bread alone, and is therefore able "to pursue development goals that possess a more humane and humanizing value."[29] In other words, because it understands man in light of his creation by God and vocation to union with God, charity offers the only path to fulfillment that truly meets our human needs. Or, to put it in the language of John Paul II, the way to guarantee a true sense for man in our world is to not lose our sense of God.[30] Benedict states this same truth with a slightly different nuance when he says, "The greatest service to development, then, is a Christian humanism.... A humanism which excludes God is an inhuman humanism."[31]

When it fails to keep the truth of God and man in view, Benedict laments that charitable efforts to achieve social justice end up degenerating into a misguided sentimentality.

---

28. Ibid., §9.
29. Ibid.
30. John Paul II, *Evangelium Vitae* (1995), §21, http://w2.vatican.va/content/john-paul-ii/en/encyclicals/documents/hf_jp-ii_enc_25031995_evangelium-vitae.html.
31. Benedict XVI, *Caritas in Veritate*, §78.

Love becomes an empty shell, to be filled in an arbitrary way. In a culture without truth, this is the fatal risk facing love. It falls prey to contingent subjective emotions and opinions, the word "love" is abused and distorted, to the point where it comes to mean the opposite. Truth frees charity from the constraints of an emotionalism that deprives it of relational and social content, and of a fideism that deprives it of human and universal breathing-space.[32]

Innumerable examples of such misguided attempts at charity are plain to see in today's world. Benedict does not mention this particular instance here, but the institution of marriage and the family has been a significant casualty of the divorce of truth from charity. Benedict correctly diagnoses the problem underlying so much of our current debates in the realm of human sexuality: they are not governed by reason and truth, but by an emotionalism and a fideism that seeks to engineer social change without accounting for the nature of the human person, his ends, and what God might have to do with it all. One of Benedict's central concerns throughout his career was to safeguard the place of God in the public sphere, the public dimension of faith. While we should not need direct recourse to the truths of the faith in order to know the nature of human sexuality, the reality is that the God of Christian faith is both *Agape* and *Logos*, Charity and Truth. If we really believe that he is these things, then how could this datum not be supremely relevant to the business of seeking justice in our world?[33]

That said, one of the greatest dangers confronting the person who thinks he has the truth is the temptation to turn that truth into an all-too-easy and comfortable ideology, to lose sight of what Benedict said earlier: we do not indeed possess the truth, but rather it possesses *us*. When we fail to attend to this reality, it is easy also to forget the dignity of the other person with whom we are communicating and from whom we stand to learn so much. So if charity is authentically practiced only in the truth, then we may say that the converse also

---

32. Ibid., §3.
33. Ibid.

holds: truth is rightly pursued only when sought and expressed in the economy of charity (cf. Eph 4:15). Benedict argues that seeking the truth in charity actually ends up lending it more credibility. The power of truth, he says, is authenticated only in the practical setting of social living. Perhaps Pope Paul VI best captured this point decades ago when he said, "Modern man listens more willingly to witnesses than to teachers, and if he does listen to teachers, it is because they are witnesses."[34]

Trinitarian Relationality and the Integral Good of Man

Having established the reciprocal relationship of truth and charity as a basis for our endeavor of enacting God's love in the world, Benedict returns to the Trinity as the primordial truth that undergirds and ought to guide all our charitable efforts. In Benedict's own words, "The Christian revelation of the unity of the human race presupposes a metaphysical interpretation of the *humanum* in which relationality is an essential element."[35] What Benedict is trying to convey here in his philosophical and foreign vocabulary is that the Christian vision of human fulfillment is based above all on the reality of the Trinity. In the Trinity, the pontiff says, relationality is essential. The three divine persons are pure relationality and are indeed distinct from one another precisely by virtue of the unique relationship each has with the others.

If God himself is a relationship of family love, then we manifest God in the world by living out our vocation as families—both as the nuclear family and human family as a whole. Indeed, Benedict begins the practical section of his *Deus Caritas Est* by citing this line from Augustine: "If you see charity, you see the Trinity."[36] The entire work of the Church is an expression of this Trinitarian love that seeks what Benedict and the tradition of Catholic social thought call the "inte-

---

34. Paul VI, *Evangelii Nuntiandi* (1975), §41, http://w2.vatican.va/content/paul-vi/en/apost_exhortations/documents/hf_p-vi_exh_19751208_evangelii-nuntiandi.html.
35. Benedict XVI, *Caritas in Veritate*, §§54–55.
36. Augustine, *De Trinitate*, VIII, 8, 12, cited in Benedict XVI, *Deus Caritas Est*, §19.

gral good of man" or "integral human development." As I mentioned above, the pope does not merely have in mind here man's bodily good, the "bread" we provide to people for their survival. Of course, service of this good does comprise a part of the Church's mission, but the enterprise of charity, such as it is commonly understood, is in reality only one of three ministries by which the Church expresses her love for the needy. Benedict writes of their relationship in this way: "The Church's deepest nature is expressed in her threefold responsibility: of proclaiming the word of God (*kerygma-martyria*), celebrating the sacraments (*leitourgia*), and exercising the ministry of charity (*diakonia*). These duties presuppose each other and are inseparable. For the Church, charity is not a kind of welfare activity which could equally well be left to others, but is a part of her nature, an indispensable expression of her very being."[37] The foundations of this threefold service of charity date all the way back to the life of Jesus and the apostles, a life perhaps best summarized by St. Luke when he writes that the first believers in Jesus "devoted themselves to the apostles' teaching and fellowship, to the breaking of bread and the prayers," that they "were together and had all things in common" and "sold their possessions and goods and distributed them to all, as any had need" (Acts 2:42–44). Benedict takes these verses as "a kind of definition of the Church" and insists that the Church "cannot neglect the service of charity any more than she can neglect the Sacraments and the Word."[38]

How to Achieve Man's Integral Good: Solidarity and Subsidiarity

The Church's mission of charitable service to society which I have just introduced is grounded on twin principles whose ramifications reach into all areas of life, from economics to bioethics to how we relate to the environment and even to how we preach the gospel.

---

37. Benedict XVI, *Deus Caritas Est*, §25.
38. Ibid., §§20–22.

The first of these is *solidarity*, which the *Catechism* calls "an eminently Christian virtue" and Pope Francis describes as "something more than a few sporadic acts of generosity … a new mindset which thinks in terms of community and the priority of the life of all over the appropriation of goods by a few."[39] In solidarity, we put ourselves in the shoes of the poor and suffering, making their needs our own and loving them as ourselves (Lv 19:18; Mk 12:31; Rom 13:9).

Solidarity is at the heart of the effort to foster what Catholic social teaching calls *the common good*, the good of individuals, families, and intermediate groups who together constitute society.[40] While Catholicism acknowledges the right to personal property, gainful employment, and other private goods, the Church's emphasis on the common good is a reminder that every right also presupposes a corresponding duty. If we have a right to the basic good things of life, then we have the duty to order what we have been given to the good of all, since everything we have ultimately belongs to and is a gift from God.[41] Benedict concisely states one key implication of this truth: "Purchasing is always a moral—and not simply economic—act."[42] For this reason, Catholic teaching speaks frequently of the "universal destination of the earth's goods," a "social dimension of property," and even of a "preferential option for the poor" which, while by no means excluding service toward other groups, occupies a "special form of pri-

---

39. *Catechism of the Catholic Church*, §1948; Francis, *Evangelii Gaudium* (2013), §188, http://w2.vatican.va/content/francesco/en/apost_exhortations/documents/papa-francesco_esortazione-ap_20131124_evangelii-gaudium.html.

40. Benedict XVI, *Deus Caritas Est*, §26; Benedict XVI, *Caritas in Veritate*, §7; Vatican Council II, *Gaudium et Spes*, §§26, 75.

41. John Paul II, *Centesimus Annus* (1991), §6, http://w2.vatican.va/content/john-paul-ii/en/encyclicals/documents/hf_jp-ii_enc_01051991_centesimus-annus.html; Benedict XVI, *Caritas in Veritate*, §43. In this regard, Paul VI, in a text cited by Francis, writes that "the more fortunate should renounce some of their rights so as to place their goods more generously at the service of others." Paul VI, *Octogesima Adveniens* (1971), §23, http://w2.vatican.va/content/paul-vi/en/apost_letters/documents/hf_p-vi_apl_19710514_octogesima-adveniens.html; Francis, *Evangelii Gaudium*, §190.

42. Benedict XVI, *Caritas in Veritate*, §66; Francis cites this text in his *Laudato Si'*, §206.

macy in the exercise of Christian charity."[43] What this means is that, all things being equal, our charitable efforts ought to focus above all on those who lack the necessities of life—this includes food, shelter, basic health care, and other bodily goods, and it also includes the spiritual goods of education, companionship, and religious formation.[44]

Most people have a general understanding of what the above principle of solidarity means and requires of us. It is a teaching enshrined at least partially in religions and philosophies the world over, as in Confucianism's saying, "Do not do unto others as you would not have them do unto you" or Immanuel Kant's categorical imperative, "Act only according to that maxim whereby you can, at the same time, will that it should become a universal law."[45] But the Christian principle of solidarity, the Golden Rule, is unique in that it is first of all positive (it includes a "do" and not just "do not") and moreover it intrinsically paired by Jesus with the prior commandment to "love the Lord your God with all your heart, and with all your soul, and with all your mind, and with all your strength" (Mk 12:30). The fullness of solidarity thus flows from one's love of God and includes concern not only for our neighbor's bodily good but also that he be given the highest of goods: divine friendship and eternal life. From the perspective of the New Testament, you simply cannot have true love of God without love of neighbor and vice versa. Perhaps no one has stated this more starkly than St. John: "If any one says, 'I love God,' and hates his brother, he is a liar; for he who does not love his brother whom he has seen, cannot love God whom he has not seen" (1 Jn 4:20).

The second core principle of Catholic social teaching is *subsid-*

---

43. John Paul II, *Centesimus Annus*, §§11, 30; John Paul II, *Sollicitudo Rei Socialis* (1987), §42, http://w2.vatican.va/content/john-paul-ii/en/encyclicals/documents/hf_jp-ii_enc_30121987_sollicitudo-rei-socialis.html; Francis, *Evangelii Gaudium*, §§188–89.

44. Pope Francis has rightly emphasized these latter points, namely that the preferential option for the poor "must mainly translate into a privileged and preferential religious care." Francis, *Evangelii Gaudium*, §200.

45. Immanuel Kant, *Grounding for the Metaphysics of Morals* (Indianapolis: Hackett, 1993), 30.

iarity, a term rarely heard of by Catholics in the pew and poorly understood in our culture as a whole. If solidarity with our fellow men is our goal, then subsidiarity is the proper means to achieving it. In *Deus Caritas Est*, Benedict begins his discussion of subsidiarity with the comment that the personal service of love—*caritas*—will always prove necessary, even in the most just of societies. Even if we were able to meet people's material needs adequately through governmental initiatives of solidarity, there will always remain suffering, loneliness, and other situations where help in the form of concrete love of neighbor is indispensable. This observation leads Benedict to stake out a strong position against big government with a great emphasis on subsidiarity as the means to avoid its dangers:

> The State which would provide everything, absorbing everything into itself, would ultimately become a mere bureaucracy incapable of guaranteeing the very thing which the suffering person—every person—needs: namely, loving personal concern. We do not need a State which regulates and controls everything, but a State which, in accordance with the principle of subsidiarity, generously acknowledges and supports initiatives arising from the different social forces and combines spontaneity with closeness to those in need.[46]

In this paragraph, we get an initial description of what Benedict understands by the term subsidiarity. In contrast with a government which would subsume all aspects of social charity under its own umbrella, subsidiarity entails service at all different social levels, not preplanned by the state but arising from the initiative of individuals and intermediate groups who are closest to those in need and therefore know each of their particular situations best.

By intermediate groups, the pontiff has in mind all manner of community organizations which are not state-run. To name just a few in my own community with which I have had some involvement, there is Catholic Charities (a large organization that provides emergency assistance to the poor, refugee, and immigration services, family strength-

---

46. Benedict XVI, *Deus Caritas Est*, §28.

ening services, hospice and health care, and more), Uplift (a group that brings meals and other material goods to the homeless in vans that travel across the Kansas City metro area), our college's Hunger Coalition (which delivers sack lunches to the poor throughout the city of Atchison on Saturdays all year long), and Unbound (an international aid organization based in Kansas City which allows us to sponsor a child's education in the developing world). My local parish and archdiocese also fall under the umbrella of this category of intermediate organizations which provide an immense variety of services to those most in need: recent immigrants from Spanish-speaking countries, children with disabilities, mothers experiencing troubled pregnancies, those living in the poorer areas of the urban core, and so many others.

Unlike the government when it sends help in the form of a check, individuals and intermediate groups such as the ones I just mentioned are in a position to offer the needy "something which often is even more necessary than material support" precisely because they are so close to them, namely, "refreshment and care for their souls." I think of it this way based on my own experience of serving the poor: which method better serves them—sending them an anonymous government check with which they can buy a meal, or sending them a person with a meal to share and some conversation? For the Christian, to ask the question is to answer it. But Benedict is aware that not everyone thinks this way, that there exist ideologies which mask "a materialist conception of man: the mistaken notion that man can live 'by bread alone' (Mt 4:4; cf. Dt 8:3)—a conviction that demeans man and ultimately disregards all that is specifically human."[47] In the same vein, John Paul II writes that the guiding principle of the Church's entire social doctrine is a correct view of the human person. If we get man wrong, then of course we are going to end up not knowing what he needs and how best to help him achieve fulfillment.[48]

---

47. Ibid. As Benedict's predecessor puts it, modern atheism is the "first cause" of this mistaken materialist conception of man. John Paul II, *Centesimus Annus*, §13.

48. John Paul II, *Centesimus Annus*, §11.

In his *Caritas in Veritate*, Benedict writes similarly and more extensively on subsidiarity, arguing that it respects human dignity more than an approach wherein big government tries to take care of all our needs from the top:

> Subsidiarity respects personal dignity by recognizing in the person a subject who is always capable of giving something to others. By considering reciprocity as the heart of what it is to be a human being, subsidiarity is the most effective antidote against any form of all-encompassing welfare state.... In order not to produce a dangerous universal power of a tyrannical nature, the governance of globalization must be marked by subsidiarity, articulated into several layers and involving different levels that can work together. Globalization certainly requires authority, insofar as it poses the problem of a global common good that needs to be pursued. This authority, however, must be organized in a subsidiary and stratified way, if it is not to infringe upon freedom and if it is to yield effective results in practice.[49]

Clearly, Benedict and his predecessors upon whose work he is drawing are at pains to warn us against the perils of an all-encompassing state—and how could they not be leery of this, given the oppressive regimes under which each once lived? Subsidiarity, having people closest to the needy take responsibility for their care, is thus prescribed as the "antidote" to totalitarian governments which easily take on a tyrannical nature.

Yet more is at work here than a warning against totalitarianism, important as that caution is. Catholic social teaching is concerned about the virtue and happiness of individuals, and Benedict thinks that excessive centralization leads to a loss of personal responsibility which is necessary for the attainment of these. In the end, the waning of subsidiarity leads to less holistic care for the needy, for the state that makes decisions for individuals takes away the decision-making capacity of those who know their needs best. Likewise, it takes away the dignity that comes when the needy exercise discretion over the

---

49. Benedict XVI, *Caritas in Veritate*, §57.

affairs of their own lives, becoming artisans of their own destiny.[50] Additionally, if the state does for people what they can do for themselves (for example, by routinely giving financial assistance to those who are able but choose not to work), it actually detracts from their flourishing. The reason for this is that the Catholic Church sees dignity in work itself, that human beings are made happy by doing honest work and earning bread by the sweat of their brow. Finally, a loss of subsidiarity affects not only those in need but also those who are best positioned to provide for them, for a government that takes over all charitable functions deprives the populace as a whole of opportunities for the exercise of virtue. In summary, then, we can say that subsidiarity is the proper means for achieving solidarity with our brethren, the virtue by which we respect people's dignity by reaching them at the most local level possible and letting them have a hand in shaping their own destiny as much as possible.

Of course, to affirm the principle of subsidiarity is not to say that government assistance is never appropriate. According to Catholic social teaching, a higher order of society can intervene in the affairs of lower orders if those at the local level either *cannot* or *will not* help those in need. For this reason, Benedict writes: "The principle of subsidiarity must remain closely linked to the principle of solidarity and vice versa, since the former without the latter gives way to social privatism, while the latter without the former gives way to paternalist social assistance that is demeaning to those in need."[51]

Here we see two opposite extremes that are opposed to authentic Catholic social teaching, which Benedict calls "social privatism" and "paternalist social assistance," respectively. In the age of Pope Leo XIII, whose pontificate inaugurated systematic Catholic social teaching as we now know it, what Benedict calls social privatism went by

---

50. Paul VI, *Populorum Progressio* (1967), §289, http://w2.vatican.va/content/paul-vi/en/encyclicals/documents/hf_p-vi_enc_26031967_populorum.html; Francis, *Evangelii Gaudium*, 190.

51. Benedict XVI, *Caritas in Veritate*, §58.

the name of "liberalism" (an economy that was too free of regulation), while the paternalist state went by the more familiar names of socialism and Marxism.[52]

We have already dealt with Benedict's critiques of socialism in some detail, but it is also crucial that we emphasize the proper role government and other higher authorities play in the enactment of solidarity within society. While subsidiarity is important for creating favorable conditions for the free exercise of economic activity, solidarity sometimes requires that governments place limits on the autonomy of corporations for the sake of defending the basic human dignity of their employees and for providing the necessary minimum support for those who are unable to secure employment.[53] Moreover, the state is authorized at times to intervene and break up monopolies or other obstacles to authentic human development. The state can even serve what John Paul II calls a "substitute function" when social sectors are dangerously weak or just getting under way.[54] In principle, then, a government can "bail out" the private sector in certain desperate cases. Whether it is right to do so in a given situation is where matters get extremely thorny, as the recent history of American politics has demonstrated well.

In any event, John Paul makes it clear that, when a higher authority intervenes in the affairs of a lower order for the sake of the common good, it has the duty to do so as briefly as possible so as to avoid the permanent loss of that dignity which comes from individuals exercising their economic and civil freedoms. Unfortunately, John Paul notes that in recent years the range of government intervention has vastly expanded, to the point of creating the so-called "Welfare State" or "Social Assistance State." In the following text, John Paul describes the

---

52. Leo XIII, *Rerum Novarum* (1891), §42, http://w2.vatican.va/content/leo-xiii/en/encyclicals/documents/hf_l-xiii_enc_15051891_rerum-novarum.html; John Paul II, *Centesimus Annus*, §10.

53. John Paul II, *Centesimus Annus*, §15.

54. Ibid., §48.

deleterious effects of this approach along with a reaffirmation of what the proper path to solidarity looks like:

> By intervening directly and depriving society of its responsibility, the Social Assistance State leads to a loss of human energies and an inordinate increase of public agencies, which are dominated more by bureaucratic ways of thinking than by concern for serving their clients, and which are accompanied by an enormous increase in spending.
>
> In fact, it would appear that needs are best understood and satisfied by people who are closest to them and who act as neighbors to those in need. It should be added that certain kinds of demands often call for a response which is not simply material but which is capable of perceiving the deeper human need. One thinks of the condition of refugees, immigrants, the elderly, the sick, and all those in circumstances which call for assistance, such as drug abusers: all these people can be helped effectively only by those who offer them genuine fraternal support, in addition to the necessary care.[55]

To state the matter concisely, state intervention may at times be necessary, but Christianity sees the role of government as only instrumental to realities which are more fundamental: the human person, the family, and society. Governments exist in order to foster the good of people—not vice versa.

Another way of looking at the above principle is to remember that the state is not the same as "society." Does society have the obligation to provide people with the necessities for basic human fulfillment? Yes, but this does not necessarily mean that the *government* has the responsibility to provide these things to people. If we grasp the twin principles of solidarity and subsidiarity aright, then we know that, while the state may need to intervene at times if we are unable or unwilling to bring about justice in our world, it is primarily we as real human beings who have the duty to supply our fellow real human beings with what they need.

55. Ibid.

Conclusion

Benedict's teaching on solidarity and subsidiarity in relation to charity may be summed up in his conviction that Christian charity is our simple response to real people with immediate needs and specific situations that require the personal touch that only we their brothers and sisters can give.[56] But the difference that Christianity makes in this regard—the difference between true Christian charity and mere almsgiving—is something that can only be appreciated fully in the living of it. Moreover, it is one thing to preach the values of subsidiarity and solidarity and to understand them on an academic level, but, if Benedict is right, the Church's wisdom on these is ultimately perceived only if we commit to the "experiment" of charity in its fullness. In this next chapter, we will approach the experience of charity from one last angle which in papal language goes by the name "integral ecology."

56. Benedict XVI, *Deus Caritas Est*, §§29, 31.

9

CHARITY (II)

Integral Ecology and Man's Place in Creation

What Does Ecology Have to Do with Charity?

In this book, we have been concerned with articulating a robust understanding of the theological virtues of faith, hope, and charity and how one fully appreciative of Nietzsche's critique can continue to live them in our secular age. In the last chapter, we focused on the nature of love and what a Christian response to God's love looks like in society today. In this chapter, we will conclude our meditations on charity by turning to the Catholic Church's vision for an "integral ecology." While perhaps at first glance seemingly unconnected with it, this dimension of the Church's mission is in reality a critically important extension of the virtue of charity, the proclamation of how the truth of Christ's love impacts everything in our lives, from how we treat our fellow man to how we live within the created world God has entrusted to us.

Since Benedict does not have a single encyclical dedicated to integral ecology, in this chapter we will glimpse the emeritus pontiff's crucial ecological insights by seeing how Pope Francis has woven them into his encyclical *Laudato Si'* whose theme is "on care for our common home." This expansive document relies heavily on Benedict's thought to frame its picture of what the authentic Christian moral life looks like in relation to the environment.[1] I recall feeling almost depressed on the day that Pope Francis's encyclical was first released back in 2015. I was excited to read the document, not only because I am into biology and gardening, but also because I knew that Benedict himself had written a lot about the environment. A flood of commentary on the encyclical had already been published online, yet I knew that it would be weeks before I would have the time to finish reading the lengthy text. After finally completing the text a couple of months later, I started to survey the blogosphere and, unsurprisingly, encountered a wide range of reactions. There were those on the left who cheered the Church for finally having gotten with the times and accepted the human causes behind climate change. And there were those on the right who dismissed the entire document, moved by their skepticism of this same claim. It turns out, however, that the question of climate change holds a minor place within the scope of the encyclical and of the Church's ecological thought as a whole. While it is certainly an issue raised by Francis, climate change is largely irrelevant to his overarching message. In other words, the text is not "an encyclical on climate change," as some have called it. Like Catholic social thought on the subject of the environment in general, it treats a number of other scientific issues and much more besides that. In this chapter, I will sidestep the issue of climate change which I see as a

---

1. The thought of Pope John Paul II is also highly significant for the enterprise of articulating the Church's vision of the environment in relation to man and God. As citing the work of three popes would be overly burdensome for most readers, in keeping with this book's overall theme I have chosen to keep the focus on the thought of Benedict itself such as it has been developed by Pope Francis. For the teaching of John Paul II on ecology, see his encyclicals *Redemptor Hominis* (1979), §§15–16, http://w2.vatican.va/content/john-paul-ii/en/encyclicals/documents/hf_jp-ii_enc_04031979_redemptor-hominis.html; *Centesimus Annus*, §§37–40; and *Evangelium Vitae*, §42. For what came to be known as his manifesto for Green Catholicism, see his message for the twenty-third World Day of Peace (January 1, 1990), http://w2.vatican.va/content/john-paul-ii/en/messages/peace/documents/hf_jp-ii_mes_19891208_xxiii-world-day-for-peace.html.

distraction for our present project. Instead of getting caught up in this debate, what I would like to do is offer a reflection on what I take to constitute the heart of Benedict's and Francis's vision for an "integral ecology" and how to live the experiment of faith by means of the "ecological virtues" demanded by it.

The Pontiffs' Vision for an Integral Ecology

If there is one theme that runs throughout Francis's encyclical on the environment, it is his repeated insistence that everything in the world is "interconnected" or "interrelated." This thought is expressed dozens of times throughout the text, and it is probably the most concise way to capture the core conviction undergirding the pontiff's vision for what he terms an "integral ecology." According to Francis, the problem is that we have forgotten that we ourselves are dust of the earth. Echoing St. Francis and St. Bonaventure, the pontiff does not shy away from speaking of all creatures as our brothers and sisters. But in invoking this turn of phrase from the Franciscan tradition, the pope is by no means denying the uniqueness of man and his place in the cosmos—far from it, as we shall see below. Rather, the thrust behind this expression is to emphasize that the natural environment (focused upon in this chapter) and man's social environment (which was in focus in the latter half of the previous chapter) are really two sides of a single reality in crisis today. This is expressed well in the following paragraph:

When we speak of the "environment," what we really mean is a relationship existing between nature and the society which lives in it. Nature cannot be regarded as something separate from ourselves or as a mere setting in which we live. We are part of nature, included in it, and thus in constant interaction with it.... We are faced not with two separate crises, one environmental and the other social, but rather with one complex crisis which is both social and environmental. Strategies for a solution demand an integrated approach to combating poverty, restoring dignity to the excluded, and at the same time protecting nature.²

This text is of paramount importance, especially since I have heard a number of traditionally minded Catholics claim that the environment is a secondary issue and that the pope has more important things he should be talking about. On this score, we should recall that Francis inherited his office from two predecessors who thankfully talked much on the subjects that these Catholics want to hear about. Francis's own view on the matter is perhaps best expressed in his first major interview as pope:

> We cannot insist only on issues related to abortion, gay marriage, and the use of contraceptive methods. This is not possible. I have not spoken much about these things, and I was reprimanded for that. But when we speak about these issues, we have to talk about them in a context. The teaching of the Church, for that matter, is clear and I am a son of the Church, but it is not necessary to talk about these issues all the time.³

Francis's encyclical, therefore, is not focused on your typical pro-life issues but on care for the common good under the aspect of our common home—the earth. Yet, despite Francis not insisting *only* on the immorality of abortion, gay marriage, and the use of contraceptive methods, we will see below that he does indeed address these issues rather forcefully.

The irony is that some people get caught up on the climate change question and miss the fact that *Laudato Si'* is in fact a deeply pro-life encyclical that ought to be applauded by all Catholics, including those who love the tradition handed down to us by John Paul II and Benedict XVI. Specifically, Francis's insistence upon environmental issues offers an exceptional backdoor entry into issues concerning human dignity and what the Church's social doctrine tradition calls integral

---

2. Francis, *Laudato Si'*, §139.
3. Francis and Spadaro, "A Big Heart Open to God."

human development, a topic discussed in the previous chapter. To be sure, Francis is not simply using environmental issues as a means to talk about thorny social problems, but since we human beings are inextricably connected with the rest of nature, to talk about how to treat the environment is also to talk about ourselves.

An illustration of this point can be seen in what Francis has to say about cruelty toward animals. While we certainly ought to respect God's creatures and see in all of them a ray of God's infinite wisdom and goodness, Francis emphasizes that the abuse of God's creation is "contrary to human dignity."[4] Or, as Benedict puts it, "The way humanity treats the environment influences the way it treats itself, and vice versa."[5] Regardless of whether Francis is right on every last scientific point in the encyclical, he and Benedict are making the more fundamental argument that it is in the first place bad *for us* as human beings to treat the environment how we carelessly often do. As in the Catholic moral tradition broadly speaking, so here the moral issue at stake concerns the habits we are creating in ourselves. Francis wants us to ponder these questions: In a world where people have grown accustomed to disrespecting the natural environment, why should we expect them to respect man's nature? Or, conversely, in a world where we habitually manipulate our own bodies without any concern for their nature, why should we expect people to respect the non-human environment around us?

Human Ecology and the Pro-life Implications of an Integral Ecology

To draw out the implications of his integral vision, Francis builds on a little understood concept introduced into Catholic social teaching by John Paul II and reiterated by Benedict XVI: human ecology

---

4. Francis, *Laudato Si'*, §§92; 130; cf. *Catechism of the Catholic Church*, §§339; 2418.
5. Benedict XVI, *Caritas in Veritate*, §51.

(or, as it is sometimes translated, ecology of man). In a 2011 address to the German parliament, Benedict pointedly stated:

> The importance of ecology is no longer disputed. We must listen to the language of nature, and we must answer accordingly. Yet I would like to underline a point that seems to me to be neglected, today as in the past: there is also an ecology of man. *Man too has a nature that he must respect* and that he cannot manipulate at will. Man is not merely self-creating freedom. Man does not create himself. He is intellect and will, but he is also nature, and his will is rightly ordered if he respects his nature, listens to it, and accepts himself for who he is, as one who did not create himself. In this way, and in no other, is true human freedom fulfilled.[6]

The encyclical *Caritas in Veritate* contains a chapter titled "The Development of People, Rights and Duties, and the Environment," wherein Benedict writes at length in a similar vein:

> There is need for what might be called a human ecology, correctly understood. The deterioration of nature is in fact closely connected to the culture that shapes human coexistence: when "human ecology" is respected within society, environmental ecology also benefits. Just as human virtues are interrelated, such that the weakening of one places others at risk, so the ecological system is based on respect for a plan that affects both the health of society and its good relationship with nature....
>
> If there is a lack of respect for the right to life and to a natural death, if human conception, gestation, and birth are made artificial, if human embryos are sacrificed to research, the conscience of society ends up losing the concept of human ecology and, along with it, that of environmental ecology. It is contradictory to insist that future generations respect the natural environment when our educational systems and laws do not help them to respect themselves. The book of nature is one and indivisible: it takes in not only the environment but also life, sexuality, marriage, the family, social relations: in a word, integral human development. Our duties towards the environment are linked to our duties towards the human person, considered in himself and

---

6. Benedict XVI, address to the Bundestag (September 22, 2011), emphasis added; cf. Francis, *Laudato Si'*, §155.

in relation to others. It would be wrong to uphold one set of duties while trampling on the other. Herein lies a grave contradiction in our mentality and practice today: one which demeans the person, disrupts the environment, and damages society.[7]

I find this to be a remarkably fresh and brilliant way to discuss pro-life issues today in the public square. We begin by recalling that man is part of nature—and every school kid these days is told that he needs to respect nature. But then it must be asked: how can we be expected to respect non-human nature if we do not even respect our own human nature? Francis invokes this argument several times in his encyclical and applies it to a wide-ranging array of issues dealing with the dignity of human life from conception until death:

When we fail to acknowledge as part of reality the worth of a poor person, a human embryo, a person with disabilities—to offer just a few examples—it becomes difficult to hear the cry of nature itself; everything is connected.[8]

Since everything is interrelated, concern for the protection of nature is also incompatible with the justification of abortion. How can we genuinely teach the importance of concern for other vulnerable beings, however troublesome or inconvenient they may be, if we fail to protect a human embryo, even when its presence is uncomfortable and creates difficulties?[9]

Among the vulnerable for whom the Church wishes to care with particular love and concern are unborn children, the most defenseless and innocent among us. Nowadays efforts are made to deny them their human dignity and to do with them whatever one pleases, taking their lives and passing laws preventing anyone from standing in the way of this. Frequently, as a way of ridiculing the Church's effort to defend their lives, attempts are made to present her position as ideological, obscurantist, and conservative. Yet this defense of unborn life is closely linked to the defense of each and every other human right. It involves the conviction that a human being is always sacred and in-

---

7. Benedict XVI, *Caritas in Veritate*, §51; cf. John Paul II, *Centesimus Annus*, §§38–39.
8. Francis, *Laudato Si'*, §117.
9. Ibid.

violable, in any situation and at every stage of development. Human beings are ends in themselves and never a means of resolving other problems. Once this conviction disappears, so do solid and lasting foundations for the defense of human rights, which would always be subject to the passing whims of the powers that be. Reason alone is sufficient to recognize the inviolable value of each single human life.... I want to be completely honest in this regard. This is not something subject to alleged reforms or "modernizations." It is not "progressive" to try to resolve problems by eliminating a human life.[10]

In the absence of objective truths or sound principles other than the satisfaction of our own desires and immediate needs, what limits can be placed on human trafficking, organized crime, the drug trade, commerce in blood diamonds, and the fur of endangered species? Is it not the same relativistic logic which justifies buying the organs of the poor for resale or use in experimentation, or eliminating children because they are not what their parents wanted? This same "use and throw away" logic generates so much waste, because of the disordered desire to consume more than what is really necessary.[11]

On the other hand, it is troubling that, when some ecological movements defend the integrity of the environment, rightly demanding that certain limits be imposed on scientific research, they sometimes fail to apply those same principles to human life. There is a tendency to justify transgressing all boundaries when experimentation is carried out on living human embryos.[12]

The upshot of these comments is that, rather than dismissing Francis's teaching, pro-life Catholics ought to take away from it a key to carrying the pro-life movement forward in this generation. This key consists in pressing our interlocutors on the contradiction inherent in the practice of advocating for the environment while failing to apply this concern to the most vulnerable human beings within that environment, among whom he mentions the poor, victims of crime and trafficking, the disabled, the elderly in peril of being euthanized, and the unborn (including the human embryo).

10. Francis, *Evangelii Gaudium*, §213.
11. Francis, *Laudato Si'*, §123.
12. Ibid., §136.

Moreover, Francis and Benedict both elsewhere apply similar logic to the issue of how artificial contraception, an unnatural disruption of a major bodily function, harms both people and the environment. Benedict writes that governmental policies of mandatory birth control do violence to our human nature, while Francis speaks of falling birth rates in affluent nations as an economic problem and follows Paul VI in proclaiming that "no genital act of husband and wife" can refuse to be open to life.[13] To look at the matter less in terms of an argument and more in regard to the sort of response it demands, integral ecology calls us to join others, where appropriate, in the important work of environmental stewardship. This does not mean that we should cease pouring ourselves into the traditional pro-life ministries, but it should be noted that the environmental sphere today offers a unique way to initiate a fruitful "dialogue of action" with those who would never otherwise join our efforts to save the lives of unborn children.[14]

In discussing perhaps the most controverted moral issue of today, Benedict and Francis also apply human ecology to the issue of gender identity. In his encyclical on love, *Amoris Laetitia*, Francis decries our society's prevailing ideology of gender that:

---

13. Francis, *Amoris Laetitia*, §80; Paul VI, *Humanae Vitae* (1968), §§11–12, http://w2.vatican.va/content/paul-vi/en/encyclicals/documents/hf_p-vi_enc_25071968_humanae-vitae.html; Benedict XVI, *Caritas in Veritate*, §44. Like Francis, in this last document cited Benedict discusses a host of issues relevant to human ecology: *in vitro* fertilization, embryo research, cloned and human hybrids, abortion, euthanasia, eugenic programming of births, contraception. Benedict XVI, *Caritas in Veritate*, §75. John Paul II does the same throughout his encyclical *Evangelium Vitae*.

14. A "dialogue of action" is one of four forms of inter-religious dialogue prescribed by the Church. In this form of dialogue, Christians and others (even those with no religious affiliation) collaborate for the common good in society. Christians today are not going to transform our society by ourselves; it would appear that the Church is convinced that we need to enlist the help of all people of good will, and this especially means tapping into the charity of those who adhere devoutly to other religious traditions. For more on this subject, see the Pontifical Council for Inter-religious Dialogue, *Dialogue and Proclamation*, §42, http://www.vatican.va/roman_curia/pontifical_councils/interelg/documents/rc_pc_interelg_doc_19051991_dialogue-and-proclamatio_en.html. A more contemporary application of these principles of inter-religious dialogue can be found in Francis, *Evangelii Gaudium*, §§250–58.

denies the difference and reciprocity in nature of a man and a woman and envisages a society without sexual differences, thereby eliminating the anthropological basis of the family. This ideology leads to educational programs and legislative enactments that promote a personal identity and emotional intimacy radically separated from the biological difference between male and female. Consequently, human identity becomes the choice of the individual, one which can also change over time.[15]

In response to the severing of gender identity from our God-given biology, Francis writes that "biological sex and the socio-cultural role of sex (gender) can be distinguished but not separated" and that "it is one thing to be understanding of human weakness and the complexities of life, and another to accept ideologies that attempt to sunder what are inseparable aspects of reality."[16] In a line that sounds like it could have been written by Benedict, he concludes, "Creation is prior to us and must be received as a gift. At the same time, we are called to protect our humanity, and this means, in the first place, accepting it and respecting it as it was created."[17] Without explicitly invoking the expression, this is Human Ecology 101. The environment as a whole is a gift from God, and each creature ought to be treated in accord with its nature. Human beings, too, are part of creation and thus have a nature given by God to be received as a gift and not to be manipulated at will.

As helpful as Francis's thought is on the subject of gender identity, the most important papal text on the issue that I have discovered comes from the pen of Benedict. In a 2012 speech to the Roman curia, the pontiff unmasks the unstated premises that undergird today's prevailing gender ideology:

Now we decide for ourselves. Man and woman as created realities, as the nature of the human being, no longer exist. Man calls his nature into question. From now on he is merely spirit and will. The manipulation of nature, which

---

15. Francis, *Amoris Laetitia*, §56.
16. Ibid.
17. Ibid.

we deplore today where our environment is concerned, now becomes man's fundamental choice where he himself is concerned. From now on there is only the abstract human being, who chooses for himself what his nature is to be. Man and woman in their created state as complementary versions of what it means to be human are disputed.[18]

A casual perusal of contemporary film, blogging, pop music, and other cultural media confirms Benedict's diagnosis. People today tend to think of themselves primary as spirit and will. From this perspective, the body is accidental to the human person. Thus one song says of our bodies, "We just use them for fun," while another proclaims, "It's okay if you wanna change the body that you came in." This unbridled freedom to do with our bodies as we wish (like manipulating our sexual organs or engaging in sexual acts with people of the same sex as we) sounds to many people like a recipe for liberation, but in reality it belies a lack of respect for God's gift of creation which has evolved over billions of years to produce our body with its particular biological gender which is complementary to that of the opposite sex.

Benedict warned about the repercussions of an ideology which asks people to consider their God-given genders as accidental, a society in which the words "male and female he created them" (Gn 1:27) no longer apply:

18. Benedict XVI, Christmas address to the Roman Curia (December 21, 2012). In accord with the design of this book, the remarks I have noted here come from Benedict, but I find psychologist Jordan Peterson to be the most articulate contemporary thinker on the subject of gender issues. Criticizing the inconsistency of those who wish to maintain that gender is not innate while simultaneously claiming that a person can be trapped in the body of the wrong gender, Peterson writes, "Gender is constructed, but an individual who desires gender re-assignment surgery is to be unarguably considered a man trapped in a woman's body (or vice versa). The fact that both of these cannot logically be true, simultaneously, is just ignored (or rationalized away with another appalling post-modern claim: that logic itself—along with the techniques of science—is merely part of the oppressive patriarchal system)." Jordan Peterson, 12 Rules for Life: An Antidote to Chaos (Toronto: Random House of Canada, 2018), 310. In his many publically available lectures and interviews, and elsewhere in his book, Peterson weaves together insights from fields including psychology, evolutionary biology, and religion to demonstrate that gender identity is not a social construct and that "this isn't a debate—the data are in." Ibid., 293.

But if there is no pre-ordained duality of man and woman in creation, then neither is the family any longer a reality established by creation. Likewise, the child has lost the place he had occupied hitherto and the dignity pertaining to him. Bernheim shows that now, perforce, from being a subject of rights, the child has become an object to which people have a right and which they have a right to obtain. When the freedom to be creative becomes the freedom to create oneself, then necessarily the Maker himself is denied and ultimately man too is stripped of his dignity as a creature of God, as the image of God at the core of his being. The defense of the family is about man himself. And it becomes clear that when God is denied, human dignity also disappears. Whoever defends God is defending man.[19]

Paradoxically, then, the effort to free ourselves from the constraints of our biological gender ends up doing violence to our nature in a way that vastly transcends the individual involved in the particular choice in question. As Benedict has it in the above paragraph, the denial of male and female complementarity entails a rejection of the family as a reality established by creation, grounded in ecology. Innocent children suffer in their own turn, for now they become objects to which parents have a right to create and manipulate with unlimited freedom—including the freedom to choose (and change) a child's gender for him or her, to create as many embryos as it takes to yield one that is genetically superior while discarding the rest, and to abort those that are expected to have a handicap. It should not require religious doctrine to see that these things run directly contrary to human ecology, but the reality observed by Benedict is that, when "God is denied, human dignity also disappears" and so "Whoever defends God is defending man."

---

19. Benedict XVI, Christmas address to the Roman Curia (December 21, 2012). On defending the family as necessary for defending human dignity itself, see also Benedict XVI, *Caritas in Veritate*, §44, where the pontiff calls the family, "founded on marriage between a man and a woman, the primary vital cell of society."

Toward an Integral Ecology: The Ecological Virtues and an Ecological Spirituality

If you read the encyclical *Laudato Si'* or Francis's prior apostolic exhortation *Evangelii Gaudium*, oddly enough one of the things that stands out most is their footnotes. More than any pontiff before him, Francis grounds his teaching by citing extensively from bishops' conferences throughout the world, a distinguishing feature of his governing style marked by an attempt to exercise greater collegiality and synodality. One fruit of this approach comes in section 88 of the encyclical, where Francis echoes the Brazilian bishops' call for the cultivation of "ecological virtues," a category that does not fit neatly within any single category of traditional virtue theology but which are an extension especially of the virtue of charity. Along the way, Francis also gives us the bad news, commenting extensively on vices which are prevalent in our culture and contrary to the development of ecological virtue. Perhaps the most helpful way to lay out these virtues and vices is by means of the following bullet points, compiled from *Laudato Si'*:

Vices opposed to the ecological virtues:

- Consumption, greed, and wastefulness (§9)
- A throwaway culture in which many resources we could reuse are discarded and reduced to rubbish (§§16, 22, 43)
- Obstructionist and evasive attitudes—"pretending that nothing will happen" if we ignore the present ecological crisis (§§14, 59)
- Building cities where people—often the poor—are "inundated by cement, asphalt, glass, and metal, and deprived of physical contact with nature" (§44)
- Letting "the great sages of the past ... [go] unheard amid the noise and distractions of an information overload (§47)
- Confusion caused by being inundated with "a mere accumulation of data"—"mental pollution" (§47)

- With the rise of Internet communication, real relationships with others are treated as commodities to be chosen and eliminated at whim (§47)
- Contrived emotion is produced through this means of communication, leading to "deep and melancholic dissatisfaction with interpersonal relations, or a harmful sense of isolation" (§47)
- "Fragmentation of knowledge and the isolation of bits of information ... often lead to a loss of appreciation for the whole, for the relationships between things, and for the broader horizon"; it "can actually become a form of ignorance, unless they are integrated into a broader vision of reality" (§§110, 138)
- A culture of relativism wherein "the culture itself is corrupt and objective truth and universally valid principles are no longer upheld" (§§122–123)
- "Life gradually becomes a surrender to situations conditioned by technology, itself viewed as the principal key to the meaning of existence" (§110).
- Frenetic activity makes people "feel busy and in a constant hurry, which in turn leads them to ride rough-shod over everything around them"; "nature is filled with words of love, but we cannot listen to them amid constant noise, interminable and nerve-wracking distractions, or the cult of appearances" (§225).

The ecological virtues and ecological spirituality:

- In a culture of relativism, remembering that "political efforts and the force of law [are not] sufficient to prevent actions which affect the environment ... when the culture itself is corrupt and objective truth and universally valid principles are no longer upheld, then laws can only be seen as arbitrary impositions or obstacles to be avoided" (§§122–123)
- Ecological education aimed at creating an "ecological citizenship" that instills good habits; "Laws and regulations [are] insufficient in the long run to curb bad conduct, even when

effective means of enforcement are present. If the laws are to bring about significant, long-lasting effects, the majority of the members of society must be adequately motivated to accept them, and personally transformed to respond. Only by cultivating sound virtues will people be able to make a selfless ecological commitment" (§211)
- Replacing consumption, greed, and wastefulness with sacrifice, generosity, and a spirit of sharing (§9)
- Cultivating "an asceticism [whereby we learn] to give and not simply to give up ... mov[ing] away from what I want to what God's world needs" (§9)
- Taking time for physical contact with nature—"to recover a serene harmony with creation, reflecting on our lifestyle and our ideals, and contemplating the Creator who lives among us and surrounds us" (§§44, 49, 225)
- Cultural ecology: not "tearing down and building new cities, supposedly more respectful of the environment yet not always more attractive to live in"; rather, development should come through "incorporate[ing] the history, culture, and architecture of each place, thus preserving its original identity ... [and] protecting the cultural treasures of humanity" (§143)
- Development and welfare not only of individuals and society but also of intermediate groups; applying the principle of subsidiarity wherein problems are treated at the most local level possible by those who know their communities' needs best; foremost among these intermediate groups in need of development is the family "the basic cell of society" (§158)
- "Intergenerational solidarity, ... [wherein] we think about the kind of world we are leaving to future generations" and adjust our behavior accordingly (§§59–62). This same theme is developed by Benedict when he writes of the environment as part of the common good: "The environment is God's gift to everyone, and in our use of it we have a responsibility towards the

poor, towards future generations and towards humanity as a whole"[20]
- Fostering an ecological spirituality and conversion with respect to our stewardship of God's creation (§216)
- Practicing the "little way" of St. Thérèse in matters ecological, with "simple daily gestures which break with the logic of violence, exploitation and selfishness"; "there is a nobility in the duty to care for creation through little daily actions, and it is wonderful how education can bring about real changes in lifestyle" (§§211, 230). Here are some examples mentioned by Francis:

  - "A person who could afford to spend and consume more but regularly uses less heating and wears warmer clothes"
  - "Avoiding the use of plastic and paper"
  - "Reducing water consumption"
  - "Separating refuse"
  - "Cooking only what can reasonably be consumed"
  - "Showing care for other living beings"
  - "Using public transport or car-pooling"
  - "Planting trees"
  - "Turning off unnecessary lights"
  - Reusing something instead of immediately discarding it"

According to Francis, all the above examples and any number of similar practices reflect a generous creativity which brings out the best in human beings. When done for the right reasons, these can become acts of love which express our own dignity. To be sure, "we must not think that these efforts are not going to change the world, they [do] benefit society [in ways] often unbeknown to us, for they call forth a goodness which, albeit unseen, inevitably tends to spread."[21] This

20. Benedict XVI, *Caritas in Veritate*, §48.
21. Francis, *Laudato Si'*, §211.

point is all the more powerful if we recall that, for better or worse, every one of our actions has an effect on the entire Mystical Body.

It is significant once again that Francis here insists upon an ecological spirituality not only for the sake of the environment, but above all for what it means for us. He insists that true freedom, peace, and joy come through conversion of heart, not only in big matters but also in small ways when we give up our obsession with consumption and learn the lesson that "less is more":

> Such sobriety, when lived freely and consciously, is liberating. It is not a lesser life or one lived with less intensity. On the contrary, it is a way of living life to the full. In reality, those who enjoy more and live better each moment are those who have given up [running] here and there, always on the look-out for what they do not have. They experience what it means to appreciate each person and each thing, learning familiarity with the simplest things and how to enjoy them. So they are able to shed unsatisfied needs, reducing their obsessiveness and weariness. Even living on little, they can live a lot, above all when they cultivate other pleasures and find satisfaction in fraternal encounters, in service, in developing their gifts, in music and art, in contact with nature, in prayer. Happiness means knowing how to limit some needs which only diminish us, and being open to the many different possibilities which life can offer.[22]

In short, Francis is calling us all to return to the gospel simplicity of learning how to moderate our desires and be happy with little, to "appreciate the small things of life, to be spiritually detached from what we possess and not to succumb to sadness for what we lack."[23]

Integral Ecology as the Virtuous Mean in the Landscape of Contemporary Environmentalism

For those who have ever been involved with environmentalist groups or know someone who has, perhaps you may have noted that

---

22. Ibid., §222–23.
23. Ibid., §222.

conservationist movements sometimes almost take on the status of a religion. Think about what a religion does. It directs us outside of ourselves, toward some higher purpose. It encompasses all of our life, involving moral precepts, liturgies, feasts, and even its own form of sacrifices and indulgences. It has an eschatology or prophetic dimension, one that is often apocalyptic. It is evangelical, eager to gain converts and confident in its truth claims even as this confidence easily begets self-righteousness. I bring these examples up because environmentalism can easily become a quasi-religion, something which is both good and bad in different respects. In reading *Laudato Si'*, one can see that Francis too is aware of this phenomenon and eager to offer a balanced response that recognizes the good of environmentalism while cautioning against its excesses.

On the one hand, our recent popes' condemnation of the dominant technocratic paradigm is abundantly clear throughout the encyclical *Laudato Si'*. As they clearly teach, we ought to act as the earth's stewards rather than its omnipotent masters, and we should not blindly embrace new technologies just because we have the power to do so. The world around is not just "stuff" to be manipulated and exploited at will. Rather creation is exalted because it has been willed into being by God himself and is not just the product of chaos or chance.[24] In this regard I think Wendell Berry was correct in writing that the indictment of Christianity by anti-Christian conservationists is in many respects warranted. Neither the Church nor the Bible endorses this sort of dualism, but unfortunately Christians sometimes have the idea that the only holy place is the church—and that the natural world is "just matter," which we must despise for Heaven's sake.[25]

---

24. Ibid., §77.

25. Wendell Berry, *Sex, Economy, Freedom & Community* (New York: Pantheon Books, 1993), 94, 109. Berry describes this substance dualism as "the greatest disease that afflicts us." According to Berry, by denying spirit and truth to the nonhuman creation, we have legitimized a form of "blasphemy," a "rape" of the earth. Ibid., 104–5. Francis certainly does not used such charged rhetoric in his encyclical, but I think that the blasphemy charge merits a good deal of reflection for Christians living in the industrialized world today.

On the other hand, the Church's integral ecology also staunchly opposes the sort of substance monism common among those who deny the importance of man's place in the cosmos:

> This is not to put all living beings on the same level nor to deprive human beings of their unique worth and the tremendous responsibility it entails. Nor does it imply a divinization of the earth which would prevent us from working on it and protecting it in its fragility. Such notions would end up creating new imbalances which would deflect us from the reality which challenges us. At times we see an obsession with denying any pre-eminence to the human person; more zeal is shown in protecting other species than in defending the dignity which all human beings share in equal measure.[26]

Francis brings us right to the heart of the matter in citing a speech from Benedict emphasizing that a refusal to acknowledge man's special place within creation (here called "biocentrism") is incompatible with the insistence that we ought to be responsible for the environment:

> There can be no ecology without an adequate anthropology. When the human person is considered as simply one being among others, the product of chance or physical determinism, then "our overall sense of responsibility wanes." A misguided anthropocentrism need not necessarily yield to "biocentrism," for that would entail adding yet another imbalance, failing to solve present problems and adding new ones. Human beings cannot be expected to feel responsibility for the world unless, at the same time, their unique capacities of knowledge, will, freedom, and responsibility are recognized and valued.[27]

If human beings are not special among God's creatures, ask the pontiffs, then why should we be expected to behave any differently toward them than they would toward us? Why can we not just invoke the survival of the fittest principle, do whatever we want since we are strongest, and be on our merry way? The answer, of course, is that even though the Catholic Church is open to the scientific theory of

---

26. Francis, *Laudato Si'*, §90.
27. Ibid., §118; Benedict XVI, message for the forty-third World Day of Peace (January 1, 2010), 2.

evolution, we also profess that human beings have a uniqueness which cannot be fully explained in evolutionary terms.[28] Thus the ecological imperatives so championed in our culture today are groundless in the absence of a deeply anchored anthropology. Thankfully, though, there is an outstanding basis for such an anthropology readily available in the Christian tradition, wherein man is the image of God charged with the command to "keep" (preserve) and "till" (make fruitful) the earth.[29]

This forceful argument is not something mentioned only once by Benedict. Indeed, Francis's integral theology is drawn in large part from Benedict's *Caritas in Veritate*, whose most poignant section for our purposes merits to be cited in full:

> When nature, including the human being, is viewed as the result of mere chance or evolutionary determinism, our sense of responsibility wanes. In nature, the believer recognizes the wonderful result of God's creative activity, which we may use responsibly to satisfy our legitimate needs, material or otherwise, while respecting the intrinsic balance of creation. If this vision is lost, we end up either considering nature an untouchable taboo or, on the contrary, abusing it. Neither attitude is consonant with the Christian vision of nature as the fruit of God's creation.
>
> Nature expresses a design of love and truth. It is prior to us, and it has been given to us by God as the setting for our life. Nature speaks to us of the Creator (cf. Rom 1:20) and his love for humanity. It is destined to be "recapitulated" in Christ at the end of time (cf. Eph 1:9–10; Col 1:19–20). Thus it too is a "vocation." Nature is at our disposal not as "a heap of scattered refuse," but as a gift of the Creator who has given it an inbuilt order, enabling man to draw from it the principles needed in order "to till it and keep it" (Gn 2:15).
>
> But it should also be stressed that it is contrary to authentic development to view nature as something more important than the human person. This position leads to attitudes of neo-paganism or a new pantheism—human salvation cannot come from nature alone, understood in a purely naturalistic sense. This having been said, it is also necessary to reject the opposite posi-

---

28. Francis, *Laudato Si'*, §81.
29. Ibid., §124; cf. Gen 2:15.

tion, which aims at total technical dominion over nature, because the natural environment is more than raw material to be manipulated at our pleasure; it is a wondrous work of the Creator containing a "grammar" which sets forth ends and criteria for its wise use, not its reckless exploitation.[30]

It is significant that Benedict uses the terms "neo-paganism" and "new pantheism" to describe the dangers of an environmentalism that easily turns into its own religion. Francis for his part recalls that pantheism (the belief that all things are divine) was part and parcel of the pagan worldview to which the biblical view of creation arose as the antidote. While continuing to admire the grandeur and immensity of creation, the Judeo-Christian tradition demythologized nature. In doing so, Francis argues, our tradition emphasizes all the more our human responsibility for nature. In light of divine revelation we know that creation is not divine and not immortal; thus we have a grave responsibility to protect it.[31]

According to Francis, the correct view of creation's relationship with God is expressed in the Catholic mystical tradition:

> The universe unfolds in God, who fills it completely. Hence, there is a mystical meaning to be found in a leaf, in a mountain trail, in a dewdrop, in a poor person's face.... Saint John of the Cross taught that all the goodness present in the realities and experiences of this world "is present in God eminently and infinitely, or more properly, in each of these sublime realities is God." This is not because the finite things of this world are really divine, but because the mystic experiences the intimate connection between God and all beings, and thus feels that "all things are God."[32]

---

30. Benedict XVI, *Caritas in Veritate*, §48.
31. Francis, *Laudato Si'*, §78. For an excellent short book (itself a collection of homilies) that deals with this demythologization of pagan religion achieved in the biblical creation accounts, see Joseph Ratzinger's book *In the Beginning* referred to earlier in this volume.
32. Francis, *Laudato Si'*, §§233–234. It is fascinating that in addition to John of the Cross, Francis cites the Muslim mystic Ali al-Khawas to impress this point. Referencing a Muslim source approvingly is hardly a mainstay of the Catholic magisterial tradition, but it accords perfectly with the aim of this particular encyclical whose audience is not just Catholics but men of all faiths as well as those who claim to have none.

The Catholic mystic St. John of the Cross senses that, in some way, all things are God. Yet at the same time, unlike many major religious traditions throughout history which consider the created world to be divine, Christianity has always held there to be a distinction between creature and Creator, between human nature and the elevation of man to God through his gift of grace. As the ancient Christian formula has it, the Son of God became man so that the sons of men might become God. But this process of *theosis* is not something that occurs in us automatically by virtue of our coming into existence. How, then, are we to achieve it?

In a sublime move toward the end of *Laudato Si'*, Francis points to the sacraments as the privileged path by which nature is taken up into God. Once again drawing upon Benedict— indeed upon some texts we reflected upon earlier in our discussion of the virtue of hope—the pontiff writes that in the Eucharist, "creation is projected towards divinization, towards the holy wedding feast, towards unification with the Creator himself."[33] Or, as Benedict writes elsewhere, "The transubstantiated Host is the anticipation of the transformation and divinization of matter in the Christological fullness.... The Eucharist provides the movement of the cosmos with its direction; it anticipates its goal and at the same time urges it on."[34] Yet again, years before becoming pope Ratzinger wrote that man's divinization through Eucharistic communion is part of God's plan for "the *resubstantiation* of the whole of earthly reality."[35]

If St. Paul is right in teaching us that all of creation is eventually to be set free from decay and obtain the glorious liberty of the sons of God (Rom 8:21–23), then the miraculous transformation of matter into God that we witness in the Eucharist ought to be a source of inspiration for an integral ecology, directing us all to be stewards of the great gift that is our common home. The Church professes that the world in which we live has been created good by God, and that he has graced it with the dignity of being capable of transformation into him-

---

33. Ibid., §235; Benedict XVI, homily for the Mass of Corpus Domini (June 15, 2006).
34. Ratzinger, *Spirit of the Liturgy*, 29.
35. Ratzinger, *Pilgrim Fellowship of Faith*, 78; cf. 118.

self. But for Benedict and Francis this does not mean that we ought to leave the earth alone and never touch it. On the contrary, the pontiffs affirm that developing the created world in a prudent way is the best way of caring for it. In other words, by participating in God's own providential care for the world, we become instruments in the hands of God to bring out the potential which he himself has inscribed in all things. Indeed, Francis calls the idea of seeing manual labor as spiritually meaningful "revolutionary," adding that seeking personal growth and sanctification in the interplay of recollection and work changes the overall way we live in the world and "makes us more protective and respectful of the environment."[36]

The question that remains is: what are we going to do with the great gift that these popes have given us in their proposals for an integral ecology? To echo what Francis said about his first major document, "I fear that these words too may give rise to commentary or discussion with no real practical effect." In concluding this chapter, I therefore invite you, the reader, to prayerfully consider how you can live out the Christian "experiment" we have been discussing in this book with an eye to implementing the Church's vision for an integral ecology, and practice the ecological virtues in your own homes, schools, parishes, and local communities.[37] One of the simplest steps of this experiment

---

36. Francis, *Laudato Si'*, §§124, 126. As one who works at a Benedictine institution, I appreciated the nod Francis gives here to St. Benedict and his "revolutionary" move of seeing manual labor as spiritually meaningful. Rather than leaving the earth alone, through the past two millennia Benedictine monks have been developing the earth's potential in fruitful, even civilization-saving ways. Not only did the Benedictines do arguably more than anyone else to preserve the intellectual tradition of Western civilization in the wake of the fall of Rome, their work with various crops and industries, and their invention of new production methods also proved invaluable. It may not seem that important at first, but one particularly interesting example consists in the monks' efforts to transform the fruit of the earth into beer. Not only did beer help the monks maintain their health during long periods of fasting, it was often served to visitors in the absence of available uncontaminated water.

37. A good place to start is the USCCB environmental justice website: http://www.usccb.org/issues-and-action/human-life-and-dignity/environment/index.cfm. The Archdiocese of Washington also has a helpful list of parish resources on *Laudato Si'*: https://adw.org/living-the-faith/social-concerns/care-for-creation/.

is to follow the "Little Way" of St. Thérèse in regard to the environment, as Francis described it above. Another key to consider is a common theme in this book taught by Benedict: that belief itself means handing ourselves over to the other in love, recognizing the one who needs me as Christ coming to meet me here and now.

Conclusion: A Practical Way to "Run the Experiment" of Integral Ecology in Daily Life

One of the major stresses in this book has been upon the necessity of running "the experiment" of faith if one wishes to know its truth. When it comes to integral ecology, a helpful way of distilling the Church's message into a practicable habit in daily life has been provided by Pope Francis in his introduction of care for our common home as a new work of mercy in the Catholic Church. In addition to the traditional seven corporal and seven spiritual works of mercy, Catholics are now called to practice care for our common home as a *corporal* work of mercy through small daily gestures that come to the aid of the earth, which Francis personifies as "among the most abandoned and maltreated of our poor" who cries out to us for help.[38] But Francis does not stop there: he also inaugurates care for our common home as a *spiritual* work of mercy. By engaging in "grateful contemplation of God's world," says Francis, we "discover in each thing a teaching which God wishes to hand on to us."[39] Practicing these works of mercy is something everyone can do each in his own way: it could be a simple lifestyle change of reducing or reusing goods we would oth-

---

38. Francis, *Laudato Si'*, §2; Francis, message for the celebration of the World Day of Prayer for the Care of Creation (September 1, 2016), §5, http://w2.vatican.va/content/francesco/en/messages/pont-messages/2016/documents/papa-francesco_20160901_messaggio-giornata-cura-creato.html. The seven traditional corporal works of mercy are feeding the hungry, giving drink to the thirsty, clothing the naked, welcoming the stranger, visiting the sick, visiting the imprisoned, burying the dead. The seven spiritual works of mercy prior to Francis's addition are counselling the doubtful, instructing the ignorant, admonishing sinners, consoling the afflicted, forgiving offenses, bearing patiently those who do us ill, praying for the living and the dead.

39. Francis, *Laudato Si'*, §§85, 214.

erwise throw away, cultivating the habit of composing, planning and maintaining a backyard garden, or even simply purchasing a plant and nurturing it. There is no one-size-fits-all recipe here, but that is part of the beauty of it. The key is that we see the importance of taking care of the earth, and even more fundamentally to be in touch with nature because of what that encounter does to our soul.

It might seem odd that contemplation of nature should be considered a work of mercy, for it could rightly be asked: how does this contemplation serve the earth? Here I think lies one of Francis's deepest insights, not only in the realm of ecology but also in the perennial tradition of Catholic moral and spiritual theology. Indeed, it is true that contemplating God's gift of the earth does not directly impact the planet itself, but it does something far more powerful with much wider implications: our contemplation and thankfulness for the immense gift of God's creation changes *us*, leading us further along the path of divinization and, with us, drawing all of creation closer to its consummation in God. I cannot think of a more timely and easy way to engage our present secularized culture and show forth the power of the gospel than to begin the sincere practice of this new work of mercy with a Christian charity grounded in the allegiance of faith to our God and the hope for the renewal of the entire cosmos in him.[40]

---

40. In addition to the good that the works of mercy do for those who are the recipients of our charity, Pope Francis cites the following text from St. Augustine in order to demonstrate the great benefit that they bring for their doers: "If we were in peril from fire, we would certainly run to water in order to extinguish the fire.... in the same way, if a spark of sin flares up from our straw, and we are troubled on that account, whenever we have an opportunity to perform a work of mercy, we should rejoice, as if a fountain opened before so that the fire might be extinguished." Augustine, *De Catechizandis Rudibus*, I, XIX, 22, quoted in Francis, *Evangelii Gaudium*, §193. Francis also makes the helpful point that, as we serve the poor, we are also "evangelized by them." Ibid., §198.

Part 3

Benedict XVI in Dialogue with Other Contemporary Thinkers

10

SALVATION BY ALLEGIANCE, NOT CERTAINTY

How to Believe Biblically

To Think How the Bible Thinks

In this last section of our book, we will develop Benedict's thought on how the Christian is to navigate the faith in the context of today's secularized world by putting the pontiff into conversation with other current thinkers on the same subject. The authors we are engaging in these two chapters do not cite Benedict or otherwise demonstrate familiarity with his thought, and for this reason I believe their distinct approaches serve all the more to illumine the contours of the pontiff's project. In a way similar to Benedict but using fresh language, these authors converge in advocating a shift away from traditional Christian apologetics and toward answering secularism's master narrative with a story of our own, especially as told through the lens of those exemplars which we call the saints. Further, these authors agree with Benedict in acknowledging the contestability of faith in our secular age, a scenario in which serious objections will be successfully outflanked only when we cease being spectators of our own faith and embrace its practice wholeheartedly.

In this chapter we will be focusing on contemporary approaches to religious epistemology from three thinkers in the field of biblical studies: Dru Johnson, Peter Enns, and Matthew Bates. If the goal of this book is to offer a narrative of what it looks like for one to live an authentically Christian existence in postmodernity or a "secular age," then it is only fitting that we ground our approach not only in the best of what contemporary thought has to offer but above all in the foundational text of the Christian tradition: the Bible. We want, in other words, not just to think correctly about the Bible, but to think how the Bible thinks. Accordingly, I contend in this chapter that Christian living in our secular age will not be compelling unless it is profoundly informed by the very biblical narrative that reveals how to peer through the glass, darkly.

Biblical Knowing

The first of the three sources we will be engaging in this chapter is Dru Johnson's book *Biblical Knowing: A Scriptural Epistemology of Error*.[1] Johnson is a helpful dialogue partner for Benedict, for he is not only a professor of biblical studies, but he is also conversant with movements in contemporary philosophy of religion. Moreover, as we saw in chapter 4, Benedict places great importance on recovering a proper understanding of biblical belief (the Hebrew verb *'āman*, Greek noun *pistis*). Most biblical instances of these terms, notes Johnson, mean something like "trusting belief" rather than the act of accepting true statements or propositions. Like Benedict, Johnson asks us to think of the Christian faith less as an intellectual affair (though certainly granting that it does by its very nature include important truth claims, not the least of which we find in the Creed) and more along the lines of a metaphor common from ancient Israel through the New Testament era: faith as a walk, the peripatetic life.

1. Dru Johnson, *Biblical Knowing: A Scriptural Epistemology of Error* (Eugene, Ore.: Cascade Books, 2013).

If the faith is a walk and a life of trust, Johnson insists that the next natural question to ask is, "Trust whom?" For, faith is not just a matter between me and Jesus which I am able to access and live independently of other human beings. As Benedict emphatically insists, so in Johnson's view faith is inextricably bound up with community and with authority. Faith is a social reality. It involves recognizing the docents through whom God speaks and embodying the actions they prescribe. St. Paul says that we walk by faith, not by sight (2 Cor 5:7), a line which Johnson glosses accordingly: "We walk by trusting authentic authority and not merely by sight" (2 Cor 5:7).[2] As a Protestant, Johnson will surely disagree with Benedict on the question of what precisely this authority ultimately is, but that a non-Catholic says this much I consider a valuable step in the right direction toward articulating an understanding of faith that resonates with all Christians.

In addition to discussing the biblical word that we conventionally render "belief," Johnson spends a considerable portion of his text parsing the Hebrew word *yada'*, typically translated as "to know." In the Bible, argues Johnson, God is not concerned that his people know objective facts so much as that they act rightly.[3] As an indication of this, consider that Genesis 1–4 employs the verb *yada'* not to denote the attainment of factual knowledge but rather to denote awareness and familiarity, even sexual intimacy. When Adam "knew" Eve his wife who in turn bore sons (Gn 4:1, 25), Genesis is not saying that new human beings came into existence because Adam learned correct information about his wife! And when a new pharaoh arose in Egypt who did not "know" Joseph (Ex 1:8), it stretches the imagination to conceive that he had never heard of this guy who had once been the number two man in the entire land. Rather, what is being asserted here is that the new king did not have *covenantal intimacy* with Joseph. I like how the NIV translation non-literally but accurately captures

---

2. Ibid., 1–3.
3. Ibid., 16–23.

this verse: the new king was a man "to whom Joseph meant nothing." As a result, this pharaoh immediately set out to enslave all of Joseph's people.

Johnson builds on the above perspective on biblical knowing by suggesting that we think of knowing more as a process of intellectual virtue building rather than as a series of discrete cognitive acts. Knowing is "a fundamentally historical function."[4] Johnson's emphasis upon the historical process of our knowing likewise coheres with Benedict's hermeneutic of divine pedagogy, by which the pontiff means that we—like God's people of old as depicted in Scripture—are able to arrive at the fullness of truth only gradually over the course of our lives.

Another insightful dimension of Johnson's is derived from the work of Eleonore Stump. In particular, he makes much of her diagnosis of contemporary blindness to the truth of Christianity's claims as the result of *hemianopia*—a blind spot to a fuller reality caused when we limit our intellectual vision to the domain of the brain's left hemisphere that houses analytic and scientific thought—while ignoring the right half that deals holistically with the complexities of imagination, intuition, and relations of persons.[5] This critique could just as well have been issued by Benedict, for whom we have seen it is not rational argumentation but rather the experience of the faith's beauty and holiness that constitutes the ultimate *apologia* for Christianity. It might even have been leveled by Nietzsche, who berates philosophers for their "Egyptianism"—thinking that they are honoring an object of study by mummifying it for the sake of conceptual precision.[6] John-

---

4. Ibid., 36. On Johnson's "virtue epistemology" and a thoughtful critique of Alvin Plantinga's epistemology as suffering from the *hemianopia* described here, see ibid., 173–75. Despite the great value I find in Plantinga's notion of properly basic beliefs (beliefs we cannot justify but which we must hold in order to navigate), I appreciate Johnson's point that perhaps it focuses too much on the single belief of a single person at a single time (as opposed to viewing our knowledge as a process of virtue building grasped only diachronically).

5. Ibid., 152; Eleonore Stump, *Wandering in Darkness* (Oxford: Oxford University Press, 2010), 25.

6. Johnson, *Biblical Knowing*, 154; Nietzsche, *The Twilight of the Idols*, in *Complete Works*.

son agrees with Michael Polyani that, at the end of the day, human knowledge is not fundamentally propositional. While we can certainly speak about our knowledge, he rejects the notion that articulation can exhaust our knowledge. Words are the means to get to meaning, but the meaning is not the words themselves.[7]

Returning once again to Scripture as his source, Johnson argues that an impoverished epistemology myopically centered on propositional knowledge is itself the precise target of Scripture's repeated critiques. To be sure, precision and clarity are concerns for Yahweh and his prophets, yet the Scriptures nonetheless tend to shy away from propositional affirmations in favor of phenomenal *experience* as constitutive of knowledge. Accordingly, when the Book of Judges laments that the new generation of Israelites did not "know" (*yada'*) Yahweh (Jgs 2:10), the author was not saying merely that his people lacked propositional knowledge of God's attributes—though he does also mention that they did not know Yahweh "or the work which he had done for Israel." In the Gospels, meanwhile, Jesus acts as if the Jewish authorities have blundered *precisely because* they narrowly focused on the propositions of the prophets as the objects of their knowledge. The rich young man knew how to recite the commands perfectly, yet he nevertheless lacked that which was essential to life: *experience*, a personal encounter with God in the flesh (Mk 10:17–22). Jesus habitually employs this type of hermeneutical reorientation throughout the Gospels, taking propositions from Israel's history and re-nestling them within the new order of grace in order to point beyond their superficial meaning and toward the grander reality of his kingdom: "You have heard that it was said to the men of old.... But I say to you...." (Mt 5:17–48).[8]

The First Complete and Authorised English Translation, vol. 16, ed. Oscar Levy (New York: Russell & Russell, 1964), 17. In this connection, it is interesting to note that Nietzsche also laments the loss of religion (insofar as it leads men to lose their will for greatness). Nietzsche, *On the Use and Abuse of History*, 43–44.

7. Johnson, *Biblical Knowing*, 158, 165. Michael Polyani, *Personal Knowledge: Towards a Post-Critical Philosophy* (Chicago: University of Chicago Press, 1974), 91.

8. Johnson, *Biblical Knowing*, 186.

Johnson brings his project to a close with a chapter detailing implications of his thought for theologians and the Church today. Here too we find some striking points of contact with Benedict XVI's religious epistemology. Already in his dissertation on the theology of St. Bonaventure, Ratzinger had emphasized that the biblical text is not an end in itself but rather the "witness" to divine revelation which precedes it, exceeds it, and occurs in our encounter with God mediated by it.[9] In a similar vein, Johnson writes, "Texts alone are incapable of rendering knowledge of a person. However, the text can act as an objective referent to the community's encounter with the God as His subject."[10] This also aligns with Johnson's affirmation that we can never grasp God as an "object" and pin him down in the first place. What we can indeed do, he maintains, is to gaze, to study, to be self-critical, and to respond obediently to God.[11] And this is what Benedict says: God is not a "thing" we can grasp. On the contrary, God grasps *us*; the truth possesses *us*.[12]

And how do we let God take hold of us? According to Johnson, we can only come to know a person by dwelling in his or her story, by becoming part of it. For the Christian, I think that this must include getting to know some theology, to know something of the inner life of God who, as Trinity, is a boundless communion of life and love. To appropriate the language of Benedict deployed in chapter 4, it also involves gaining an increasing familiarity with the story of God's "struggle" with mankind over the course of salvation history as recorded in Scripture. But the way to gain the sort of knowledge of which we are speaking here is ultimately encapsulated best in one word: discipleship. By following Jesus as his disciple, the Christian gains access to knowledge that simply cannot be had apart from participation in his

---

9. For a discussion of this term in Benedict, see Ramage, *Dark Passages of the Bible*, 66.

10. Johnson, *Biblical Knowing*, 205. For Ratzinger's theology of revelation based on Bonaventure, see Ramage, *Jesus, Interpreted*, 73–75.

11. Johnson, *Biblical Knowing*, 207.

12. Benedict XVI, *Last Testament*, 241.

master's life. Moreover, Johnson concurs with Benedict's insistence in chapter 5 that discipleship is not merely an individual but also a social affair. In short, since the epistemological process is fundamentally social, "theological knowledge requires fiducial binding to a peculiar society: the Church."[13] Again, as a Protestant, Johnson will have a different view from the Catholic as to the precise nature of the Church's hierarchical structure, but it is significant that Catholics and Protestants can agree that some authoritative entity is in fact indispensable for today's believer.

Before moving on to our next author, I think it is worth pausing for just a moment to take note of a comment from Johnson on the pivotal issue of religious authority that has long divided Catholics and Protestants. Observing that thoughtful Protestants and Catholics both have to grapple with the question of why their respective religious authorities (Scripture and the Magisterium, respectively) ought to be considered ultimate, Johnson makes the following comment intended to remind Catholics that the Church's hierarchical teaching office is not self-evidently the definitive voice instituted by Christ to speak in his name for all time: "Claiming the Magisterium as our prophetic voice makes for a rather tidy epistemological process, but it does not actually help one to adjudicate between prophetic voices. Rather, it calls for basic genuflection to the voice of the Magisterium."[14]

---

13. Johnson, *Biblical Knowing*, 209.
14. Ibid., 204. For what I consider to be one of the most helpful arguments in favor of the Catholic magisterium, see Newman, *Essay on Development of Christian Doctrine*, 88–90. "Some authority there must be if there is a revelation given," declares Newman (ibid., 88). In other words, he is arguing here that, if there is no authority around to guarantee that the Christian revelation has occurred, then in effect we today have no good epistemological warrant for affirming the alleged revelation in the first place. Newman continues: "The absolute need of a spiritual supremacy is at present the strongest of arguments in favor of the fact of its supply. Surely, either an objective revelation has not been given, or it has been provided with means for impressing its objectiveness on the world" (ibid., 89). If we grant that the nature of revelation demands an earthly guarantor of it, how do we know that the Catholic Church of all churches is this guarantor? After all, I do think Johnson is correct in asserting that the Magisterium's voice ought not to be considered self-authenticating any more than the Bible

I think Johnson is right to remind Catholics that we cannot casually assert the Magisterium as the ultimate religious authority any more than the Protestant can assert the same regarding Scripture. It is not my aim here to convince non-Catholics of my position on what or who constitutes Christianity's ultimate authority, though of course it should go without saying that I do not think that this authority lies in Scripture alone. My goal here, rather, is to drive home from another angle the point that, just as the truth of Christianity cannot be arrived at "cold" from the outside apart from a wholehearted commitment to discipleship, so too the truth of the Catholic Church in particular is unlikely to be grasped fully by the non-Catholic unless he embarks on a life of allegiance to Christ as mediated through this same Church.

The Sin of Certainty

Let go from his former academic institution for being too theologically edgy, Peter Enns has developed a unique reputation—and a significant following—among evangelical Christians over the past several years. Like Johnson whose work we just discussed, Enns's book *The Sin of Certainty: Why God Desires Our Trust More Than Our "Correct" Beliefs* may be considered controversial by some Christians, yet I find his approach to be invaluable for the enterprise of this book.[15] Over the course of the following several pages, I hope to capture some of Enns's refreshing insights and discuss how they may work in concert with consideration of Benedict XVI's approach to refine our picture of

---

is. In response to this question, Newman observes that the Catholic Church alone of all the historical churches dares to claim this authority, and that for many of the faithful "this is not the least persuasive argument for her infallibility" (ibid., 88). I do not find that Newman's words constitute a failsafe argument for Catholicism, but, as far as I can tell, they lead to the conclusion that either the Catholic Church has been instituted by Christ to guarantee the truths of the faith with certitude, or else we mortals simply do not enjoy the sort of certitude that Newman and many others seek.

15. Peter Enns, *The Sin of Certainty: Why God Desires Our Trust More Than Our "Correct" Beliefs* (New York: HarperOne, 2017).

what an intelligent and vibrant Christian faith looks like in our secular age.

Enns begins his popular book *The Sin of Certainty* with a series of statements designed to strike right at the heart of the existential crisis of faith in which so many contemporary Christians find themselves entrenched. To begin, it should be observed that Enns is by no means opposed to Christians holding that faith and reason align with each other. He does not countenance the proposition that faith is absurd, that we believe *because* it contradicts what we can know through human reason. Yet Enns nevertheless has a problem with the way many Christians think about the relationship between faith and reason: many Christians are preoccupied by thinking that our relationship with God is only healthy if we have absolute certainty about what we believe. Enns labels this notion the "sin of certainty," and he thinks that it compromises the integrity of the gospel itself.[16] Indeed, Enns goes so far as to commend doubt as a "sacred" experience, "God's instrument" for our sanctification, and "divine tough love."[17]

In contrast with the way many Christians are accustomed to thinking, Enns contends that faith ought not to be defined primarily by *what* we believe but rather in *whom* we trust. Put simply, "We have misunderstood faith as a *what* word rather than a *who* word—as primarily *beliefs about* rather than primarily as *trust in*"—as having a relationship with God.[18] This sentence might as well have been penned by Benedict, who, as we have seen, thinks of belief less as the accep-

---

16. Ibid., 18.
17. Ibid., 165. If I had not known it was Enns who penned the above words, I would have expected it to have been Pope Francis, who states quite bluntly, "If a person says that he met God with total certainty and is not touched by a margin of uncertainty, then this is not good." Francis and Spadaro, "A Big Heart Open to God.". Francis has emphasized that doubt is present in every believer's life, and that this is sometimes even a good thing. The pontiff maintains that doubt is present in every true discernment and that authentic Christian leadership is of a sort that takes seriously the positive or at least inescapable role doubt plays in our lives as believers in a postmodern or "secular" context.
18. Enns, *Sin of Certainty*, 22.

tance of true propositions and more as a total way of life in which we hand ourselves over to the other in charity. Moreover, like Benedict, Enns appeals to the biblical concept of belief (Hebrew ʾāman, Greek *pistis*) to back up his claim. *Pistis* is also an action word, he observes, and as such it often means being faithful, being trustworthy. Christianity, then, is not primarily about us "having faith." Above all, Christianity is about Christ's being faithful *to us*, and then by extension how he elicits us to faithfulness and trust in him (cf. Gal 2:16).[19] In a rather comical comment with which I cannot help but basically agree, Enns remarks, "If I were king of Christianity, after limiting church services to forty-five minutes and sermons to ten.... I would proclaim a kingdom-wide decree that, at least for a while until we get it, 'believe' should be stricken from all of our Bibles and replaced with *trust*."[20]

To drive home his point that faith is at bottom a dynamic relationship of trust, Enns asks us to consider the experience of belief in analogy with marriage. Those of us who are married often hold mistaken beliefs regarding our spouses, notes Enns, yet thankfully this skewed knowledge does not nullify our marriage. This is because our vows are based on a mutual commitment to a lifelong gift of self, not on whether we understand one another correctly at all times. The same is the case when it comes to our relationship with God, Enns argues. We tend to think of "strong" faith as faith that is free from uncertainty and existential crises, but in reality deep faith—like a solid marriage—can and often does coexist with these. To anticipate something I will discuss below (on the subject of the saints), it may even be the case that endurance of the crucible of uncertainty and existential crisis is precisely what makes development of mature faith possible.

---

19. On Enns's point about the faithfulness of Jesus, see ibid., 98–102. In recent decades, Pauline scholars have been reconsidering how best to translate Galatians 2:16 ("A man is not justified by works of the law but through faith in Jesus Christ," often cited by the Reformers as evidence for justification by faith alone. Enns embraces the current trend of translating διὰ πίστεως Ἰησοῦ Χριστοῦ as "through the faithfulness of Jesus Christ" rather than "through faith in Jesus Christ."

20. Enns, *Sin of Certainty*, 112.

One of the great strengths of Enns's approach to faith is he grounds it in some of the Bible's most poignant, existentially challenging texts. I agree wholeheartedly with the conviction with which he begins his reflections on these passages: "I believe the Bible does not model a faith that depends on certainty for the simple fact that the Bible does not provide that kind of certainty. Rather, in all its messy diversity, the Bible models trust in God that does not rest on whether we are able to be clear and certain about what to believe."[21] For Enns, the Bible is a book of diverse voices that speaks to the myriad situations in which we human beings find ourselves. It sometimes disturbs Christians when they discover the extent to which the Bible contains raw expressions of fierce doubt, but the fact that the ancient Israelites embraced this as part of their faith ought instead to be a consolation for us. Like Enns, I am thankful that we have the Bible as it is "rather than a sanitized one where spiritual struggles of the darkest kind are brushed aside as a problem to be fixed rather than accepted as part of the journey of faith."[22]

Enns's expression of gratitude extends to the entirety of Scripture, but he has especially the Old Testament in mind. Sometimes we Christians living in this secularized world find it hard to relate to the New Testament's clarity and sense of urgency. In this respect, Enns observes: "Christians today have more in common with the Israelites wandering through a lonely and threatening desert or exiled to a hostile land than with Paul and most other New Testament writers. The Old Testament doesn't speak in the booming voice of imminent triumph. It speaks of generation after generation of the faithful and not so faithful, of successes and failures, of God's presence and God's absence."[23] This depiction of the Bible as the messy story of Israel's triumphs and defeats reminds us of Benedict's depiction of Scripture from chapter as the narrative of Israel (whose Hebrew name literally

21. Ibid., 53.
22. Ibid., 195.
23. Ibid., 197.

means "struggles with God") struggling to grasp hold of God and of God struggling to make himself known to his people throughout the ages. The Bible is not a monolith, and, according to Benedict, not all of its passages are true in their bare literal meaning apart from their relationship with Christ.[24]

One of our best illustrations of Enns's (and Ratzinger's) point is found in the Book of Ecclesiastes, sometimes referred to by its Hebrew name, Qoheleth. As far as Ecclesiastes is concerned, there is not much of a difference between human beings and the animals. They have the same breath, they both die, and they both return to the dust from which they came, not knowing whether anything is left afterwards (Eccl 3:19–21). Moreover, those who have died are not long remembered (1:11; 9:5). Sure, those who are closest to us will remember us for a while after we die, perhaps even until the time of their own death. All the same, life goes on as time marches on, and the immediate demands of daily life inexorably cause us to think of our departed loved ones less and less. In all likelihood, as our children and grandchildren think of us ever more infrequently, the point will come when our descendants—perhaps beginning already with our own great-grandchildren—will have forgotten even our names. As Dale Allison puts it in his rumination upon this relentless sequence of events, "Absence makes the heart grow harder."[25]

In light of this unsettling observation about our humanity, Enns replies that the Book of Ecclesiastes teaches us a critically important lesson. All our lives we run around desperately trying to make sense of everything, but in the end our efforts always end in futility. This is why the epilogue of Ecclesiastes concludes with the pragmatic words, "Fear God, and keep his commandments; for this is the whole duty of man" (Eccl 12:13). As Enns parses him, Ecclesiastes's message is for us to stop obsessively trying to work everything out in words and con-

---

24. Ratzinger, "Farewell to the Devil?" in *Dogma and Preaching* (San Francisco: Ignatius Press, 2011), 200.

25. Allison, *Night Comes*, 87–88.

cepts. We cannot figure everything out, cannot have perfect certitude in our faith. Indeed, it is a distinct possibility that our past certitudes will one day vanish like vapor in the wind (In fact, Ecclesiastes's favorite word *hevel*, typically translated as "vanity," literally means vapor or breath). Yet for Ecclesiastes this is no warrant for a plunge off the cliff of despair. Ecclesiastes's final exhortation is to fear God, not to give up on God. He is telling us—and struggling believers of all ages—how we can continue to live in a world wherein all we thought we knew about God is suddenly ripped away from us. When this inevitably happens, he says, keep being faithful anyway. Continue obeying God anyway. I really appreciate how Enns describes the character of the person who perseveres in this way: "When we have stared into the pit of despair over God and his world, and our thoughts about God don't line up at all, and then we trust God anyway, enough to continue living in the hope that trusting God is worth it—even just the faint hope of having hope—well, you can't kill someone like that."[26] Enns's portrayal of the longsuffering man reminds me of a line uttered by the master tempter in C. S. Lewis's *Screwtape Letters*: "Our cause is never more in danger than when a human, no longer desiring, but still intending, to do our Enemy's will, looks round upon a universe from which every trace of Him seems to have vanished, and asks why he has been forsaken, and still obeys."[27]

The plight of the desperately tortured man is captured in unparalleled fashion by the biblical book of Job, another text explored by Enns. Enns is probably right in identifying Job as the most miserable man in the Bible. The book goes to great lengths to emphasize that

---

26. Enns, *Sin of Certainty*, 80. For a related discussion of the meaning of vanity as deployed by Ecclesiastes, see Ramage, *Dark Passages of the Bible*, 245–49. One of my emphases over the course of those pages is that Ecclesiastes's darkness is a sort of foil for the rest of the Bible. It is important for painting a picture of what life without God looks like, and it has helped countless people who feel similarly that their lives are vanity, to realize that they can continue to love God and persevere anyway despite the chaos in which they find themselves immersed.

27. C. S. Lewis, *The Screwtape Letters* (San Francisco: HarperCollins, 2001), 40.

its protagonist's suffering—the loathsome sores all over his body, the death of his children, a wife who wishes he would die—is not due to his own fault (cf. Jb 1:22 and 2:10, for example). In fact, it would appear that Job's suffering actually comes at the behest of Yahweh through a gamble he makes with Satan or, more properly, "the satan" (*ha-satan* in Hebrew).[28] At any rate, most of the book is occupied with recounting back-and-forth lectures by Job to his friends and his friends to him. Job's friends hold to the ancient Israelite view that one's personal suffering is the result of disobedience. Job himself, meanwhile, claims that he is innocent and that his suffering is unjustified.

At the end of the book (chaps. 38–42), Yahweh finally chimes in with his explanation, or, rather, non-explanation. What he does is remind Job that he and only he is the Creator. Not without an obvious hint of sarcasm, Yahweh thus questions Job, "Where were you when I laid the foundation of the earth? Tell me, if you have understanding" (Jb 38:4). Yahweh has no patience for mere mortals who are in no position to question him. "Gird up your loins like a man," he commands Job, continuing, "I will question you, and you declare to me" (Jb 40:7). God's words in this passage remind me of Benedict's emphasis in chapter 4 that the Christian life does not consist in questioning God so much as in letting ourselves be questioned and called to an account for our existence by God.[29] At the end of the day, Yahweh's answer to the innocent sufferer is a non-answer, but according to Enns that is okay for Job, and we need to accept that it should be sufficient for us as well: "When we come to our own Job-like moments, the way forward isn't to expect God to give us some additional piece of information to make everything fall into place. The answer that people like Job and his friends want—because they've got to 'know what they believe'—is precisely the answer God keeps hidden. No special bit of knowledge for you. Rather, God exposes the limitations of our think-

---

28. For a discussion of the difference between the two and its theological significance, see Ramage, *Dark Passages of the Bible*, 185–87.

29. Benedict XVI, "The Virgin Mary, Icon of Obedient Faith."

ing."[30] In sum, Job shows us that the point of divine revelation is not to give us a complete explanation of the inner workings of God—it is to put us into *relationship* with God.

A final biblical book profitably mined by Enns is the Book of Psalms. In a terrific little chapter titled "Parts of the Bible We Don't Read in Church (but Should)," the author treats a sampling of texts, some of which have been excised from the Catholic liturgy, others of which have not. For example, the very dark Psalm 88 may not be pondered frequently in other Christian communities, but it is quite appropriately read in the compline liturgy of the Catholic Church every Friday night. Like Job, the petitioner of this psalm feels himself as utterly cut off from God. He clearly has his doubts as to whether his last end will be a happy one, yet he keeps going back to God anyway. Is this psalm preserved as an example of what *not* to think, say, and feel regarding the things of God? According to Enns, the answer to this is a resounding "Nah." The experience of feeling like we are dead to God is part of the Bible and cannot simply be brushed aside.

Another psalm mentioned by Enns and prayed frequently in the Catholic Church is Psalm 22, which we hear every Palm Sunday (and on Friday, Week III, of the Liturgy of the Hours). In praying this psalm (or at least the part of it he managed to utter aloud while asphyxiating), Jesus reveals that he experienced the same phenomenon of abandonment described by the psalmist.[31] As part of his *kenosis* or self-emptying, Jesus went through the entire human experience, albeit without sin. In undergoing the experience of darkness, he thereby re-

---

30. Enns, *Sin of Certainty*, 91. Here I have discussed suffering in the context of Enns's recent commentary on Job and Ecclesiastes. These receive a more extensive treatment in my *Dark Passages of the Bible*, 237–73.

31. Of course, it is possible, as some have supposed in the past, that Jesus was simply uttering these words for our sake or merely to evoke the psalm's deeply positive ending. To be sure, Jesus was indeed uttering these words for us, and I am certain that he (and the evangelists who wove his words into their narratives) had in view the psalm's ending, which envisions all the nations of the earth turning toward the Lord (Ps 22:27). I think that more is going on here, though.

veals that our own experiences of feeling abandoned are not godless moments, evidence that something is wrong in our spiritual lives. Indeed, in a passage whose truth has been affirmed by countless Catholic spiritual masters throughout the ages, Enns observes, "Feeling abandoned by God may make us more like Jesus than when things are floating along swimmingly."[32] Stated in another way, "When we are in despair or fear and God is as far away from us as the most distant star in the universe, we are at that moment with Christ more than we know—and perhaps more than we ever have been—because when we suffer, we share in and complete Christ's sufferings."[33]

In one of the best moves made in his book, Enns reaches beyond the Bible and ties his biblical reflections into the broader Catholic spiritual tradition (For Catholics reading this book, please take a moment to appreciate that there are non-Catholic brethren who appreciate the wisdom of the Catholic saints). Enns shows a deep esteem for the likes of Mother Teresa, whom he admires for lightheartedly acknowledging that she never had clarity, only trust. He likewise finds great edification in Thomas Merton's prayer that begins, "My Lord God, I have no idea where I am going."[34] More importantly still, Enns recounts his own journey of encountering the writings of the sixteenth-century Spanish mystics John of the Cross and Teresa of Avila. As we learn from great men and women such as these, the "dark night of the soul" is not a sign that we are far from God, but rather the opposite: it is a special sign of the divine presence and an indication that we are firmly on the road of purification and preparation for union with God. Another insight from the Spanish mystics is that the measure of man's holiness is not to be found in clear thoughts or lofty sentiments, but rather in the depth of our charity. We are most like God when we are loving God. Or, as Enns puts it, "Being like God. That's the goal. And we are most like God not when we are certain we are right about God, or when we tell others

32. Enns, *Sin of Certainty*, 167.
33. Ibid., 200.
34. Ibid., 111.

how right we are, but when we are acting toward one another like the faithful Father and Son."³⁵

If his turn to the saints is one of the best parts of Enns's work, for me the absolute best moment in his book comes in his excursus on the liturgy. Again, Enns is not Catholic—he currently worships in an Episcopalian community. That said, both Catholics and Protestants stand to benefit from his understanding of liturgy's primacy within the Christian faith:

> I need to be in a place where the pulpit was off to the side and the table was central, symbols for me of letting go of old patterns, where lengthy sermons were the center of worship. I need. Others may not. I like a prayer book and liturgy to guide me in my faith rather than falling back into my comfort zone of controlling reality with my learned and carefully chosen words.³⁶

Enns is only speaking for himself in the above passage, but I think that he is putting his finger upon a truth that applies across the board to all Christians, whether we realize it or not. As the Second Vatican Council tells us, the liturgy of the word and the liturgy of the Eucharist are so closely connected that they form a single act of worship. Nevertheless, the same council identifies participation in the Eucharistic sacrifice as the source and summit of Christian life.³⁷ On the one hand, this is the case because Christ is eminently present—body, blood, soul, and divinity—in the sacrament of the Eucharist. But I think that there is another aspect of the liturgical sacrifice that lends it its primacy. Liturgical worship of Christ requires us to set aside our rational attempts to circumscribe God if only for a few moments in order to bow down before the ineffable divine mystery. As we have emphasized throughout the present volume, this humble apophatic homage is by no means an anti-intellectual act of resignation, much

---

35. Ibid., 101–2.
36. Ibid., 193.
37. Vatican Council II, *Sacrosanctum Concilium* (1963), §56, http://www.vatican.va/archive/hist_councils/ii_vatican_council/documents/vat-ii_const_19631204_sacrosanctum-concilium_en.html; Vatican Council II, *Lumen Gentium*, §11.

less an endorsement of a fideism that would ask Christians to believe things that go *against* reason. On the contrary, liturgical worship is the epitome of an intelligent faith's actualization. It is the most concrete spiritual and physical instantiation of our profession that God is God and we are not. Liturgical worship inscribes into our very being and actions the truth that, while we cannot even come close to fully understanding God, we can indeed engage him in a profound relationship of love, trust, and allegiance.

Conclusion: If You Would Believe, Act as Though You Believe

I would like to draw this chapter to a close with the help of a few insights from Matthew Bates's recent book *Salvation by Allegiance Alone: Rethinking Faith, Works, and the Gospel of Jesus the King.*[38] As in the case of the above authors whom we have surveyed, Bates's project has a deep affinity with the thought of Benedict XVI. Like Enns and Benedict, Bates advocates a move away from faith as acceptance of noetic content and toward faith as a relationship of love and trust. In fact, Bates prescribes a "surgery" wherein we revise our vocabulary along the lines envisioned by Enns, replacing salvation by faith with salvation by *allegiance*. Just as Enns proposed a retranslation of Galatians 2:16, Bates suggests that we render Ephesians 2:8 as follows: "For by grace you have been saved through *allegiance*; and this is not your own doing, it is the gift of God—not because of works [of the Jewish law], lest any man should boast."[39]

---

38. Matthew Bates, *Salvation by Allegiance Alone: Rethinking Faith, Works, and the Gospel of Jesus the King* (Grand Rapids, Mich.: Baker Academic, 2017).

39. Ibid., 2–4. Like others who follow the New Perspective on Paul (for example, N. T. Wright), Bates does not consider the "works" of good deeds as irrelevant to salvation. Rather, I believe that this theological approach rightly understands Paul's condemnation of "works" as an attack on those who considered that salvation came through continued adherence to all the legal precepts of the Jewish law. Ibid., 20–22. For another insightful analysis of faith in terms of allegiance, see James Prothro, *Both Judge and Justifier: Biblical Legal Language and the Act of Justifying in Paul* (Tübingen: Mohr Siebeck, 2018), 212–16.

Responding to the simplistic supposition one sometimes finds among the Christian faithful, Bates insists that faith is not the opposite of evidence-based inquiry and reasoned judgment. We do not believe totally apart from publicly available evidence, much less because the evidence points in the opposite direction of faith's claims. What we have noted before can therefore easily be applied to situations in which two or more religious traditions offer mutually contradictory takes on reality: some interpretations can definitively be ruled out, but it is more difficult to make a compelling argument that only this or that interpretation is right. Returning to Bates's line of thought, religious faith is thus not an irrational leap into complete darkness or the arbitrary choice to accept a particular set of claims over others but instead "a reasonable, action-oriented response grounded in the conviction that God's invisible underlying realities are more certain than any apparent realities."[40]

As in the case of a quote from Enns which we discussed above, this last sentence might just as well have been penned by Benedict, for whom we have seen in chapter 4 that one of the most essential characteristics of faith is its profession that what cannot be seen by man in fact represents true reality. Moreover, Bates's insistence that faith is irreducible to intellectual assent is something with which Benedict (and Newman) would wholeheartedly concur. According to both, intellectual acceptance of the truths of the faith is a necessary but not sufficient condition of faith. At the same time, neither thinker countenances fideism by telling us that our beliefs ought to go against our reason's dictates—in other words, what our brains tell us is right. But what I find most insightful and most congenial to Benedict's project is Bates's central contention that we use the word *allegiance* to render the biblical *pistis* and *'āman*. It captures in one word the essential truth that salvation occurs in a dynamic and enduring relationship of both faith and love. Benedict himself says that one can profess that salva-

---

40. Bates, *Salvation by Allegiance Alone*, 17, 20.

tion comes by faith alone or by charity alone, so long as one understands the terms aright.⁴¹ Bates's choice of the word *allegiance* helps us to thread this theological needle.

Finally, one of the most refreshing parts of Bates's project, once again intimately related to Benedict's concerns while at the same time carrying them forward, lies in his discussion of the following question: How intellectually certain does one have to be for his faith to "count"? As Christians inhabiting this secular age, many of us have wondered at one time or another whether we still have faith. I mean, we may say the words of the Creed, but is this the same as actually believing them? Bates's answer to this query is remarkably simple and profound: "Fortunately, we do not have to speculate about what level of intellectual certainty is required for salvation, because the flip side of the allegiance-alone coin spells out the boundary for us—*we must be intellectually certain enough that we are willing to give our allegiance* (pistis) *to Jesus as our true king.*"⁴² Or, as Richard John Neuhaus wisely put it, "If you would believe, act as though you believe, leaving it to God to know whether you believe, for such leaving it to God is faith."⁴³ In short, to believe in Jesus is to swear fealty to him, to submit to the reign of God that Jesus is effecting. The answer to the question of whether or not we believe in Jesus boils down to whether or not we have committed our entire lives to *following* him. If we can answer this allegiance question in the affirmative, then despite all our frailty and sin, we are on the right Way.

---

41. See Benedict XVI, "The Doctrine of Justification: From Works to Faith"; and Ramage, "Reception of St. Paul in the Works of Joseph Ratzinger/Benedict XVI," 147–71.
42. Bates, *Salvation by Allegiance Alone*, 94–95.
43. Cited in Randy Boyagoda, "Cordially, Richard John Neuhaus," *First Things* (August 2012): 18.

11

"IRONIC" BELIEF

The Christian Story and Apologetics in a Secular Age

Countering Secularism's Master Narrative with a Hopeful One of Our Own

Why do we believe in the Christian faith? How certain are we of its truth? And what if it turns out that it is wrong to place our hope in its expectation for the resurrection of the body on the last day? These are questions that we have touched on in various ways throughout this volume, but as we approach the end of our journey we will bring them existentially into focus as we complete our work of putting Benedict XVI into dialogue with other contemporary thinkers whose projects converge with his in important ways. I will be framing the chapter in light of three works in the field of contemporary philosophy of religion: James Smith's *How Not to Be Secular*, John Cottingham's *Philosophy of Religion: Towards a More Humane Approach*, and Myron Penner's *The End of Apologetics*. Along the way, we will bring a number of other authors of the past and present into the conversation in order to help flesh out the implications of Benedict's approach for living the "experiment of faith" in today's world. One of the key proposals that I will be making in this chapter and the next is that the Christian faith—and its hope in the resurrection in particular—is "ironic," meaning that it is normative and certain notwithstanding the inherent inability of our finite intellect to know much about what God is or about what happens after we die. Another key feature of this chapter and the next will be the suggestion that we stop taking a primarily defensive posture and instead direct our apologetic efforts towards answering secularism's master narrative with a story of our own, especially as told through the lens of the saints and our own wholehearted practice of the faith.

James Smith, *How Not to Be Secular*
The Religious Quest in Our Secular Age, the Age of Authenticity

One of the most oft-recurring questions in my adult life as a follower of Christ has centered on the relationship of faith and doubt. My sense is that most believers think that their faith is supposed to be "certain," meaning that the believer cannot be wrong. But what concerns me is the reality of belief as experienced in the actual lives of adults today: for a great many of us, the certainty we had as children and which we think we still ought to have now eludes us.

James Smith's book *How Not to Be Secular* addresses precisely the phenomenon of which I am speaking here: "Faith is fraught; confession is haunted by an inescapable sense of its contestability. We don't believe instead of doubting; we believe while doubting. We're all Thomas now."[1] This depiction of believing while doubting rings true to my experience. It also reminds me of the desperate father's works from Mark 9:24: "Lord, I believe; help my unbelief!" This was a man who did not have a clear faith that we would tend to look upon as being rock-solid. It was a faith that acknowledged its own lack of faith—which paradoxically only showed the man's faith all the more strongly.

Instead of reproving people like us and this man for our skepti-

---

1. Smith, *How Not to Be Secular*, 4.

cism, James Smith simply wants us to acknowledge it as the reality of our lives and to see that real good can be made of it. Smith's book, itself a lucid distillation of the thought of philosopher Charles Taylor, describes our present time as a "secular age." By this he means something different from what the reader might at first expect. In Taylor's sense of the term, "secular" does not refer to a society comprised largely of non-religious people but rather to a society in which "belief in God is understood to be one option among others, and thus contestable (and contested)."[2] Why was it virtually impossible not to believe in God just a few centuries ago in our Western society, whereas now many find this not only easy, but even inescapable? The difference between the two ages, Taylor maintains, is not the catalogue of available beliefs but rather our default assumptions about what is believable.[3]

We live today in what Taylor calls an *age of authenticity*, which he describes as the "understanding ... that each one of us has his/her own way of realizing our humanity, and that it is important to find and live out one's own, as against surrendering to conformity with a model imposed on us from the outside."[4] The prime value of this society is choice, the decision of the individual freed from any external constraints (think Pinckaers's freedom of indifference) to embark on his own personal quest for meaning. Religion cannot be imposed on those who inhabit this age. We demand that religion speak to us, helping us to make sense of our own experience and to express who we understand ourselves to be. Religion is no longer a given, a tradition we inherit from our parents—we think that we have to "find" our faith and forge our own "spiritual" path even if it is not "religious."[5]

While the religious seeker in our age of authenticity may appear indulgent and self-centered, the fact is that we cannot escape the

2. Ibid., 21.
3. Ibid., 19.
4. Taylor, *A Secular Age*, 475.
5. Smith, *How Not to Be Secular*, 90.

quest-like shape of our religious search today. There is no turning back the clock on disenchantment with the old ways of religion. In an interesting and I think very valuable move, Smith sees in this situation something deeply positive: "The burden of proof, indeed the burden of belief, for so long upheld by society, is now back on the believer, where it belongs."[6] Although there may be fewer Christians in Western society than in years past, it is increasingly becoming the case that those who call themselves Christian do so out of a conscious, free decision that they know is one of many available offers on hand. Writing this brings to mind these words penned by Ratzinger decades ago:

> From the crisis of today the Church of tomorrow will emerge—a Church that has lost much. She will become small and will have to start afresh more or less from the beginning.... As a small society, it will make much bigger demands on the initiative of her individual members.... But in all of the changes at which one might guess, the Church will find her essence afresh and with full conviction in that which was always at her center: faith in the triune God, in Jesus Christ, the Son of God made man.[7]

As for Taylor, so for Ratzinger, our Western society's present religious situation is not an unmitigated disaster. While we wish that belief were easier and that more people accepted the faith, those of us who are trying "the experiment" know what we are getting into and find ourselves faced with no other choice but to pursue the path of discipleship with an intentionality that might be easier to neglect in a more favorable cultural climate.

Challenging Secularism's Master Narrative

What is the believer to do in a secular age in which the atheistic narrative appears authentic and attractive while that of religion comes across as canned, unoriginal, and repulsive? Taylor thinks that the Christian needs to go on offense, not in the apologetic mode of over-

---

6. Ibid., 11.
7. Joseph Ratzinger, *Faith and the Future* (San Francisco: Ignatius Press, 2009), 116.

confidently "proving" the faith to be true but rather in attacking the smug secular spin on reality that so many unwittingly imbibe as if it were obviously the way things are. The "master narrative" of the West's prevailing atheistic humanism paints a picture of religion as a repressive, mythical relic of the past from the grips of which we are finally on the brink of evolving. As Taylor neatly summarizes it, this is "a story of great moral enthusiasm at a discovery, at a liberation from a narrower world of closer, claustrophobic relations, involving excessive control and invidious distinctions."[8]

If we were to ask Benedict what he finds most problematic in the secularist story, he would certainly make mention of its assumption that the universe is a "closed" system, that God—if such a being exists—certainly cannot enter into human history through miracles such as the Incarnation and Resurrection.[9] Taylor, like Benedict, wants to drill into us the truth that the secular, atheist gospel narrative is itself merely one take on reality. It is one reading of the way things are—a construal, moreover, that is frequently espoused and preached in a condescending, "holier-than-thou" fashion. Taylor wants to level the playing field by getting both the believer *and* non-believer to accept the truth that our understanding is underdetermined, that going in either direction—theism or atheism—requires a "leap of faith."[10]

Answering Atheism by Telling a Different Story

In this last section, we saw how Taylor attacked the false secularist premise that its narrative is obviously the only rational account of

---

8. Taylor, *A Secular Age*, 575; Smith, *How Not to Be Secular*, 102.
9. On Ratzinger's famous "critique of the critique" which bears directly upon this assumption of the atheist, see his "Biblical Interpretation in Conflict: On the Foundations and the Itinerary for Exegesis Today," in *Opening Up the Scriptures: Joseph Ratzinger and the Foundations of Biblical Interpretation*, ed. José Granados, Carlos Granados, and Luis Sánchez-Navarro (Grand Rapids, Mich.: Eerdmans Publishing Co., 2008), 1–29.
10. Taylor, *A Secular Age*, 550; Smith, *How Not to Be Secular*, 110. For a similar discussion regarding the truth of the Gospels and whether they ought to be read through a hermeneutic of faith or suspicion, see my *Jesus, Interpreted*, chap. 7, especially its conclusion.

things. We might think of that as the "negative" side of his offensive, but there is also a "positive" one. Like Benedict, Taylor thinks that we can do more than simply point out flaws in atheistic assumptions. As we saw above, the secular story is just that—a story, an enthusiastic master narrative of liberation, of discovery, of beating the bad guy (old religion). For most people, stories are more powerful than meticulously crafted arguments. Consequently, Taylor believes that our response to modern atheism's master narrative must also be deployed in narrative form. Christians need not merely make different arguments, we need to tell a different story than that of the secularist.

Of course, the Christian tradition has one really important story, the greatest story ever told. This master narrative extends from the universe's creation, to the creation of human beings in God's image along with our (repeated) fall, our cries for redemption, and our eventual salvation from sin and death by the resurrection of God himself incarnate in the flesh. This is a magnificent story indeed, and as a Christian I believe one with a beauty that bespeaks its truth. But this is not actually the precise story Taylor has in mind.

Aware that Christians cannot offer a simple solution to the dilemma in which we find ourselves caught within this secular age, Taylor suggests that the path forward is to be found by meeting our contemporaries where they are, latching on to what is good in the age of authenticity. Seeing as people today so greatly value personal choice and the sincerity of those who follow their convictions no matter the cost, we should be pointing them to stories of exemplars of Christians who have done precisely this. To synthesize Taylor's thought with that of Benedict which we have encountered before in chapter 2 and which will conclude our book in the next chapter, encounters with the saints—Christians who have "lived the experiment"—provide points of contact with a fullness that the secular worldview cannot begin to provide. Arguments may be included, but here the portraits themselves are the *apologia* or argument for faith. The life of the Christian living his faith in its fullness is a demonstration in the sense that it offers a better account of our experience, yet one that has to be experienced to be seen for what it is.[11]

In any event, neither I nor any of the authors discussed here are under any illusion that the endeavor we are talking about will convince everybody, or even a great number of people. As Smith puts it, what is hoped for is the following:

> In that cross-pressured space, some will begin to feel—and be honest about—the paucity of a closed [secularist] "take." And in ways that they never could have anticipated, some will begin to wonder if "renunciation" isn't the way to wholeness, and that freedom might be found in the gift of constraint, and that the strange rituals of Christian worship are the answer to their most human aspirations, as if, for their whole lives, they've been waiting for Saint Francis.[12]

Taylor's exemplar in the text I have just cited was a saint who lived eight centuries ago. He is an important figure in Christian history, and rightly taken as an inspiration for countless Christians over the ages. However, one would also do well to recall that, for Benedict, the power of the saints' lives is often most evident in the ordinary living saints, that is, those who are "experimenting" in the faith now to the best of their ability, even amidst great limitations and failures. In the Bible, the term "saints" refers to these living Christians (see, for example, Acts 9:13ff).[13]

St. Paul, who penned a great deal of the New Testament, calls upon the Christian community to "be imitators of me, as I am of Christ" (1 Cor 4:16; 11:1). Paul knew that he was a frail, sinful human being, yet he encouraged the faithful to look at him as an example anyway. I do not think that this was hubris; in light of our discussion in this chapter, perhaps we can better see that Paul was onto something. Christian belief does not take place in a vacuum, and it is not a mere intellectual affair. It is a total way of life, an apprenticeship of disci-

---

11. Taylor, *A Secular Age*, 643, 729; Smith, *How Not to Be Secular*, 133, 137.
12. Smith, *How Not to Be Secular*, 138.
13. Benedict XVI, "Holiness."

pleship that is best endeavored in the presence and with the example of those who have been living the experiment long before we came along. I myself am no canonized saint, but I do (usually) try to walk the path of Christ amidst the community of saints on earthly pilgrimage toward our heavenly homeland. One of my small hopes in this book is that, weaving in a little of my personal story and struggles into the narrative provides an example of the Christian life that may help some readers deal with doubt and darkness. I hope that one finds in these reflections something beautiful and compelling that is lacking in the jaded picture painted by a disillusioned former believer or by the naïve and arrogant overconfidence sometimes projected by devout Christians. Echoing a homily that greatly moved my family the week of my father's death, I would say that this book contains the confessions of a "practicing" Catholic, meaning that neither I, nor my father, nor any of us have perfected the faith. Yet the very effort of Christians to practice, to experiment, to fight the good fight, to run the race—or whatever other expression one might choose to describe it—can itself be an *apologia* for the truth of the Christian way of life.[14]

John Cottingham, Philosophy of Religion: *Towards a More Humane Approach*

Like Smith and Taylor, John Cottingham contends that we need to rethink how one would go about providing rational justification for religious truth claims such as that of the Resurrection. Cottingham suggests that we take our cue from Aristotle, according to whom one's philosophical methods have to be suited to the subject matter under investigation. When it comes to the realm of religion, argues Cottingham, mere "spectator evidence" is not sufficient. As our authors above have emphasized that the truth of the Christian faith can be seen for

---

14. The homily to which I refer here was delivered by Fr. Paul Scalia at the funeral mass for his father Justice Antonin Scalia on February 20, 2016. The transcript can be accessed through any number of sites online.

what it truly is only through experience, so Cottingham argues that religious discourse is inherently multilayered. It resonates with human beings on many different levels, not all of which are grasped by the reflective, analytic mind. As a result, he maintains, "Any plausible account of the human condition must make space for the crucial role of imaginative, symbolic, and poetic forms of understanding in deepening our awareness of ourselves and the reality we inhabit."[15] Imagine, Cottingham continues, if an endeavor in the philosophy of music were to confine itself to abstract theories and arguments, paying no attention to the transforming power that music has in the lives of those who experience it. This is what it is like when we try to philosophize about religion and weigh its truth claims without attempting to experience it. What we need, then, is "to develop a more 'humane' model for philosophy of religion: one that preserves the virtues of a critical philosophical methodology, but connects the subject more closely with the moral and spiritual sensibilities that have shaped religious belief over the centuries, and which continue to inform the lives of believers today."[16]

Cottingham invokes the work of several contemporary and past thinkers to develop his "more humane" approach to religion. For example, he points to Eleonore Stump's recent book in which she argues that the problem of evil cannot be addressed properly by maintaining constant critical detachment from the issue. According to Stump, philosophical reflection of suffering is best carried out with the help of story, and moreover the sort of story in which we see ourselves as personally involved. She proposes that we engage such narratives in an "antiphonal" fashion, which I take to mean as a dynamic of call and response wherein we converse with a text, letting it speak to us and change us rather than probing it as an inanimate object. In a similar vein, Martha Nussbaum insists that one cannot appreciate a great

---

15. John Cottingham, *Philosophy of Religion: Towards a More Humane Approach* (New York: Cambridge University Press, 2014), 8.
16. Ibid., 11.

literary text (for example, the Bible) unless we allow ourselves to be receptive and "porous" to its intended effect.[17] These approaches cohere nicely with Benedict's approach to the truth claims of religion and of suffering in particular. For the pontiff, it is also stories—the lives of the saints, living and deceased—which convey the truth of the faith most powerfully. Additionally, these authors share Benedict's contention unfolded in chapters 6 and 7 on hope that the problem of suffering is not something that can be understood fully from the outside. Rather, it is only from the inside—by living a life of intentional discipleship and offering our sufferings in union with Christ on the cross—that we perceive the truth of the Christian message about his death and resurrection.

In chapter 4 on the virtue of faith, we saw that the emeritus pontiff had recourse to the thought of Pascal to help him explain the nature of Christian faith. Cottingham also invokes the French polymath to further his cause, in particular the latter's contention that it is our heart, not our reason, that senses God.[18] Like the other authors whose thought we have been exploring, Cottingham does not envision the Pascalian approach as one of mere sentimentalism but rather one that demands a holistic process in interior transformation, which in Christianity we refer to by such terms as discipleship and redemption. Paul Moser coined the term "kardiatheology" to denote the approach, while Cottingham himself describes it as an "epistemology of involvement" and a call to "allegiance." We get a sense for what is required here by looking to the Greek words *askesis* (training) and *mathesis* (learning), which in the Latin is rendered *disciplina* (discipline). To be religious is not just to espouse certain doctrines but to take up the commitments or practices enshrined in these words.

However one wants to describe this dynamic of belief, the point is that genuine evidence for religious truth claims is indeed available,

---

17. Ibid., 7; Stump, *Wandering in Darkness* 24–27; Martha Nussbaum, *Love's Knowledge* (Oxford: Oxford University Press, 1990), 281–82.

18. Pascal, *Pensées*, no. 913.

but it is evidence that it is accessible only by those who are willing to embark upon a path of formation and a relationship with the truth.[19] Pascal says as much in his eloquent commentary on the *Deus absconditus* of Isaiah 45:15. The "hidden God," insists Pascal, is not utterly unknowable by man. God cannot be directly known in this life, but he does provide signs to those who seek relationship with him with all their heart. Indeed, he provides just enough light for those who wish to see, and enough darkness for those who do not.[20] In another fascinating point of contact with Benedict's thought, Cottingham points out that his approach is the same as what we find in Scripture: "Unless you believe, you will not understand" (Is 7:9).

A great many things change once we make the commitment to believe. It is not that all uncertainties fade or that all our dreams come true, but things previously opaque gain some light because the faith provides us with a setting for our inquiry and our living. Take for example seemingly mistaken biblical or doctrinal passages. Unlike the fundamentalist, the informed believer does not read his tradition's authoritative texts as a blueprint or manual that is perspicuous apart from reference to an interpretative framework. In a timely and illuminating analogy, Cottingham compares our religion's sacred pages to hyperlinks in a computerized text. In pursuing the "link" to the entire Christian community and tradition, the believer gains access to an entire network of connections hitherto unknown and unavailable. Once engaged, these connections are precisely what render otherwise isolated and seemingly untrue propositions such as the Resurrection meaningful.[21] The believer now sees set before him the entire breadth

---

19. Cottingham, *Philosophy of Religion*, 20–23; Paul Moser, *The Evidence for God: Religious Knowledge Reexamined* (Cambridge: Cambridge University Press, 2010), 26, 172. On the subject of allegiance, seeing it as an illuminating translation of the term "faith," see Bates, *Salvation by Allegiance Alone* which was discussed in detail in the prior chapter.

20. Pascal, *Pensées*, nos. 427, 149.

21. Cottingham, *Philosophy of Religion*, 150–51; Sandra Lee Menssen and Thomas Sullivan suggest evaluating revelatory claims by an appeal to what they call conditional-upon-explanation facts (CUE-facts). These are putative truths that "one does not accept as true but

of reason—"an ever present net of moral understanding and illumination"—from which he may draw the fullness of understanding and life if only he is willing to reach out and participate in it. Cottingham's exhortation captures well Benedict's famous call from many years ago: "The courage to engage the whole breadth of reason, and not the denial of its grandeur—this is the program with which a theology grounded in biblical faith enters into the debates of our time."[22]

Myron Penner, The *End of Apologetics*

The End of Apologetics as We Know It

When I first picked up Myron Penner's book with a title that seemed to signal the end of apologetics, I did not know precisely what to expect. Published as it was by Baker Academic, one thing I did have confidence in was that the author would not be arguing that we ought to be indifferent to Christianity's truth claims. To my great delight, the book struck a chord within me almost immediately after beginning to peruse its first pages. As I expected, Penner's call to end apologetics was not being proffered as an excuse for complacency; instead, he was diagnosing a deep-seated problem that I too had long noticed without being able to put my finger on in the way this author had.

All too often, when Christians today try to convince others (or themselves) of our faith's truth claims, we do so using language that our interlocutors simply no longer understand. It is not that arguments for God's existence such as Aquinas's traditional five ways are invalid—I myself find them profoundly helpful—but rather that peo-

---

would accept, provided they are appropriately linked to a plausible explanation." Cast in Cottingham's terms, the "plausible explanation" described by Menssen and Sullivan would come from the whole web of factors that comprise the Christian tradition and experience, many of which I have discussed: personal experience of beauty in the Church, the freedom and happiness that come through obedience to the Church's moral teachings; encounters with living saints, etc. Sandra Lee Menssen and Thomas D. Sullivan, *The Agnostic Inquirer: Revelation from a Philosophical Standpoint* (Grand Rapids, Mich.: Eerdmans Publishing Co., 2007), 211.

22. Benedict XVI, "Faith, Reason and the University."

ple today lack the philosophical vocabulary requisite for seeing the cogency of the arguments. Without special training, people today do not grasp the same thing Aquinas understands with terms such as potency, act, nature, and the like. In other words, we have lost the context that made the arguments meaningful and relevant. Penner here makes a fascinating move by recalling Alasdair MacIntyre's famous "disquieting suggestion" and extending it to the realm of apologetics. In brief, MacIntyre suggested decades ago that moral discourse in our contemporary world is in a state of disarray wherein everyone continues to use the same traditional language of moral concepts such as "good" while lacking understanding of what the terms meant in their proper context—and, to make matters worse, almost no one recognizes the discrepancy. For Penner, the same acute disorder is prevalent in our speaking and thinking about God in modern culture, wherein believers and non-believers alike continue to use the same verbiage ("God," "truth," "proof," etc.) while intending fundamentally different things both from one another and at times from the Christian tradition itself.[23]

Connected with Christians' failure to acknowledge the incommensurability of our God language with the understanding of those whom we wish to evangelize, Penner laments that we often overestimate the rational warrant for our beliefs. Just as it is for anyone else, it is easy for the Christian to suppose that his analysis of the universe is impartial and ought to be understood by anyone who sincerely hears him out. Because we enjoy the benefit of divine revelation, it is even understandable that Christians sometimes suppose that our own arguments are intrinsically superior to those of our interlocutors. Yet Penner thinks that our apologetic arguments in favor of the faith often end up being more a curse than a blessing. Taking his cue from Søren Kierkegaard, he goes so far as to speak of the misguided apologist as a

---

23. Penner, *End of Apologetics*, 4. For MacIntyre's "disquieting suggestion" told through a metaphor about the collapse of the natural sciences, see his *After Virtue: A Study in Moral Theory* (Notre Dame, Ind.: University of Notre Dame Press, 1984), 1–5.

"second Judas" who betrays Christ with "the treason of stupidity."[24] Penner maintains that, contrary to popular perception, Kierkegaard was not a fideist who saw faith and reason as fundamentally opposed to each other; instead, his criticism targeted the truncated *modern* conception of reason which Christians today unwittingly assume. We are crippled, he argues, by a "debilitating forgetfulness" of our own unconscious presuppositions about the way things must be—and it is this blindness that renders us unable to speak to our contemporaries in a convincing manner. But the only way to get past our modernity, so to speak, is to first go *through* it. We simply cannot return to an alleged "golden age" of Christianity wherein belief was a much more cut-and-dry proposition.[25]

Outflanking Objections through the Practice of the Faith, Telling a Different Story

Rather than *arguing* for the superiority of Christianity in such a way that any rational inquirer ought to be able to conclude that it is true, Penner's strategy resembles that of Taylor and Smith in that he aims to "outflank" objections by shifting the discussion away from the proof and toward the *picture* or *story*. In this important respect, Penner's project also closely resembles that of Pope Benedict, for whom (as we will discuss in more detail in the concluding chapter) the truth of the Catholic faith is seen best in the beauty that the Church has produced over the ages and in the concrete stories of countless lives lived for and in Jesus Christ. Moreover, just as Benedict spoke in chapter 4 of our Christian task as one of letting ourselves be grasped by the truth rather than grasping it ourselves, Penner insists that our focus ought to be less on knowing truth than on *becoming* the truth by living it: "Christianity, then, is much more a way or an invitation to live

---

24. Penner, *End of Apologetics*, 8; cf. Søren Kierkegaard, *Sickness unto Death*, ed. and trans. Howard V. Hong and Edna H. Hong (Princeton: Princeton University Press, 1980), 87.
25. Penner, *End of Apologetics*, 11–13.

(walk, grow) in the truth than it is a doctrine."[26] This is not to say that Penner or Benedict thinks that our doctrines are unimportant or untrue. The question here is rather on how we are able to establish or confirm these truths in our own lives as inhabitants of the contemporary world.

In order to refine his account of Christian belief in the world today, Penner turns to Alasdair MacIntyre's concept of a "practice" within tradition-based inquiry, aptly summarized here as "a conception of rational inquiry that is embodied in a tradition and in which the standards of rational justification emerge from the history and practice of interpretation within the rational community itself."[27] MacIntyre would agree with Benedict in holding that the truth of the faith can be grasped only within the context of living in the Christian community. Indeed, MacIntyre's work highlights that human reason itself is caught up in the traditions we inhabit: the web of commitments, practices, and language that makes it possible for us to make sense of the world. This fiduciary framework, as Penner calls it, provides for us the basic

26. Ibid., 66.
27. Penner refers here to MacIntyre's *Whose Justice? Which Rationality?* (Notre Dame, Ind.: University of Notre Dame Press, 1988), 7. For MacIntyre's classic definition of a practice, see his *After Virtue*, 187: "By 'practice' I mean any coherent and complex form of socially established cooperative human activity through which goods internal to that form of activity are realized in the course of trying to achieve those standards of excellence which are appropriate to, and partially definitive of, that form of activity, with the result that human powers to achieve excellence, and human conceptions of the ends and goods involved, are systematically extended." MacIntyre offers the game of chess as an example of one such practice. In a similar vein, Bishop Robert Barron illustrates with a sport: "To learn basketball, one has to play it, and in order to play it, one must surrender to its rhythms, rules, practices, and basic moves. The person who continues to stand on the sideline, analyzing the game in terms of its analogous relation to similar games or in the light of the generic experience of playing 'sports,' will never know it. The learner must trust those who have fallen in love with basketball and who have played it with an abandon made possible by certain definite rules that circumscribe and direct their movement. This, I suggest, is similar to the way that one learns the practices and doctrines of Christianity: through apprenticeship, obedience, and embodied imitation." Barron, "A Reflection on Christ, Theological Method, and Freedom," in *How Balthasar Changed My Mind: 15 Scholars Reflect on the Meaning of Balthasar for Their Own Work*, ed. Rodney A. Howsare and Larry S. Chapp (New York: The Crossroad Publishing Company, 2008), 23.

context in which we think, act, and believe; and it "can no more be avoided by a cognitively functioning human being than breathing by a living one."[28]

Alongside MacIntyre, Penner holds up the thought of G. K. Chesterton as a model for how to overcome the shortcomings of modern apologetics. In his *Orthodoxy*, Chesterton locates his own reason for accepting Christianity less in its ability to say objectively true things about the universe as in his experience of the faith as "a truth-telling thing."[29] As Chesterton further expounds, Christianity teaches some ideas which are *prima facie* incredibly unattractive, such as original sin (we could also add such things as the faith's insistence on mortifying our desires, a very unpopular concept today). The doctrine of original sin might initially give one the impression that the Church has a very negative anthropology. Yet in reality, this apparently unreasonable doctrine is able to elicit a remarkably beautiful quality of life in those who accept it, for the other side of the coin of original sin is our redemption from it through the grace of Christ. As St. Paul has it, the paradox of sin is that, where it abounds, grace abounds all the more (Rom 5:20). Still, the apostle's claim remains an affirmation of *faith*—that is, we cannot prove the datum to a disinterested third-party observer.

As in Benedict's analogy of the stained-glass window from chapter 4, so too for Penner the truth of the faith is discernible only from the inside, by living it. And what does the faith do for us once we are on the inside? Penner suggests that a very good reason to be a Christian is that the faith builds us up, makes us happy, and helps us make sense of the world as a whole. He summarizes this position as follows: "The reason I accept Christian faith, then, is it enables me to interpret my life fruitfully and the world meaningfully through the practices, categories, and language of Christian faith, so that I have a more authentic

---

28. Penner, *End of Apologetics*, 183n159. Penner compares his understanding of fiduciary frameworks to Wittgenstein's concept of "forms of life."
29. Ibid., 75; G. K. Chesterton, *Orthodoxy* (San Francisco: Ignatius Press, 1995), 163–64.

understanding of myself and a sense of wholeness to my life."[30] I do not think that Penner means here to dismiss the importance of Christian doctrines any more than Benedict does. To the contrary, the very language and categories of these truth claims comprise an integral part of what helps the Christian to make sense of his life and of reality as a whole. On this point, I have met a number of non-Catholics over the years who expressed amazement at how the Church has thought through everything and has a reason for everything she professes. Whatever they may have thought about the truth of the Catholic Church's claims, these individuals could not help but be impressed at the sheer magnitude of the project we call Catholicism. Yet being impressed by a religion is clearly not the same as having faith, and we should not expect one to accept individual Christian doctrines outside the context of the lived practice of the faith.

Becoming an Apprentice in "Ironic" Belief

One final concept from Penner will help us to arrive at a practical application of his thought here at the end of this chapter. Taking a page from philosopher Richard Rorty, Penner describes the sort of view I am espousing here in this chapter—and indeed in this book as a whole—as "ironic." In the author's own words: "My ironist, like Rorty's, is someone who acknowledges the contingency of all our descriptions and our vocabularies and acknowledges that all our objective attempts to know reality and justify our beliefs about it are mere 'approximations.' I do not take this, however, as a thesis about the possibility of truth for humans but as a commentary on its availability."[31] Penner's calculated use of the term "ironic" is very different from the way the pragmatist Rorty deploys it. Whereas Rorty recommends that the ironist give up the search for truth and God and focus instead on edification and consensus building, Penner's self-described "Kierkeg-

30. Penner, *End of Apologetics*, 76.
31. Ibid., 99; Richard Rorty, *Philosophy and the Mirror of Nature* (Princeton: Princeton University Press, 1979), 357.

aardian" approach to ironic faith is profoundly realist and cares deeply for attaining the truth about God. For Penner, Christian doctrines really do give us insight into the objective reality of things, even though they are inherently limited, crafted as they are by finite intellects. They are, in other words, "the best rendering a Christian community could give, given their concerns and interests within the specific contexts and Christian practices in which they formulated the truth claims."[32] The irony is consists in the reality that, despite their intrinsic limitations and the fallibility of our finite human intellect apprehending them, these same doctrines remain certain and "normative"—that is, authoritative—for Christians.

Summarizing what he takes the general character of Christian truth claims to be, Penner writes, "To say it in a sentence, they are second-order, contingent, perspectival truths that do not give us God's perspective on himself, but nevertheless are normative for us."[33] This reminds us of Benedict's approach to the Trinity unfolded in chapter 5, wherein the pontiff sees the creedal affirmations as normative albeit not exhaustive signposts to the inscrutable reality of God. Moreover, we have seen how Benedict admits that the doctrine itself reflects the historical circumstances and cultural milieu of the early Church. Sure, he says, the Trinity could have been formulated somewhat differently, and yet it has providentially served for two millennia to unite people in the community of the confessing word. Today, Christians would do well to consider ourselves as part of this great community spanning across the globe, across the ages. Our belief necessarily occurs within the conversation of a hermeneutical tradition with its sacred texts and sacred authority who interprets them.

Penner employs an interesting expression to describe the individual believer's precise role within the great community of faith on its quest for truth and union with God. Rather than thinking of ourselves

---

32. Penner, *End of Apologetics*, 121.
33. Ibid., 123.

as possessors of truth, he suggests that it might be better to think of ourselves as "apprentices to truth."

To speak of an apprentice to truth in this way is to acknowledge that truth is not our possession but something by which we must be possessed. I do not have the truth and cannot get it on my own. Instead, I must apprentice; I must submit myself to the tutelage of those who have mastered the requisite skills— or what the Greeks call *techne*, the knowledge that comes through exercising an *art*—in which I am not proficient.[34]

A person familiar with the corpus of Pope Benedict might suppose that this paragraph had been authored by the pope rather than by the evangelical Penner. The importance of placing ourselves under the tutelage of truth, to gradually learn to let ourselves be possessed by it—these are indeed important themes in our book. One of Penner's contributions is that he brings to the table a helpful down-to-earth touch that complements Benedict's approach. In what I take to be one of his most important thoughts, and in turn one of the most important points in this volume, Penner writes:

As with any apprenticeship, there will be setbacks and failures as I learn how to be in truth's possession, and at times it may even appear I do not have much faith at all. The important thing will be that I maintain an essential interest in or fundamental concern with my life and its relation to truth (God), and that I never stop working this out in dialogue with the texts, practices, community, and relationships (that is, the Church) that present me with the concepts and categories to interpret my life in relation to God.[35]

---

34. Ibid., 107.
35. Ibid. Penner adds a couple of accents to his point about dialogue with the tradition that may catch some Catholics off guard but are nevertheless worth pondering: "I am placed in question by the Truth, and I in turn place the practices and beliefs of my community in question.... It is precisely because they are so committed to their tradition and believe in its deepest impulses that prophets sometimes attack it. The prophetic call is always to a deeper fidelity to the founding event of the tradition, but not in such a way that controls it or even tries to make it into a univocal, monochromatic tradition." Ibid., 167-68. The Catholic may not dissent from the magisterium's authoritative pronouncements, an aspect of the faith that does not directly concern the evangelical Penner. All the same, there is truth in his insistence

To maintain the Christian faith over the entire course of one's life, to persevere in dialogue with the texts, practices, community, and relationships of the Church, requires a substantial amount of virtue. Indeed, it is rightly described by Penner as "agonistic"—a risk, a contest, a struggle in which I as a disciple have to place my entire life on the line while not enjoying the luxury of perfect rational justification for every last one of my faith convictions taken individually.[36] As a Catholic, I do not sit in authority over Scripture, tradition, or the Magisterium. Our exploration of Benedict's thought thus far has driven home this point forcefully. Since God's truth precedes and far exceeds the limits of my finite intellect's reach, there are therefore going to be certain teachings of the Church that I simply just do not get, teachings which for me derive their own rational warrant by virtue of their connection to the edifice of the Catholic faith as a whole to which they are attached.

The resurrection itself may even be glimpsed from this perspective. Perhaps I cannot rationally verify the truth of the resurrection when considered as a proposition isolated from the practice of Christianity, but the fact that the resurrection is the most important historical claim of the religion that has given me such a beautiful life is certainly a worthy reason for giving it serious consideration. Interestingly, both Benedict and Penner evoke the story of the patriarch Jacob to make the point about what I can do as an individual when faced with propositions such as the Resurrection that seem to elude the grasp of my intellect: I can "wrestle with God," struggling to make his truths mine, to let myself be ever more possessed by him and molded into an instrument of his grace.[37]

To the extent that we attempt the Christian quest of expressing the truths we profess in real life, Penner thinks that we have present-

---

that challenging certain negotiable aspects of our tradition can be a good thing and indeed be expressive of great reverence for the tradition itself.

36. Ibid., 125.
37. Ibid., 123.

ed proof for Christianity: "The proof of Christian witness is always in the pudding. The pudding in this case is the lives of Christian witnesses—our overall patterns of action and behavior."[38] Accordingly, if what I proclaim is really true, then it ought to be evident in how I live and act. Indeed, according to Penner, "To have faith is to express it in one's life—the essence of Christianity. It is, in other words, to be Christian."[39] Here again, Penner is saying something remarkably similar to that of Benedict, for whom belief is not primarily an intellectual act but rather the total exercise of handing ourselves over in self-gift to the other, of making the truth of God's love the core of our existence.

Conclusion

In this chapter, I have sought to develop Benedict's thought on how the Christian might navigate the faith in the context of today's secular age by putting the pope into conversation with other current thinkers on the same subject, particularly in the domain of philosophy of religion. These authors have converged with Benedict in advocating a shift away from traditional Christian apologetic concerns and towards answering secularism's master narrative with a story of our own, especially as told through the lens of the saints and our own wholehearted practice of the faith. Now it is time to bring our book to a close with a final chapter that raises the question of what, ultimately, it is that constitutes the true *apologia* for the Christian faith in the eyes of Benedict XVI. In drawing the book to a close, I will lay out his thoughts and then add a few of my own on why I have chosen to follow Christ in this secular age where he appears to many as just another option among many.

38. Ibid., 124.
39. Ibid., 95.

12

CONCLUSION

The Beauty of Life in Christ: Faith's Ultimate Apologia

A Privileged Way to Run the "Experiment" of Faith

"I have often affirmed my conviction that the true apology of Christian faith, the most convincing demonstration of its truth ... are the saints and the beauty that the faith has generated."[1] Throughout his career, Joseph Ratzinger/Benedict XVI, time and again, emphasized that the *via pulchritudinis*, the way of beauty, is a privileged path by which men of today are able to "run the experiment" of a relationship with God and be given strength to fight the good fight of faith in our secular age. In a de-Christianized society characterized by indifference to the Church's truth claims and hostility toward its moral norms, Benedict believes that recourse to the universal language of

---

1. Ratzinger, "Feeling of Things, the Contemplation of Beauty." Other formulations of Ratzinger's leading apologetics principle are found in *Feast of Faith* (San Francisco: Ignatius Press, 1986), 124; *Ratzinger Report*, 129–30; *Principles of Catholic Theology* (San Francisco: Ignatius Press, 1987), 373; *Truth and Tolerance*, 226; Benedict XVI, meeting with the clergy of the Diocese of Bolzano-Bressanone (August 6, 2008). An initial version of this chapter was published under the title "Pope Benedict XVI's Theology of Beauty and the New Evangelization," *Homiletic and Pastoral Review* (January 2015), https://www.hprweb.com/2015/01/pope-benedict-xvis-theology-of-beauty-and-the-new-evangelization/. Portions of it also appear in Ramage, *Jesus, Interpreted*, chap. 7.

beauty is indispensable if the Christian is to compellingly present the Gospel to would-be disciples of Jesus. In affirming this, of course, Benedict is by no means saying that we do not need to make arguments in favor of individual doctrines of the faith, much less alleging that the faith is a mere experience or blind leap devoid of intellectual content. He means, rather, that rational arguments for the faith are not enough to convict people of the truth found within the Church. For most people, something further is needed to bring about conversion to Christ and a commitment to discipleship in our secular age.

In this concluding chapter, I would like to reflect on the concept and role of beauty in Benedict's theology and suggest areas in which it may be fruitfully applied in the quest to live an intelligent faith in today's world—to see through the glass, even if darkly. I have been contending all along in this book that the way to live the experiment of Christian faith credibly in our secular age is to embrace the theological virtues as envisioned robustly by Benedict. I have also emphasized that, if it is to survive Nietzsche's critique in the lives of intelligent people today, the Christian faith is going to have to stand out and challenge the bourgeois morality of our own age. The domain of beauty is the linchpin of this endeavor in Benedict's view, for he is convinced that the Christian faith has an unparalleled beauty that bespeaks its truth in a way that no rational argument, no matter how ably articulated, can achieve. And, above all, it is in the beauty of a life well-lived—the beauty of the theological virtues of faith, hope, and charity experienced in practice—that the truth of Christianity is best glimpsed. In short, for Benedict the truth and goodness of the Christian faith is seen most clearly under the aspect of its beauty.

If I had to pick one chapter that stands out as the most crucial in the present volume from an existential standpoint, this would be it. In particular, my hope is that this culminating chapter's applied existential reflections on why I myself follow Christ and profess hope in the resurrection of the body will prove beneficial to those readers who find themselves struggling with acceptance of one or more of Christianity's core doctrines. In short, my hope that telling something of my own story of striving to see through the glass, darkly, will help cast into relief what the experience of faith, hope, and love looks like in our secular age—how a person fully appreciative of the Nietzschean critique can live the Christian faith to the full in our society.

The Nature of Beauty and Its Power to Convert

It is commonly said that "beauty lies in the eye of the beholder." There is certainly some truth to this saying. When it comes to some matters (say, whether you like a particular song or movie), there is considerable room for debate among people of good will as to whether a given work of art should be called beautiful. Yet to relegate beauty solely to the realm of the subjective gives rise to grave problems when pushed to its logical conclusion. This can be seen by the fact that there exist certain realities that any sane person would recognize as *not* beautiful. For an extremely obvious example, take the carnage of Auschwitz—not the acts of heroism by those imprisoned, but the brutal acts of aggression perpetrated upon them. If one is to call *that* beautiful, then one has clearly emptied the word "beauty" of all meaning.

So what is beauty? As we will discover below, Benedict provides us with something different from a textbook definition of beauty. But for now a good starting point is St. Thomas Aquinas whose thought reflects a large part of the tradition of reflection upon the subject. Within the tradition, beauty is described as having three hallmarks: integrity, proportion, and clarity or luminosity. A piece of art possesses *integrity* when it is whole (a painting is not ripped in half); *proportion* occurs when a thing's various parts are all in proper relation with one another (the painting has *not* been drawn with twig-like limbs); *clarity* is that "shine" that allows for the self-revelation of the beautiful (a painting could possess integrity and proportion but lack adequate light).

For his part, Benedict draws on Plato to give us more of a phenomenological account describing the experience of beauty rather than seeking to define its precise nature. He teaches us that the dominant effect of beauty is to give us a healthy "shock" that draws us out of ourselves and the rut in which we sometimes find ourselves entrenched throughout our daily routine. Beauty gives us wings, lifting us up so that we may soar to the transcendent and rise to greatness. It "disturbs" us and even causes us suffering.[2] Writing in a similar vein, Fr. Jacques Philippe reminds us that the Greek patristic tradition connected the beautiful, *kalos*, with the verb *kalein*, which means to call or summon. For Church Fathers such as Dionysius the Areopagite, beauty thus beckons us to truth, to goodness, and to unity.[3]

C. S. Lewis, to whom Benedict himself refers in this connection, gets to the heart of the matter when he says that created beauty provokes in us a longing to be united with, to receive into ourselves, and to enter into that infinite Beauty of which all created beauty is but a reflection.[4] One of Benedict's favorite illustrations of this point can be seen in the medieval cathedral and its power to draw one toward the infinite. Upon crossing the threshold of God's house, one enters a space and time set apart from ordinary life. The upward thrust of the Gothic cathedral's walls is an invitation to prayer, intended to express in its architectural lines the soul's longing for God, while its stained-glass windows flood the building with the light of God.[5]

---

2. Ratzinger, "Feeling of Things, the Contemplation of Beauty"; Benedict XVI, meeting with artists (November 21, 2009).

3. Jacques Philippe, *Called to Life* (New York: Scepter Publishers, 2008), 102.

4. Lewis, "Weight of Glory," 42.

5. Benedict XVI, "The Cathedral from the Romanesque to the Gothic Architecture: The Theological Background," general audience (November 18, 2009). For its part, the Pontifical Council for Culture points to three areas in which we can be moved by beauty in the created world. First of all, it discusses beauty in creation. Think of John Paul II leading his students on outdoor hikes, catechizing them, celebrating Mass, and simply getting to know them as people. The council also discusses beauty in the arts. This involves such things as offering beautiful liturgies, and forming the faithful to appreciate great art. Finally, there is the beauty that comes through an encounter with Christ himself. We meet Christ especially in his word, in the liturgy, and in the saints. These are merely a few indications of areas in which we all can have

The Universal Language of Beauty and Its Visible Manifestations

In his lifelong process of meditating on beauty, Benedict has repeatedly touched on the various arts of painting, iconography, architecture, sculpture, music, film, and literature as vehicles for communicating the message of the Gospel—or, in keeping with the vocabulary we have been employing—"experiments" we can run to help people test the truth of the Christian message. Benedict tells us that the power of art lies in its ability to speak a universal language, a language of parables. This is a language uniquely capable of speaking to those who seek God but who initially may not be open to hearing the Gospel message more directly. This is by no means to say that dogma is irrelevant. It simply means that for some people the path leading to the fullness of truth might first be entered through the door of an experience of beauty.[6]

Why this is the case can be readily understood upon a moment's reflection. How many times in our lives have we found our attempts to engage people on a moral or dogmatic issue stymied before the discussion even got off the ground? For many of us, this has also been our experience when attempting a dialogue with fellow Catholics on such issues. If it is a matter of politics, morals, or religion, we are told that we should not impose our views on other people.

With this picture in mind, now consider a different scenario. Over the years how many amicable conversations have you had with people about movies? When it comes to my experience in classroom teach-

---

transformative encounters with the beautiful in our Church today. On this point and for an excellent overview of beauty in relation to belief, see the Pontifical Council for Culture, *The Via Pulchritudinis, Privileged Pathway for Evangelization and Dialogue* (2006), http://www.vatican.va/roman_curia/pontifical_councils/cultr/documents/rc_pc_cultr_doc_20060327_plenary-assembly_final-document_en.html.

6. Benedict XVI, address to participants in the plenary assembly of the Pontifical Council for Culture (November 13, 2010).

ing and parish evangelization, people who would otherwise be reluctant to discuss a moral issue with me are much more open to doing so when it emerges from a discussion of a film that broached the topic. Most recently I have been showing people *The Lives of Others*, a German film that marvelously illustrates the power of beauty to convert souls. A benefit of the work is that it is not even implicitly Christian. The key line at the crucial point of the movie comes when one of its grieving characters plays a sonata and then asks, "Can anyone who has heard this music, I mean truly heard it, really be a bad person?" In the following scenes, the audience watches as the effects of this music are played out in the life of the film's protagonist. I use this illustration as a way to raise the question of whether there is such a thing as objectively good or bad music—and, more importantly, whether one can say there are objectively good and bad things. One of my main goals in doing this is to challenge the widespread assumption that certain things "may not be good for me, but I can't say they are bad for someone else."

While my above comments focused on film, Benedict also spends considerable time reflecting on images as outstanding means for communicating the Gospel. His words introducing the *Compendium to the Catechism of the Catholic Church* are especially illuminating. The section of the work dedicated to artistic images is dear to Benedict because he sees in great art an antidote to what he calls today's "culture of images." Especially for young people who become estranged from the faith, Benedict tells us that "a sacred image can express much more than what can be said in words, and be an extremely effective and dynamic way of communicating the Gospel message."[7] When teaching morality I myself make abundant use of images such as Caravaggio's *Calling of St. Matthew* to reflect upon our vocation to holiness and how Christ wishes to "re-create" us through the gift of his grace.

---

7. Benedict XVI, "The Approval and Publication of the *Compendium of the Catechism of the Catholic Church*," moto proprio (June 28, 2005), §5.

I also catechize my students through outstanding frescos by Raphael, medieval stained-glass windows, and Renaissance sculpture. People today relate well to images, and it is relatively easy to comb the tradition and find compelling art to meet them where they are and balance their daily aesthetic experience with a sacred or at least wholesome perspective. To paraphrase the great author Flannery O'Connor, this art does not even have to be Christian, but it does have to be good art. Mediocre Christian art is not what Benedict has in mind in claiming that beauty has the power to convert souls.

The same principles apply to music. I often have my students listen to two different pieces one after another, my favorite pair being ACDC's *Highway to Hell* followed by the theme to *Jurassic Park*. Again, neither of these is even Christian, but the key is that a reaction is elicited in everyone who hears these two very different pieces. It is fascinating to ask people what happens in their souls when hearing each of them. The majestic orchestral piece by John Williams draws us out of ourselves, giving us a sense of awe, reverence, even nostalgia. It puts us in touch with our humanity, and makes us ponder higher things. Heavy metal music on the other hand, hardly inspires an impulse for contemplation or charity. In Benedict's own words, rock music "is the expression of elemental passions, and at rock festivals it assumes a cultic character, a form of worship, in fact, in opposition to Christian worship."[8] While Benedict's analysis may not cause us to give up all our rock music, it does provide us with important food for thought, helping us to reflect upon why we listen to our music and what we can do to better immerse ourselves in an aesthetic environment that will lift us up rather than imprison us in a perpetual cycle of self-gratification.

In a couple of places Benedict gives us an autobiographical glimpse into how the beauty of music bolsters his faith. One time after attending a Bach concert with a Lutheran bishop, the two sponta-

---

8. Ratzinger, *Spirit of the Liturgy*, 147–48.

neously looked at each other and said, "Anyone who has heard this, knows that the faith is true." Benedict later reflected on the experience, saying, "The music had such an extraordinary force of reality that we realized, no longer by deduction, but by the impact on our hearts, that it could not have originated from nothingness, but could only have come to be through the power of the Truth that became real in the composer's inspiration."[9]

The Beauty of Religious Experience

In saying these lofty words about the power of beauty in art, one should not get the false impression that only art connoisseurs can come to God through the experience of beauty. There are many times in my life when I have looked out on the world and said something similar to what Benedict is reporting here: the beauty of encountering a friend in deep conversation, the beauty of a film that brought tears (my favorite is the 2012 *Les Misérables*), the beauty of my newborn children, the beauty of finding redemption through immense physical suffering, the beauty of witnessing my dad's holy death—these are just a few experiences which I think merit to be called "religious." These are some of the times when I, like Benedict, have had occasion to say: "This could not have originated from nothingness." Of course, religious experiences can also include witnessing the miraculous, but what I have in mind here is actually the more ordinary or seemingly mundane experiences of God that more than just a privileged few have witnessed. I myself am not conscious of ever having witnessed a grandiose physical miracle in my own life, but I have certainly experienced innumerable moments of grace such as the ones I just mentioned.

---

9. Ratzinger, "Feeling of Things, the Contemplation of Beauty." See also his account of this experience in Benedict's catechesis "Art and Prayer," general audience (August 31, 2011).

The Beauty of a Life Well Lived: Spiritual Beauty

Benedict's theology of beauty embraces much more than the arts. It embraces a wide variety of religious experiences that have the power to convert us ever closer to Christ. Even more than art, the beauty nearest and dearest to the emeritus pontiff's heart lies in the beauty that shines forth in the lives of the saints. After praising the ability of artistic beauty to convert, Benedict adds:

> Yet the beauty of Christian life is even more effective than art and imagery in the communication of the Gospel message. In the end, love alone is worthy of faith and proves credible. The lives of the saints and martyrs demonstrate a singular beauty which fascinates and attracts, because a Christian life lived in fullness speaks without words. We need men and women whose lives are eloquent and who know how to proclaim the Gospel with clarity and courage, with transparency of action and with the joyful passion of charity.[10]

In connecting the lives of the saints with beauty as the primary *apologia* for the Christian faith, Benedict echoes the understanding of beauty that we find in St. Thomas Aquinas. The Angelic Doctor applies the three properties of beauty (integrity, proportion, and clarity) to the spiritual realm: "Spiritual beauty consists in a man's conduct or actions being well-proportioned in respect of the spiritual clarity of reason."[11] For St. Thomas this all-important beauty lies precisely in *the life well-lived, the life of the virtues*. To live virtuously is to live a life of balance, to live in the clarity of right reason integrated into all our actions. Accordingly, the habits of character treated in this book, which go by the name of the theological virtues, form what Benedict calls a "mosaic of holiness" by which the Christian disciple shines the light of Christ upon the world around him.

Benedict thinks that we will find the truth of Christianity by striv-

---

10. Benedict XVI, address after screening the film *Art and Faith–Via Pulchritudinis* (October 25, 2012).
11. St. Thomas Aquinas, *Summa Theologiae*, II-II, q. 145, a. 2.

ing to live the Gospel generously and to cultivate the virtues discussed in this book. Moreover, our endeavor to live them exudes its own beauty that shines through without a contrived effort on our part to put on a show and "attract" others by our Christian joy. That said, beginning in his very first papal homily Benedict emphasized the need for consciously making the effort to speak to others of our friendship with Jesus, a task he described in terms of beauty: "There is nothing more beautiful than to know Him and to speak to others of our friendship with Him."[12] At the conclusion of this same text, Benedict advances a point which reflects a recurring theme in his thought: we who love Christ need to share with people the good news that our friendship with Jesus does not hold us back from fulfilling our deepest desires. On the contrary, as we discussed in chapter 3 above on the nature of true freedom, living a life in conformity with the demands of the Gospel actually makes us happy! As Benedict puts it, it is only in this friendship that we experience beauty and liberation.

A final, important word on the subject of the beauty that we find in a life well-lived: when Benedict speaks of the spiritual beauty of the saints as an apology for the truth of the Christian faith, he actually thinks that it is a particular sort of saint who most exudes that beauty which has the power to convert souls:

> Actually I must say that also for my personal faith many saints, not all, are true stars in the firmament of history. And I would like to add that for me not only a few great saints whom I love and whom I know well are "signposts," but precisely also the simple saints, that is, the good people I see in my life who will never be canonized. They are ordinary people, so to speak, without visible heroism but in their everyday goodness I see the truth of faith. This goodness, which they have developed in the faith of the Church, is for me the most reliable apology of Christianity and the sign of where the truth lies.[13]

---

12. Benedict XVI, homily at the Mass for the inauguration of his pontificate (April 24, 2005).

13. Benedict XVI, "Holiness."

Here at last we come to the heart of Benedict's conviction regarding how one comes to know the truth of the Catholic faith. To be sure, the canonized saints whose lives Benedict spent years recalling have a pivotal role to play in confirming and deepening our faith. However, it is above all the well-lived life of non-canonized saints—the "simple" or "ordinary" people we know—who for Benedict and for most of us are the truest sign of where the truth of the faith lies. This claim especially makes sense in light of Benedict's above emphasis on our need to have "first-hand experience" of the faith in order to see its truth.[14] For while some souls may be granted a profound spiritual encounter with a canonized saint of ages past, for most of us it is our direct and intimate experience with a living member of the communion of saints which proves life-changing. A true witness such as this is one whose very life bids us to become personally involved with Jesus and urges us as the apostle Phillip urged Nathaniel, "Come and see!" (Jn 1:46). With my accounts of ordinary personal experience with the faith scattered here and there throughout this book, and especially in my invitation to hear why I believe in Christ and hope for the resurrection with which I am about to conclude this book, I hope to have provided the reader with small illustrations of this "come and see" approach to the faith.

Two Concrete Reasons Why I Believe in Christ and Hope for the Resurrection

As we bring this book to its climax, I would now like to apply Benedict's principles that we have been discussing to real life by considering a very practical question that has touched the life of every believer at one point or another on his faith journey: what about individual doctrines and practices within the Christian faith that are hard for us to swallow, those which are either bizarre, seemingly trivial, or are

---

14. For this precise formulation, see Benedict XVI, "Bartholomew," general audience (October 4, 2006).

simply do not ring true? When it comes to the question of how one is to arrive at belief in particular Christian doctrines, I sometimes try to put myself in the position of someone who, unlike me, grew up in a nonreligious home. What would it take for me to arrive at faith in, say, the Resurrection? Part of the Christian answer to this of course has to be *grace*. I take that for granted. But, really, how would I make the jump from non-belief to belief in the proposition that an individual human at a definite point in history achieved what as far as we can tell is scientifically impossible? After all, the Resurrection appears to defy all that science tells us about the nature of decomposing matter—namely, once the atoms of a living being begin to disperse into the universe upon its death, they are never reconfigured in the same way again. I like to think of it in this way: if a Muslim, Hindu, or Buddhist claimed that one of their own leaders had risen from the dead, would I believe their testimony? Then why, pray tell, do I believe that the historical event of Jesus' resurrection is real, and moreover what do we even mean by resurrection in the first place?

From where I stand at the moment, I would say that this cannot be known if we think of it solely as an isolated event that allegedly happened two thousand years ago. But if we let our consideration of the Resurrection's putative truth be informed by our entire life practice of the Christian "way," then I believe we can come to see it for what it truly is. This might be thought of as an indirect proof, not a step-by-step argument but instead an experiment in the laboratory of life. At least in my experience, it is difficult to describe what experience of the Resurrection means in my day-to-day life. But what I can tell you is how profoundly the teachings and practices of the Church *as a lived whole* have shaped my existence and given me joy. Cast in the terms we have been laying out this chapter, what I mean to say is that the truth of the Catholic faith reveals itself fully through the beauty of experiencing it in real life. What I would now like to do is to provide two concrete examples of this dynamic that I've experienced in my own life.

The Beauty of Holy Matrimony

For my first illustration, I would like to spend a few moments pondering the Catholic Church's theology of marriage, which for me is an eminent *apologia* for Christianity's truth as a whole and, by extension, what it considers its own core doctrines and practices. While frequently misunderstood and even despised in today's culture, I find this area of the Church's life to be one in which she shines brightest. The Christian claim is that God is Trinity, an eternal exchange of life and love wherein the mutual self-gift of Father and Son spirates a third person, whom we call the Holy Spirit. Christian marriage is a call to reflect this eternal reality in our concrete lives, to be a created reflection or "icon" of the Trinity, wherein husband and wife give themselves to each other in such a powerful way that their love flowers in the form of a third (and sometimes fourth, fifth, sixth, etc.) person.[15] This great dignity with which our Christian faith views the vocation of spouses to union and procreative love is simply without parallel in any other worldview, religion, or system that I have encountered over the course of my earthly pilgrimage.

Intimately related to the above and indeed as a consequence of it, the Catholic Church teaches that those who would wish to marry must be open to bringing forth children into this world. In another powerful theological image—this one borrowed from St. Paul—Christians are told that their sacramental relationship is to mirror that of Christ and his Church (Eph 5:32). Christ gave himself totally for his bride, becoming incarnate, living, and dying for her of his own free will. He makes her fruitful, and he will never abandon her. So, too, husbands are to love their wives freely, totally, fruitfully, and faithfully. Part of this self-gift, if it is to be complete, includes the gift of one's fertility. The Catholic Church thus teaches that any sexual act that refuses this total gift by means of contraception fundamentally

---

15. On the family as "icon" of the Trinity, see Benedict XVI, *Deus Caritas Est*, §11.

fails to mirror the love between Christ and his Church.[16] I expounded the Church's teaching on this point in greater depth in chapter 8 above. My point here is that this authoritative moral teaching, while appearing backwards and even oppressive on the outside, is in reality incredibly liberating when lived out in the context of marriage. As of my writing this book, my wife and I have been blessed with five children. If we did not have the Church's definitive teaching on the subject of artificial contraception—and live in a community that supports it in practice—we would almost certainly have fewer offspring. This is not to say that it is bad to have one or two children; much less is it a criticism of those who experience the cross of infertility. What I am trying to say is that my wife and children bring immense happiness to my life, and that the Church's ostensibly stifling teaching against contraception is in a very real sense directly responsible for my family situation. This is for me an eminent *apologia* for the truth of the Catholic faith, which stands pretty much alone in today's world in its bold proclamation that our marriages are called to reflect the Trinity—and that some of our culture's most popular practices directly contradict this meaning and ought to be avoided by followers of Jesus.

Of course, marriage and family life are not all bliss. There are always the dirty diapers, sometimes seemingly endless cycles of winter illness, and periodic sleepless nights. Further, having children means taking fewer "us" vacations than spouses otherwise would. It also usually means fewer and more expensive dates (though my wife does a good job of making sure we take them regularly!). Then there are the behavior problems, in some family situations severe, not to mention the possibility of untimely death and all that it entails. In short, the more people you have to take care of, the more sufferings—and joys—will be involved. This is especially the case when you are a man like me who suffers chronically from a number of associated ailments.

---

16. For the aforementioned characteristics of marital love, see Paul VI, *Humanae Vitae*, §9. More recently, Pope Francis put it bluntly when he stated that "no genital act of husband and wife can refuse this meaning." Francis, *Amoris Laetitia*, §80.

When I get up on a cold winter morning, I wish I could sit by the fireplace in peace and drink my coffee while reading the news or praying. Instead, as soon as I wake up my kids also burst out of bed with their various breakfast and hygienic requirements—and they need me to make the little sacrifice of setting down my coffee to turn lukewarm as I help them out. Yet even here I see our family's attempt to live the Church's teaching as an *apologia* for its truth. The little issues that I have mentioned here (and parents know that I could add many more) serve a vital purpose: they curb my selfishness. By not letting me do everything I want to do, my kids are actually doing me a favor. They are giving me the chance to offer myself as a gift and thereby to imitate Jesus Christ in my own limited way. Again, if it were not for the Church's "hard sayings" on marriage and family life, I likely would not have many of these opportunities.

Life in the Spirit and Redemptive Suffering

Related to the question of suffering I was just discussing, there is another dimension of Catholic teaching and practice that I consider a veritable *apologia* for her belief in the resurrection of Jesus: what St. Paul calls "life in the Spirit." Indeed, I think that the closest we come to a description of how the resurrection impacts our daily lives is to be found in the spiritual writings of St. Paul. As articulated in Romans 8, life in the Spirit is the life of freedom from the flesh (understood here by Paul as our selfish desires), a glorious freedom wherein we act in accord with the realization that we are sons and heirs of God, destined to be glorified with Christ provided we suffer with him. In meditative reading of the letters of St. Paul, one acquires what Smith and Taylor would call the feeling or "vibe" for how our life is changed in light of Christ's resurrection. To put it in a nutshell, it is a life of joy born from the realization that there is meaning in suffering and hope that there is light at the end of the tunnel, fulfillment on the other side of this vale of tears.

One particular aspect of life in the Spirit which I find compelling is what is commonly known as the path of redemptive suffering. In brief, the Church teaches that our sufferings are not just random, cruel occurrences that terminate in the futility of death. Rather, as Catholics we believe that suffering is actually a vehicle for union with God and even a gift from above. To the extent that we live our sufferings in the light of God, the more closely our life mirrors that of Jesus, and thus the more beautiful it is. Christ's total gift of self on the Cross is the most beautiful of human actions ever to have been performed, and it challenges the superficial notion of beauty dominant in our culture today. The beauty of our crucified Lord is not simply a harmony of proportion and form. While Christ is surely "the fairest of the sons of men" (Ps 45:2), he is also the one "who had no form or comeliness that we should look at him, and no beauty that we should desire him" (Is 53:2).

From the suffering Christ we learn one of life's most important lessons: that true beauty also embraces the ugliness of pain and even the dark mystery of death. Jesus on the cross reminds us that true beauty, true freedom, and ultimately true happiness are only found when we accept suffering as part of God's plan for our sanctification.[17] In short, the crucible of suffering with Christ on the Cross draws us away from the transitory, detaching us from what is opposed to God. In his novel *The Idiot*, one of Dostoyevsky's characters famously remarked that beauty will save the world. This is certainly a thought that we ought to be considering as Christian disciples. But here Benedict reminds us that salvific beauty is not any beauty whatsoever but specifically the redeeming beauty of Christ crucified who invites us to share in his cross.

So dignified is the vocation of sharing Christ's cross that the Church describes it as one of co-redemption, wherein we unite our sufferings to those of Christ for the benefit of others in need of his

---

17. Ratzinger, "Feeling of Things, the Contemplation of Beauty."

mercy. In a verse which I affectionately like to call the most "Catholic" in the Bible, St. Paul says to the Colossians, "I rejoice in my sufferings for your sake, and in my flesh I complete what is lacking in Christ's afflictions for the sake of his body, that is, the church" (Col 1:24). Though Paul is aware that God does not *need* us absolutely speaking, he insists that God has nonetheless *chosen* to use us as his instruments to bring about his salvation for others. I can think of nothing that more greatly extols and ennobles our human nature than the Church's teaching that we are co-redeemers with God in the flesh precisely through our sufferings. Again, the very grandeur of this claim and its resonance with my deepest aspirations contribute to its being an *apologia* for the proposition upon which it is predicated, that is, the Resurrection.

As I insist throughout this book, the truth of the Christian claim can only been seen in its doing. In other words, the beauty of the Church's teaching on this redemptive suffering made possible by the Resurrection has the force it does in my life precisely because I have had the occasion to *live* it. Not that I have done it perfectly by any means, but over the last two decades I have had plenty of opportunities to live out the reality of redemptive suffering—and I can think of nothing that has led me to confess the Christian faith more firmly than what it has done for me in my struggle with intense health problems, intellectual darkness, and death in the family.

Here is an illustration of this reality that is with me as a reminder of Christ's truth every hour of every day. After being diagnosed with systemic lupus erythematosus (sometimes called SLE or just "lupus") in early 2003, I've had to deal with daily, often immense pain. As a result of my illness, I've undergone a number of serious surgeries on my eyes in the attempt to repair my detached retina, a total hip replacement, open-heart surgery to fix my aortic valve, and—thanks to the unbelievable goodness of a dear friend—a kidney transplant. Today I continue to deal constantly with myriad lupus issues, and many of my surgeries have had life-changing consequences (like a constant tick from my mechanical heart valve, severely blurry vision from repeated eye surgeries, and a greatly compromised immune system for life as a result of the drugs I take to stop my body from rejecting my lone functioning kidney as a foreign object). This brings me to my point: I do not know how I would have endured all of this with joy apart from the grace that comes through the sacramental life of the Catholic Church and her awesome teaching on the value of redemptive suffering. At any rate, I am confident that my experience of the illness is of an immensely different sort than it would have been absent the gift of faith.

I could say the same thing about the experience of my father's sudden death a few years ago. In the middle of the night, Dad unexpectedly suffered a heart attack and passed away within hours. Although his death was probably the most earth-shattering event of my life thus far (definitely more so than all the physical pain), the week I spent at my childhood home after Dad's passing was one in which God rained down countless reminders of his love and providential care for my family. My dad had died a holy death, and everyone surrounding him at his passing and burial knew it. I was not the only one who could not stop thinking, amidst so much suffering, just *how beautiful* the whole affair was. In our pain God did not just whisper that he was still there—he shouted it, especially in the Church's liturgy throughout the week.

I would like to share just one example of how the beauty of the Church's rites for my father's funeral moved me to faith, recalling what happens in a Catholic funeral right before the Mass begins. Immediately after my father's casket was closed for the final time, I was handed the funeral pall and helped my siblings lay it over the casket. The pall is the reminder of the faithful departed's baptism into Christ—an indelible mark that he now carries into eternity. As we laid the pall over my father's casket, I could not help but draw the connection to the Catholic baptismal liturgy. After baptizing the child, the priest clothes him with a little white garment and says, "You have become a new creation, and have clothed yourself in Christ. See in this white garment the outward sign of your Christian dignity. With your family and friends to help you by word and example, bring that dignity unstained into the everlasting life of heaven." It hit me more strongly than ever before that this is what the funeral pall recalls.

My liturgical experience of Dad's death spoke volumes about the truth of Christianity in general and the Catholic Church in particular. I think Benedict captures the reason this is so: "Why, in brief, does the faith still have a chance? I would say the following: because it is in harmony with what man is."[18] The Catholic Church's doctrine and practice is in harmony with whom man is: the Church forces us to confront death in all its awfulness, but then she also gives us all the grace we need to face it well.

And here it is that I think we come even more directly to an *apologia* for the doctrine of the Resurrection in particular. The reason why redemptive suffering is redemptive is not just because it purifies us from selfishness (although it does do that), or because other people may be inspired by it (though this also happens), but rather because our suffering and death ultimately lead to resurrection. Indeed, resurrection cannot happen without it: "Truly, truly, I say to you, unless a grain of wheat falls into the earth and dies, it remains alone; but if it dies, it bears much fruit" (Jn 12:24). Is this a definitive proof that ought to convince all onlookers that the resurrection of Christ happened? By no means. However, it is the conviction of Penner, Benedict, and others like myself that the experience of beauty and wholeness made possible from this exalted teaching is itself evidence for its conformity to reality. In other words, I have to ask myself: how could it be that the religion that produced such an immensely profound, fulfilling path of life be profoundly wrong in its most fundamental affirmations upon which its way of life is predicated? I am not saying that it is impossible, but, after all my years of searching for God thus far, if

---

18. Joseph Ratzinger, "Relativism: The Central Problem for Faith Today" (May 1996), https://www.ewtn.com/library/CURIA/RATZRELA.HTM.

Jesus and his resurrection are not the way to him, then I do not know what is.[19]

But What if It Turns Out That I Am Wrong?

Given all that was said above, I nevertheless sometimes think about the whole issue in the following manner. Let us say that I wake up one day in a really weird way, and it turns out that I had died in my sleep during the night. Let us say that I then realize, "Wow, I am God!" (as is believed in certain monistic traditions such as Hinduism). Or let us say I come to the realization, "Wow, Jesus' resurrection didn't really mean what I thought it did—it was a parable not meant to be taken literally!" (as contemporary authors such as John Dominic Crossan would have it). Or let us even say that I die and never wake up—it turns out I was wrong, and there is no afterlife after all. Even if this were to occur, it still would not change the fact that, as best as I can tell standing here right now, redemptive suffering and its reward, the resurrection, provide the best account of the reality of things when considered as a whole in light of my personal experience and with an eye to the Catholic Church's comprehensive doctrine and way of life.[20]

---

19. Of course, there are always those traditions that manage to produce beautiful lives in their adherents despite being based on what many of us outsiders would consider irrational premises. On this point, see John Cottingham's observation that the validity of much religious practice "survives the inadequacy of a theoretical account of it." Cottingham, *Philosophy of Religion*, 154. If we are to follow Benedict's line of thought, the reason for this is that religion is not primarily an intellectual affair but rather an existential one with an intellectual component. Regarding how to account for the capacity of other religions to produce beauty and holiness even while being fraught with certain contradictions, the Catholic need only consult the Second Vatican Council's teaching that the truth and goodness found in traditions outside of the visible Church are a participation in Christ himself. See Vatican Council II, *Lumen Gentium*, §16; and Vatican Council II, *Nostra Aetate*, §2.

20. As I mentioned in the introduction, my point in this book is not to prove the superiority of Catholic doctrines over competitors from other traditions on a one-by-one basis. I do happen to think that Christianity is the most intellectually coherent of religions and that it stands on the right side when it comes to all the major issues that divide religions (the nature of God, the relationship of creatures to God, the afterlife, etc.). A discussion of these

On this point there is a little of Pascal in my thinking and a little of Benedict. Both speak of the need to make a "wager" in life. This gamble is unavoidable—the question concerns where we are going to place our chips. I do not thereby mean to say that I consider any of the above heterodox outcomes as likely as the orthodox Christian teaching on the Resurrection. Rather, I simply wish to say that we can be realists and even believe in the Church's infallibility while acknowledging that we ourselves are quite fallible. As John Henry Newman put it well more than a century ago, it is common to confuse infallibility (a gift pertaining to the institution of the Church) with certitude (pertaining to individual truth claims we make).

Could I be wrong about my beliefs? Can I imagine reality being different from the way I am convinced it is? Newman's musings on certitude are incredibly valuable on this point. For example, he says, I remember for certain what I did yesterday, but this does not mean that my memory is infallible; I am quite clear that two and two make four, but I do sometimes make mistakes in math. I have no doubt whatever that my best friend is a true friend and not a traitor, but in the past I have trusted those who failed me. All this goes to show that our certainty of a proposition today "is no ground for thinking that I shall have a right to be certain of that proposition tomorrow." Moreover, Newman adds to this the uncomfortable truth that no line can be drawn, no distinct test can be performed to distinguish between real and merely apparent certitudes: "What looks like certitude always is exposed to the chance of turning out to be a mistake."[21] So, to return

---

particulars—what truth and beauty Christians share in common with those of other faiths and why I believe Christianity alone contains the fullness of divine revelation—will have to wait for another book. For now, I will content myself with recalling this statement from Eleonore Stump which can easily be applied to situations in which two or more religious traditions offer mutually contradictory takes on reality, "We can definitively rule some interpretations out, but it is hard to make a compelling argument that only *this* interpretation is right." Stump, *Wandering in Darkness*, 27.

21. John Henry Newman, *Essay in Aid of a Grammar of Assent*, 227. Worth consideration here is the entirety of chap. 7, §2, on the indefectibility of certitude from which this material is drawn.

to my earlier question, is it possible that I am wrong in my conviction about Christ's resurrection? I think the answer to this question has to be "yes."

But do I have any good reason to suppose that I am indeed wrong? And do I foresee any good reason that I should change my convictions? I have been around the block quite a few times in this regard, and the answer I give to these questions is a resounding "No." And Newman agrees. If my certitude today is not guaranteed to be present tomorrow, the following is also the case: "That I am wrong in my convictions about today's proposition, does not hinder my having a true conviction, a genuine certitude, about tomorrow's proposition."[22] In light of Penner's language that we explored in the previous chapter, we might call this position "ironic" in the sense that admitting one may be wrong about something typically goes hand-in-hand with a lack of certitude regarding the issue in question. For Newman, however, admitting the theoretical possibility that our faith claims are wrong does not mean that we lack certainty in their regard. I have real certainty in my Christian faith, yet I also have to acknowledge that faith is not the same as vision. As St. Paul says, now we see through a glass, darkly (1 Cor 13:12 KJV). Our faith does not understand, it knows only in part and seeks understanding. And, as Catholics know well, our hope for salvation does not thereby guarantee our salvation, for "hope that is seen is not hope" (Rom 8:24). In any event, what am I supposed to do—turn to what I consider a much less compelling nihilist worldview just because of the theoretical possibility that I am wrong about my realist, Christian faith? A couple decades ago, one of my consecrated friends admitted to me that her knowledge of Catholicism's truth was not infallible but that she was Catholic because it was the least ridiculous of all options out there. At the time, I thought that that was a rather odd way to think about things. Twenty years later, I see the point. Being a disciple of Jesus Christ in the Catholic Church is not an

---

22. Ibid.

undertaking devoid of its own set of issues or elements that are, in my friend's words, "ridiculous." It is just that, despite the problems that certainly exist within the Church, it nevertheless remains the privileged locus willed by Jesus Christ where we can find him and, in turn, find the meaning of all things in him. I think that C. S. Lewis captures this last point well when he writes, "I believe in Christianity as I believe that the Sun has risen, not only because I see it, but because by it I see everything else."[23]

This acknowledgment of problems within Christian belief may seem a little odd in a book aimed at helping people to believe, but to me it is just a contemporary reliving of the experience of the apostles in confrontation with Jesus' great bread of life discourse. After many of his followers had left Jesus due to his "hard saying" that they were to eat his body and drink his blood (Jn 6:60), the Lord asked the twelve apostles, "Do you also wish to go away?" What interests me is that the apostles said neither yes nor no in response to this inquiry. Maybe they did entertain the possibility of leaving—maybe they were not yet certain about the truth of Jesus' saying—yet they had followed him this far and saw no better option than to stay the course: "Lord, to whom shall we go? You have the words of eternal life" (Jn 6:68).

To whom, indeed? It may be possible that Christianity's hope for the resurrection is wrong after all, but it sure would be odd if the fundamental truths of the faith that give birth to the immense riches of Christian culture and moral living—like the power of redemptive suffering and the beauty of Christian marriage, and other realties such as the respect for all human beings that Christianity so uniquely champions—were based on a grave misunderstanding of reality and it turns out that the resurrection of Jesus was a mere myth, hoax, or delusion. At the end of the day, is Christianity's hope for the resurrection right, or is Nietzschean nihilism the face of reality? To put it in Jesus' own words, "You will know them by their fruits" (Mt 7:16).

---

23. Lewis, "Is Theology Poetry?" in *The Weight of Glory and Other Addresses*, 140.

A surprising literary connection that casts light on the dynamic I am trying to describe here can be found in C. S. Lewis's fictional tale *The Silver Chair*. In his characteristically vivid and pointed prose, Lewis depicts an incisive temptation of the book's protagonists (the Pevensie children) on the part of its antagonist, the witch (representing Satan). In this passage, the witch tries to get the children to deny the existence of the spiritual world (Narnia) as well as that of the lion Aslan (its Christ figure).

> "You have seen lamps, and so you imagined a bigger and better lamp and called it the *sun*. You've seen cats, and now you want a bigger and better cat, and it's to be called a *lion*. Well, 'tis a pretty make-believe, though, to say truth, it would suit you all better if you were younger. And look how you can put nothing into your make-believe without copying it from the real world, this world of mine, which is the only world. But even you children are too old for such play.... Come, all of you. Put away these childish tricks. I have work for you all in the real world. There is no Narnia, no Overworld, no sky, no sun, no Aslan."[24]

This temptation, in which I suspect Lewis is purposefully channeling the thought of the great skeptic David Hume, is the characteristic temptation of us believers trying to live the faith in a secular age. Maybe, after all, there is no God, no Jesus, no Heaven. Maybe it is all just a fairy tale, a make-believe game and lie that we tell ourselves to avoid having to face the harsh reality of a universe without God and without hope for an afterlife.

Within the context of Lewis's story, this temptation is felt very hard by the children of Narnia, who start to succumb to the Witch's enchanting argumentation. Surprisingly, though, the usually pessimistic marsh-wiggle Puddleglum pipes up and lays out this Pascalian reply to the witch:

---

24. C. S. Lewis, *The Silver Chair*, in *The Chronicles of Narnia Complete 7-Book Collection* (HarperCollins, 2013), 632.

"One word, Ma'am.... Suppose we have only dreamed, or made up, all those things—trees and grass and sun and moon and stars and Aslan himself. Suppose we have. Then all I can say is that, in that case, the made-up things seem a good deal more important than the real ones. Suppose this black pit of a kingdom of yours is the only world. Well, it strikes me as a pretty poor one. And that's a funny thing, when you come to think of it. We're just babies making up a game, if you're right. But four babies playing a game can make a play-world which licks your real world hollow. That's why I'm going to stand by the play world. I'm on Aslan's side even if there isn't any Aslan to lead it. I'm going to live as like a Narnian as I can even if there isn't any Narnia."[25]

I love this passage, because it pretty much captures the way I think about the Christian faith (and, given how well it is articulated and how it serves as the dagger that destroys the witch, I suspect it reflects the view of Lewis himself). Lewis agrees with what we have said in insinuating that we must be open to the theoretical possibility that the whole Narnia adventure is a mere dream or fairy tale. But, as we have argued along the lines of Newman, admitting the theoretical possibility of error does not mean we have no certitude in our faith (in the existence of Narnia, to keep with Lewis's image).

Moreover, given just how *beautiful* the life of faith is in contrast with an existence lived according to the postulates of nihilism, it would be most odd if it turned out that this beauty were based on a total misunderstanding of the nature of things and in reality there is no God or hope for our final redemption. So maybe the whole thing is a dream, but all the evidence of our faith experience—from the power of redemptive suffering, to the beauty of Christian marriage, and countless other areas of life we have not explored—seems to point in the opposite direction. Accordingly, all I can do is to echo Puddleglum's saying in my own life: "I'm on Aslan's side even if there isn't any Aslan to lead it. I'm going to live as like a Narnian as I can even if there isn't any Narnia."[26]

25. Ibid., 633.
26. For a more detailed philosophical treatment of the position articulated by Puddleglum in response to the critiques of Hume, Freud, Marx, and Nietzsche, see Ramage, *Jesus*,

Conclusion: Nietzsche or Benedict (XVI)?

When you read the lesser known writings of Benedict XVI, you frequently end up discovering unexpectedly delightful gems. It is with one of these that I would like to draw my reflections on beauty—and thus this book as a whole—to a close. When he celebrated Mass in St. Patrick's Cathedral in New York, Benedict gave a fascinating homily in which he reflected upon the great building as an allegory of faith and the search for truth. Like any Gothic cathedral, from the outside its windows appear dark and heavy, even dreary. But once one enters the Church, these same windows suddenly come alive with resplendent light passing through their stained glass. The allegory is clear: "It is only from the inside, from the experience of faith and ecclesial life, that we see the Church as she truly is: flooded with grace, resplendent in beauty, adorned by the manifold gifts of the Spirit."[27] Here Benedict teaches in poetic fashion a truth we have witnessed him reiterate in many different places and ways throughout this volume: the truth and goodness of the Catholic Church ultimately can be seen only *from*

Interpreted, 240–63. Plantinga argues that, sure, it is conceivable that the Christian faith is wrong and merely the result of wish fulfillment, delusion, or some other cognitive dysfunction. However, the shoe may be on the other foot, he says. According to St. Paul, it is not belief but unbelief that is the result of wish fulfillment—the desire to suppress the truth so as to live in a world without a God to whom I owe worship and obedience. Alvin Plantinga, *Knowledge and Christian Belief* (Grand Rapids, Mich.: Eerdmans Publishing Co., 2015), 43. Connected to Puddleglum's point about believing being right notwithstanding our ability to have definitive certitude about many things concerning God, Mark Johnston offers a powerful and provocative criticism of how believers often fall into "servile idolatry" and "spiritual materialism," especially when it comes to the afterlife. He observes that there is a temptation to fall into the mentality of only doing the right thing for the sake of a reward eventually to be bestowed upon us in the form of eternal life. Although Christ reveals that we do indeed receive the crown of glory for following him, Johnston does well to remind us that "the new dispensation of Christ is founded on outpouring love, love that looks for nothing in return." Johnston, *Saving God: Religion after Idolatry* (Princeton: Princeton University Press, 2009), 182. While the views expressed in Johnston's book are certainly unconventional, his thoughts actually remind me a lot of Lewis's discussion of "proper rewards" versus "mercenary rewards" as found in "Weight of Glory," 26–28.

27. Benedict XVI, homily for votive Mass for the universal Church (April 19, 2008).

the inside when we fast from our own preconceptions and desires with a willingness to embark upon "the experiment of faith."[28]

To be sure, none of what has been said above changes the fact that we can and must always be prepared with reasonable arguments to defend the truths of the Catholic faith in the world. Yet Benedict wishes to remind us that we are rarely if ever going to argue postmodern man into believing. One thing we can certainly do every day, even on those days when the subject of faith never comes up explicitly in our conversations, is to live beautifully the life of grace within the Church. Our life well-lived in the quest for Christian holiness has great power to draw our brothers and sisters closer to God. This witness epitomizes what Benedict has in mind when he calls the Church's saints and her beauty the greatest apology for the Christian faith. It contains within itself a power to touch many of us in situations where otherwise very sound appeals to truth or moral goodness fail. But, if Benedict is right, then beauty and the saints are not going to convince anyone who is not willing to "enter into the experiment" and see what they look like from the point of view of one on the path of discipleship, the way of the Cross.

In his landmark 1981 book *After Virtue*, Alasdair MacIntyre described our present time as a new dark age in which the barbarians live not beyond the frontiers but instead among us in our own communities. In accordance with MacIntyre's diagnosis, I have argued in this book that the way forward for the Christian wishing to live an intelligent and vibrant faith under such circumstances consists in recommitting fully to immersing ourselves in the Christian tradition and to living the theological virtues of faith, hope, and charity along the lines envisioned by Pope Benedict XVI. MacIntyre famously concluded his book with a chapter insisting that today's individual is fundamentally faced with a choice between two mutually exclusive ways of life, epitomized in the figures of Nietzsche and Aristotle. Adapting MacIntyre's

---

28. Ratzinger, "Why I Am Still in the Church," 132–53.

language, in this book I have argued that our existential choice today consists ultimately in two competing worldviews represented by the figures of Friedrich Nietzsche and Benedict XVI. While acknowledging that there may be more points of contact between these two towering figures than commonly assumed, Nietzsche's incisive critique of the Christian way of life remains one of the greatest challenges to the faith and his philosophy the faith's most serious alternative in our secular age.

In the very last line of his book, MacIntyre recalled the great saint who saved civilization in the dark ages of old and wrote that we are waiting today for another, doubtless very different, St. Benedict. I have found this Benedict in the contemporary pope of the same name, and I will be forever grateful to him for helping myself and countless other believers to live the faith just a little better even if our vision still takes place through the glass, darkly. My hope is that this book has helped you to find in Benedict XVI a powerful patron for conducting the experiment of faith in our secular age.

BIBLIOGRAPHY

Note: Pope Benedict XVI's encyclicals, homilies, general audiences, etc. may be found on the Vatican website at http://w2.vatican.va/content/benedict-xvi/en.html.

Aelred of Rievaulx. *Spiritual Friendship*. Kalamazoo, Mich.: Cistercian Publications, 1974.

Alighieri, Dante. *Purgatory*. Translated by Anthony M. Esolen. New York: Modern Library, 2003.

Allison, Dale. *Night Comes: Death, Imagination, and the Last Things*. Grand Rapids, Mich.: Eerdmans Publishing Co., 2016.

Amiri, Rachel and Mary Keys. "Benedict XVI on Liberal Modernity's Need for the 'Theological Virtues' of Faith, Hope, and Love." *Perspectives on Political Science* 41, no. 1 (2012): 1–18.

Anscombe, Elizabeth. *Faith in a Hard Ground: Essays on Religion, Philosophy and Ethics*. Luton: Andrews UK Ltd., 2011.

Aquinas, Thomas. *S. Thomae Aquinatis Opera Omnia: ut sunt in Indice Thomistico, additis 61 scriptis ex aliis medii aevi auctoribus*. Edited by Robert Busa. 6 vols. Stuttgart-Bad Cannstatt: Frommann-Holzboog, 1980.

———. *Summa Theologica [Summa theologiae]*. Translated by the Fathers of the English Dominican Province. Westminster, Md.: Christian Classics, 1981.

Augustine. *Confessions*. Translated by J. G. Pilkington, edited by Philip Schaff. Nicene and Post-Nicene Fathers, 1st ser. 1. Buffalo, N.Y.: Christian Literature Publishing Co., 1887. http://www.newadvent.org/fathers/1101.htm.

Aumann, Jordan. *Spiritual Theology*. Westminster, Md.: Christian Classics, 1987.

Balthasar, Hans Urs von. *Dare We Hope "That All Men Be Saved"?* San Francisco: Ignatius Press, 1986.

———. *Mysterium Paschale*. San Francisco: Ignatius Press, 2012.

Barber, Michael. *Singing in the Reign: The Psalms and the Liturgy of God's Kingdom*. Steubenville, Ohio: Emmaus Road, 2001.

Barron, Robert. "Evangelizing the Nones." Erasmus lecture Presented at the Union League Club, New York, N.Y., October 30, 2017. https://www.wordonfire.org/resources/lecture/evangelizing-the-nones/18203/.

———. *The Strangest Way: Walking the Christian Path*. Maryknoll, N.Y.: Orbis Books, 2002.

———. "A Reflection on Christ, Theological Method, and Freedom." In *How Balthasar Changed My Mind: 15 Scholars Reflect on the Meaning of Balthasar for Their Own Work*, edited by Rodney A. Howsare and Larry S. Chapp, 9–25. New York: The Crossroad Publishing Company, 2008.

Barth, Karl. *Church Dogmatics*, vol. 3, pt. 2, *The Doctrine of Creation, Part 2*. Edinburg: T. & T. Clark, 1986.

Bates, Matthew. *Salvation by Allegiance Alone: Rethinking Faith, Works, and the Gospel of Jesus the King*. Grand Rapids, Mich.: Baker Academic, 2017.

Benedict of Nursia. *Rule*. New York: Vintage Books, 1998.

Benedict XVI. "The Approval and Publication of the *Compendium of the Catechism of the Catholic Church*." Moto proprio. June 28, 2005.

———. *Deus Caritas Est*. Encyclical letter. 2005.

———. Homily at the Mass for the inauguration of his pontificate. April 24, 2005.

———. Address at the University of Regensburg. September 12, 2006.

———. "Bartholomew." General audience. October 4, 2006.

———. "Faith, Reason and the University: Memories and Reflections." Speech to the representatives of science at Aula Magna of the University of Regensburg. September 12, 2006.

———. "James, the Greater." General audience. June 21, 2006.

———. "Judas Iscariot and Matthias." General audience. October 18, 2006.

———. Homily for the Easter Vigil. April 15, 2006.

———. Homily for the Mass of Corpus Domini. June 15, 2006.

———. "St. Paul's New Outlook." General audience. November 8, 2006.

———. *Jesus of Nazareth: From the Baptism in the Jordan to the Transfiguration*. New York: Doubleday, 2007.

———. *Spe Salvi*. Encyclical letter. 2007.

———. Address to representatives from the World of Culture in Paris. September 12, 2008.

———. Address to the United Nations. April 18, 2008.

———. "The Doctrine of Justification: From Works to Faith." General audience. November 19, 2008.

———. "The Doctrine of Justification: The Apostle's Teaching on Faith and Works." General audience. November 26, 2008.

———. Homily for the opening of the Pauline Year. June 28, 2008.
———. Homily for votive Mass for the universal Church. April 19, 2008.
———. Meeting with the clergy of the Diocese of Bolzano-Bressanone. August 6, 2008.
———. "Saint Paul's Concept of Apostolate." General audience. September 10, 2008.
———. *Caritas in Veritate*. Encyclical letter. 2009.
———. "The Cathedral from the Romanesque to the Gothic Architecture: The Theological Background." General audience. November 18, 2009.
———. First Vespers homily for the closing of the Pauline Year. June 28, 2009.
———. "Hugh and Richard of Saint-Victor." General audience. November 25, 2009.
———. "John Damascene." General audience. May 6, 2009.
———. "Monastic Theology and Scholastic Theology." General audience. October 28, 2009.
———. "Saint Anselm." General audience. September 23, 2009.
———. Homily. July 24, 2009.
———. Meeting with artists. November 21, 2009.
———. *St. Paul*. San Francisco: Ignatius Press, 2009.
———. Address to participants in the plenary assembly of the Pontifical Council for Culture. November 13, 2010.
———. *Church Fathers and Teachers: From Saint Leo the Great to Peter Lombard*. San Francisco: Ignatius Press, 2010.
———. Message for the forty-third World Day of Peace. January 1, 2010.
———. *Verbum Domini*. Apostolic exhortation. 2010.
———. Address to the Bundestag. September 22, 2011.
———. "Art and Prayer." General audience. August 31, 2011.
———. General audience. June 22, 2011.
———. "Holiness." General audience. April 13, 2011.
———. *Jesus of Nazareth: Holy Week: From the Entrance into Jerusalem to the Resurrection*. San Francisco: Ignatius Press, 2011.
———. "Meditation." General audience. August 17, 2011.
———. "The Nocturnal Struggle and Encounter with God." General audience. May 25, 2011.
———. "The Prayer and the Holy Family of Nazareth." General audience. December 28, 2011.
———. "Saint Francis de Sales." General audience. March 2, 2011.
———. "Saint John of the Cross." General audience. February 16, 2011.

———. Address after screening the film *Art and Faith–Via Pulchritudinis*. October 25, 2012.

———. Christmas address to the Roman Curia. December 21, 2012.

———. "The Desire for God." General audience. November 7, 2012.

———. General audience. February 1, 2012.

———. General audience. March 7, 2012.

———. General audience. April 25, 2012.

———. General audience. May 16, 2012.

———. General audience. May 23, 2012.

———. General audience. October 3, 2012.

———. "God Reveals His 'Benevolent Purpose.'" General audience. December 5, 2012.

———. *Holy Men and Women of the Middle Ages and Beyond*. San Francisco: Ignatius Press, 2012.

———. "How to Speak about God?" General audience. November 28, 2012.

———. "The Liturgy, School of Prayer—The Lord Himself Teaches Us to Pray." General audience. September 26, 2012.

———. *A School of Prayer: The Saints Show Us How to Pray*. San Francisco: Ignatius Press, 2012.

———. "The Virgin Mary, Icon of Obedient Faith." General audience. December 19, 2012.

———. "What Is Faith?" General audience. October 24, 2012.

———. General audience. February 6, 2013.

———. "'I Believe in God.'" General audience. January 23, 2013.

———. *Jesus of Nazareth: The Infancy Narratives*. San Francisco: Ignatius Press, 2013.

———. Address at the commemoration of the 65th anniversary of the priestly ordination of Pope Emeritus Benedict XVI. June 28, 2016. https://w2.vatican.va/content/francesco/en/speeches/2016/june/documents/papa-francesco_20160628_65-ordinazione-sacerdotale-benedetto-xvi.html.

———. "'The Church and the Scandal of Sexual Abuse." April 10, 2019. https://www.catholicnewsagency.com/news/full-text-of-benedict-xvi-the-church-and-the-scandal-of-sexual-abuse-59639.

Benedict XVI and Francis. *Lumen Fidei*. Encyclical letter. 2013. http://w2.vatican.va/content/francesco/en/encyclicals/documents/papa-francesco_20130629_enciclica-lumen-fidei.html.

Benedict XVI and Peter Seewald. *Last Testament: In His Own Words*. London: Bloomsbury, 2016.

Berry, Wendell. *Sex, Economy, Freedom & Community*. New York: Pantheon Books, 1993.
Boyagoda, Randy. "Cordially, Richard John Neuhaus." *First Things* (August 2012): 17–18.
Brown, Francis, Samuel Rolles Driver, and Charles Augustus Briggs. *Enhanced Brown-Driver-Briggs Hebrew and English Lexicon*. Oxford: Clarendon Press, 1977.
Catechism of the Catholic Church. Translated by United States Conference of Catholic Bishops. Washington, DC: Libreria Editrice Vaticana, 1994.
Chautard, Jean-Baptiste. *The Soul of the Apostolate*. Trappist, Ky.: Abbey of Gethsamani, 1946.
Chesterton, G. K. *The Everlasting Man*. In *The Collected Works of G. K. Chesterton*, vol. 2, 135–418. San Francisco: Ignatius Press, 1986.
———. *Orthodoxy*. San Francisco: Ignatius Press, 1995.
Congregation for the Doctrine of the Faith. *On Certain Aspects of the "Theology of Liberation."* Instruction. August 6, 1984.
Cottingham, John. *Philosophy of Religion: Towards a More Humane Approach*. New York: Cambridge University Press, 2014.
Enns, Peter. *The Sin of Certainty: Why God Desires Our Trust More Than Our "Correct" Beliefs*. New York: HarperOne, 2017.
Fee, Gordon. *The First Epistle to the Corinthians*. Edited by Ned B. Stonehouse et al. Rev. ed. The New International Commentary on the New Testament. Grand Rapids, Mich.: Eerdmans Publishing Co., 2014.
Francis. *Evangelii Gaudium*. Apostolic exhortation. 2013. http://w2.vatican.va/content/francesco/en/apost_exhortations/documents/papa-francesco_esortazione-ap_20131124_evangelii-gaudium.html.
———. *Laudato Si'*. Encyclical letter. 2015. http://w2.vatican.va/content/francesco/en/encyclicals/documents/papa-francesco_20150524_enciclica-laudato-si.html.
———. *Amoris Laetitia*. Apostolic exhortation. 2016. http://w2.vatican.va/content/francesco/en/apost_exhortations/documents/papa-francesco_esortazione-ap_20160319_amoris-laetitia.html.
———. Message for the celebration of the World Day of Prayer for the Care of Creation. September 1, 2016. http://w2.vatican.va/content/francesco/en/messages/pont-messages/2016/documents/papa-francesco_20160901_messaggio-giornata-cura-creato.html.
Francis and Antonio Spadaro. "A Big Heart Open to God." *America* (September 30, 2013). https://www.americamagazine.org/faith/2013/09/30/big-heart-open-god-interview-pope-francis.

Gaál, Emery de. *The Theology of Pope Benedict XVI: The Christocentric Shift.* New York: Palgrave Macmillan, 2010.

John Paul II. *Redemptor Hominis.* Encyclical letter. March 4, 1979. http://w2.vatican.va/content/john-paul-ii/en/encyclicals/documents/hf_jp-ii_enc_04031979_redemptor-hominis.html.

———. *Sollicitudo Rei Socialis.* Encyclical letter. December 30, 1987. http://w2.vatican.va/content/john-paul-ii/en/encyclicals/documents/hf_jp-ii_enc_30121987_sollicitudo-rei-socialis.html.

———. Message for the twenty-third World Day of Peace. January 1, 1990. http://w2.vatican.va/content/john-paul-ii/en/messages/peace/documents/hf_jp-ii_mes_19891208_xxiii-world-day-for-peace.html.

———. *Centesimus Annus.* Encyclical letter. May 1, 1991. http://w2.vatican.va/content/john-paul-ii/en/encyclicals/documents/hf_jp-ii_enc_01051991_centesimus-annus.html.

———. *Love and Responsibility.* San Francisco: Ignatius Press, 1993.

———. *Evangelium Vitae.* Encyclical letter. March 25, 1995. http://w2.vatican.va/content/john-paul-ii/en/encyclicals/documents/hf_jp-ii_enc_25031995_evangelium-vitae.html.

———. General audience. July 28, 1999. http://w2.vatican.va/content/john-paul-ii/en/audiences/1999/documents/hf_jp-ii_aud_28071999.html.

———. Address to the ambassador of New Zealand to the Holy See. May 25, 2000. http://w2.vatican.va/content/john-paul-ii/en/speeches/2000/apr-jun/documents/hf_jp-ii_spe_20000525_ambassador-new-zealand.html.

———. *Man and Woman He Created Them: A Theology of the Body.* Translated by Michael Waldstein. Boston, Mass.: Pauline Books & Media, 2006.

Johnson, Dru. *Biblical Knowing: A Scriptural Epistemology of Error.* Eugene, Ore.: Cascade Books, 2013.

Johnston, Mark. *Saving God: Religion after Idolatry.* Princeton: Princeton University Press, 2009.

Kant, Immanuel. *Grounding for the Metaphysics of Morals.* Indianapolis: Hackett, 1993.

———. *Critique of Practical Reason.* New York: Prometheus Books, 1996.

Kierkegaard, Søren. *Sickness unto Death.* Edited and translated by Howard V. Hong and Edna H. Hong. Princeton: Princeton University Press, 1980.

Leo XIII. *Rerum Novarum.* Encyclical letter. May 15, 1891. http://w2.vatican.va/content/leo-xiii/en/encyclicals/documents/hf_l-xiii_enc_15051891_rerum-novarum.html.

Lewis, C. S. *The Four Loves.* New York: Harcourt Brace, 1960.

———. *The Problem of Pain.* New York: Macmillan, 1962.

———. *Reflections on the Psalms.* London: Harvest Books, 1964.

———. *The Great Divorce.* San Francisco: HarperSanFrancisco, 1973.

———. *Miracles, a Preliminary Study.* New York: Macmillan, 1978.

———. *The Screwtape Letters.* San Francisco: HarperCollins, 2001.

———. *The Weight of Glory and Other Addresses.* San Francisco: HarperSanFrancisco, 2001.

———. *The Silver Chair.* In *The Chronicles of Narnia Complete 7-Book Collection.* San Francisco: HarperCollins, 2013.

Lubac, Henri de. *Teilhard de Chardin: The Man and His Meaning.* New York: Hawthorn Books, 1965.

———. *The Religion of Teilhard de Chardin.* New York: Desclee Co. 1967.

———. *Paradoxes of Faith.* San Francisco: Ignatius Press, 1987.

———. *The Drama of Atheist Humanism.* San Francisco: Ignatius Press, 1995.

MacIntyre, Alasdair. *After Virtue: A Study in Moral Theory.* Notre Dame, Ind.: University of Notre Dame Press, 1984.

———. *Whose Justice? Which Rationality?* Notre Dame, Ind.: University of Notre Dame Press, 1988.

Madden, James. *Mind, Matter, and Nature: A Thomistic Proposal for the Philosophy of Mind.* Washington, D.C.: The Catholic University of America Press, 2013.

Martin, Ralph. *Will Many Be Saved? What Vatican II Actually Teaches and Its Implications for the New Evangelization.* Grand Rapids, Mich.: Eerdmans Publishing Co., 2012.

Maximus the Confessor. *On the Cosmic Mystery of Jesus Christ.* Crestwood, N.Y.: St. Vladimir's Seminary Press, 2003.

Meconi, David. *The One Christ: St. Augustine's Theology of Deification.* Washington, DC: The Catholic University of America Press, 2013.

Menssen, Sandra Lee, and Thomas D. Sullivan. *The Agnostic Inquirer: Revelation from a Philosophical Standpoint.* Grand Rapids, Mich.: Eerdmans Publishing Co., 2007.

Merton, Thomas. *Mystics and Zen Masters.* New York: Farrar, Strauss and Giroux, 1967.

Moser, Paul. *The Evidence for God: Religious Knowledge Reexamined.* Cambridge: Cambridge University Press, 2010.

Newman, John Henry. *An Essay in Aid of a Grammar of Assent.* Garden City, N.Y.: Image Books, 1955.

———. *An Essay on the Development of Christian Doctrine.* Notre Dame, Ind.: University of Notre Dame Press, 1989.

———. *Apologia pro Vita Sua and Six Sermons*. New Haven, Conn.: Yale University Press, 2008.

Nichols, Aidan. *The Thought of Pope Benedict XVI*. New York: Burns & Oates, 2007.

Nietzsche, Friedrich. *Nachgelassene Werke: Ecce homo; Der Wille zur Macht*. Leipzig: Kröner, 1922.

———. *Thus Spake Zarathustra: A Book for All and None*. New York: Modern Library, 1940.

———. *The Twilight of the Idols*. In *Complete Works. The First Complete and Authorised English Translation*, vol. 16, ed. Oscar Levy. New York: Russell & Russell, 1964.

———. *The Will to Power*. New York: Vintage Books, 1969.

———. *On the Use and Abuse of History*. New York: Macmillan Publishing Company, 1988.

———. *Beyond Good and Evil*. Buffalo, N.Y.: Prometheus Books, 1989.

———. *On the Genealogy of Morality*. Cambridge: Cambridge University Press, 2007.

Nussbaum, Martha. *Love's Knowledge*. Oxford: Oxford University Press, 1990.

Pascal, Blaise. *Pensées*. London: Penguin Books, 1995.

Paul VI. *Populorum Progressio*. Encyclical letter. 1967. http://w2.vatican.va/content/paul-vi/en/encyclicals/documents/hf_p-vi_enc_26031967_populorum.html.

———. *Humanae Vitae*. Encyclical letter. 1968. http://w2.vatican.va/content/paul-vi/en/encyclicals/documents/hf_p-vi_enc_25071968_humanae-vitae.html.

———. *Octogesima Adveniens*. Apostolic letter. 1971. http://w2.vatican.va/content/paul-vi/en/apost_letters/documents/hf_p-vi_apl_19710514_octogesima-adveniens.html.

———. *Evangelii Nuntiandi*. Apostolic exhortation. 1975. http://w2.vatican.va/content/paul-vi/en/apost_exhortations/documents/hf_p-vi_exh_19751208_evangelii-nuntiandi.html.

Penner, Myron Bradley. *The End of Apologetics: Christian Witness in a Postmodern Context*. Grand Rapids, Mich.: Baker Academic, 2013.

Peterson, Jordan. *12 Rules for Life: An Antidote to Chaos*. Toronto: Random House of Canada, 2018.

———. Interview with Dennis Prager at the Prager University summit, May 3–4, 2019. https://www.youtube.com/watch?v=L47oJxwp6yg.

Philippe, Jacques. *Called to Life*. New York: Scepter Publishers, 2008.

Pieper, Josef. *Faith, Hope, Love*. San Francisco: Ignatius Press, 1997.

Pinckaers, Servais. "Recherche de la signification véritable du terme 'spéculatif,'" *Nouvelle Revue Théologique* 81, no. 7 (1959): 673–95.

———. *Sources of Christian Ethics*. Translated by Sr. Mary Thomas Noble, OP. Washington, D.C.: The Catholic University of America Press, 1995.
———. *Morality: the Catholic View*. Notre Dame, Ind.: St. Augustine's Press, 2003.
Pius XII. *Humani Generis*. Encyclical letter. 1950. http://w2.vatican.va/content/pius-xii/en/encyclicals/documents/hf_p-xii_enc_12081950_humani-generis.html.
Plantinga, Alvin. *Knowledge and Christian Belief*. Grand Rapids, Mich.: Eerdmans Publishing Co., 2015.
Plato. *Symposium*. Indianapolis: Hackett, 1989.
Polyani, Michael. *Personal Knowledge: Towards a Post-Critical Philosophy*. Chicago: University of Chicago Press, 1974.
Pontifical Council for Culture. *The Via Pulchritudinis, Privileged Pathway for Evangelization and Dialogue*. 2006. http://www.vatican.va/roman_curia/pontifical_councils/cultr/documents/rc_pc_cultr_doc_20060327_plenary-assembly_final-document_en.html.
Pontifical Council for Inter-religious Dialogue. *Dialogue and Proclamation*. 1991. http://www.vatican.va/roman_curia/pontifical_councils/interelg/documents/rc_pc_interelg_doc_19051991_dialogue-and-proclamatio_en.html.
Prothro, James. *Both Judge and Justifier: Biblical Legal Language and the Act of Justifying in Paul*. Tübingen: Mohr Siebeck, 2018.
Pruss, Alexander. *One Body: An Essay in Christian Sexual Ethics*. Notre Dame, Ind.: University of Notre Dame Press, 2013.
Rahner, Karl. *On the Theology of Death*. New York: Herder and Herder, 1961.
———. *Nature and Grace*. New York: Sheed and Ward, 1964.
Ramage, Matthew. *Dark Passages of the Bible: Engaging Scripture with Benedict XVI and Thomas Aquinas*. Washington, D.C.: The Catholic University of America Press, 2013.
———. "Benedict XVI on Freedom in Obedience to the Truth: A Key for the New Evangelization." *Homiletic and Pastoral Review* (May 12, 2014). https://www.hprweb.com/2014/05/benedict-xvi-on-freedom-in-obedience-to-the-truth-a-key-for-the-new-evangelization/.
———. Review of *Will Many Be Saved? What Vatican II Actually Teaches and Its Implications for the New Evangelization* by Ralph Martin. *Nova et Vetera* 12, no. 4 (2014): 1313–17.
———. "Pope Benedict XVI's Theology of Beauty and the New Evangelization." *Homiletic and Pastoral Review* (January 29, 2015). https://www.hprweb.com/2015/01/pope-benedict-xvis-theology-of-beauty-and-the-new-evangelization/.
———. "Violence Is Incompatible with the Nature of God: Benedict, Aquinas,

and Method C Exegesis of the 'Dark' Passages of the Bible." *Nova et Vetera* 13, no. 1 (2015): 273–295.

———. "The Reception of St. Paul in the Works of Joseph Ratzinger/Benedict XVI," *Letter and Spirit* 11 (2016): 147–71.

———. *Jesus, Interpreted: Benedict XVI, Bart Ehrman, and the Historical Truth of the Gospels*. Washington, DC: The Catholic University of America Press, 2017.

Ratzinger, Joseph. "The Dignity of the Human Person" [commentary on *Gaudium et Spes*]. In *Commentary on the Documents of Vatican II*, vol. 5, edited by Herbert Vorgrimler, 115–63. New York: Herder and Herder, 1969.

———. *Daughter Zion: Meditations on the Church's Marian Belief*. San Francisco: Ignatius Press, 1983.

———. *Feast of Faith*. San Francisco: Ignatius Press, 1986.

———. *Principles of Catholic Theology*. San Francisco: Ignatius Press, 1987.

———. *Eschatology: Death and Eternal Life*. Washington, DC: The Catholic University of America Press, 1988.

———. *In the Beginning: A Catholic Understanding of the Story of Creation and the Fall*. Grand Rapids, Mich.: Eerdmans Publishing Co., 1995.

———. *Nature and Mission of Theology*. San Francisco: Ignatius Press, 1995.

———. *Called to Communion*. San Francisco: Ignatius Press, 1996.

———. "Relativism: The Central Problem for Faith Today." May 1996. https://www.ewtn.com/library/CURIA/RATZRELA.HTM.

———. "Truth and Freedom." *Communio: International Catholic Review* 23, no. 1 (1996): 16–35.

———. *Salt of the Earth*. San Francisco: Ignatius Press, 1997.

———. "Crises of Law." Address to the LUMSA Faculty of Jurisprudence in Rome. November 10, 1999. https://www.ewtn.com/library/Theology/LAWMETA.HTM.

———. Address to catechists and religion teachers. December 12, 2000. https://www.ewtn.com/new_evangelization/Ratzinger.htm.

———. *The Sabbath of History*. Washington, D.C.: William G. Congdon Foundation, 2000.

———. *The Spirit of the Liturgy*. San Francisco: Ignatius Press, 2000.

———. "The Feeling of Things, the Contemplation of Beauty." Message to the Communion and Liberation meeting at Rimini. August 24, 2002. http://www.vatican.va/roman_curia/congregations/cfaith/documents/rc_con_cfaith_doc_20020824_ratzinger-cl-rimini_en.html.

———. *Introduction to Christianity*. 2nd ed. San Francisco: Ignatius Press, 2004.

———. *Truth and Tolerance*. San Francisco: Ignatius Press, 2004.

———. Homily to the College of Cardinals for the election of the Roman pontiff.

April 18, 2005. http://www.vatican.va/gpII/documents/homily-pro-eligendo-pontifice_20050418_en.html.

———. *Pilgrim Fellowship of Faith*. San Francisco: Ignatius Press, 2005.

———. *The Yes of Jesus Christ*. New York: Crossroad Publishing Company, 2005.

———. *Images of Hope: Meditations on Major Feasts*. San Francisco: Ignatius Press, 2006.

———. *Eschatology: Death and Eternal Life*. 2nd ed. Washington, D.C.: The Catholic University of America Press, 2007.

———. "Biblical Interpretation in Conflict: On the Foundations and the Itinerary for Exegesis Today." In *Opening Up the Scriptures: Joseph Ratzinger and the Foundations of Biblical Interpretation*, edited by José Granados, Carlos Granados, and Luis Sánchez-Navarro, 1–29. Grand Rapids, Mich.: Eerdmans Publishing Co., 2008.

———. *Church, Ecumenism, and Politics*. San Francisco: Ignatius Press, 2008.

———. *Faith and the Future*. San Francisco: Ignatius Press, 2009.

———. "Conscience and Truth," *Communio* 37 (2010): 529–38.

———. "Belief in Creation and the Theory of Evolution." In *Dogma and Preaching*, 131–42. San Francisco: Ignatius Press, 2011.

———. "Farewell to the Devil?" In *Dogma and Preaching*, 197–204. San Francisco: Ignatius Press, 2011.

———. "On the Understanding of 'Person' in Theology." In *Dogma and Preaching*, 181–96. San Francisco: Ignatius Press, 2011.

———. "What Comes after Death?" In *Dogma and Preaching*, 255–59. San Francisco: Ignatius Press, 2011.

———. "Why I Am Still in the Church." In *Fundamental Speeches from Five Decades*, 133–54. San Francisco: Ignatius Press, 2012.

Ratzinger, Joseph, and Vittorio Messori. *The Ratzinger Report*. San Francisco: Ignatius Press, 1987.

Ratzinger, Joseph, Heinz Schürmann, and Hans Urs von Balthasar. *Principles of Christian Morality*. San Francisco: Ignatius Press, 1986.

Rausch, Thomas. *Faith, Hope, and Charity: Benedict XVI on the Theological Virtues*. New York: Paulist Press, 2015.

Rorty, Richard. *Philosophy and the Mirror of Nature*. Princeton: Princeton University Press, 1979.

Rousseau, Jean-Jacques. *Émile: or, On Education*. New York: Basic Books, 1979.

Rowland, Tracey. *Ratzinger's Faith: The Theology of Pope Benedict XVI*. Oxford: Oxford University Press, 2008.

Rziha, John. *The Christian Moral Life: Directions for the Journey to Happiness*. Notre Dame, Ind.: University of Notre Dame Press, 2017.

Sales, Francis de. *Treatise on the Love of God*. New York: Benziger Brothers, 1884.

———. *Introduction to the Devout Life*. New York: Image Books, 1989.

Schönborn, Christoph. "The Reflections of Joseph Ratzinger Pope Benedict XVI on Evolution." In *Scientific Insights into the Evolution of the Universe and of Life*, edited by W. Arber, N. Cabibbo, and M. Sánchez Sorondo, 12–21. Vatican City: Ex Aedibus Academicis in Civitate Vaticana, 2009.

Silva, Moisés, ed. *New International Dictionary of New Testament Theology and Exegesis*. Grand Rapids, Mich.: Zondervan, 2014.

Smith, James K. A. *How Not to Be Secular: Reading Charles Taylor*. Grand Rapids, Mich.: Eerdmans Publishing Co., 2014.

Stump, Eleonore. *Wandering in Darkness*. Oxford: Oxford University Press, 2010.

Taylor, Charles. *A Secular Age*. Cambridge, Mass.: Belknap Press of Harvard University, 2007.

Tolkien, J. R. R., Verlyn Flieger, and Douglas A. Anderson. *Tolkien on Fairy-Stories*. London: HarperCollins, 2014.

Torrell, Jean Pierre. *Saint Thomas Aquinas*, vol. 2, *Spiritual Master*. Washington, DC: The Catholic University of America Press, 2005.

Vatican Council II. *Sacrosanctum Concilium*. 1963. http://www.vatican.va/archive/hist_councils/ii_vatican_council/documents/vat-ii_const_19631204_sacrosanctum-concilium_en.html.

———. *Lumen Gentium*. 1964. http://www.vatican.va/archive/hist_councils/ii_vatican_council/documents/vat-ii_const_19641121_lumen-gentium_en.html.

———. *Unitatis Redintegratio*. 1964. http://www.vatican.va/archive/hist_councils/ii_vatican_council/documents/vat-ii_decree_19641121_unitatis-redintegratio_en.html.

———. *Dei Verbum*. 1965. http://www.vatican.va/archive/hist_councils/ii_vatican_council/documents/vat-ii_const_19651118_dei-verbum_en.html.

———. *Gaudium et Spes*. 1965. http://www.vatican.va/archive/hist_councils/ii_vatican_council/documents/vat-ii_const_19651207_gaudium-et-spes_en.html.

———. *Nostra Aetate*. 1965. http://www.vatican.va/archive/hist_councils/ii_vatican_council/documents/vat-ii_decl_19651028_nostra-aetate_en.html.

Watts, John D. W. *Isaiah 1–33*. Word Biblical Commentary 24. Nashville: Thomas Nelson, 2005.

Young, Julian. *Friedrich Nietzsche: A Philosophical Biography*. Cambridge: Cambridge University Press, 2010.

INDEX

Abortion, 38n9, 172, 175, 177n13
Acts (Book of), 159
Aelred of Rievaulx, 146n8
Agape, 145–57
Apophaticism, 59–62, 83–85, 92–96, 98, 213
Authenticity, age of, 218–22
Alighieri, Dante, 116, 138
Allah, 55n5, 56
Allegiance, 101, 103n41, 193, 204, 214–16
Allison, Dale, 103n41, 113, 125n10, 129n16, 131n19, 133n25, 134n27, 137n31, 139n36, 140, 142, 208
Aman/Amen, 74–75, 198, 206, 215
Amoris Laetitia, 153n23, 177–78, 252n16
Anderson, Douglas, 133n63
Anima separata, 124–25
Annunciation, 64
Anselm of Canterbury, 58
Anthony of Padua, 29
Anthropocentrism, 187
Apologia/Apology/Apologetics, 5, 7–8, 21, 57, 77, 96n29, 112, 118, 129n16, 197, 200, 217–37
Apostles, 50, 65, 159, 261
Aquinas, Thomas, 30n17, 57–60, 62n20, 75, 102n40, 125m9, 126n11, 135–36, 143n2, 145n4, 148nn13–15, 228–29, 241, 247
Aristotle, 59n14, 135, 136n29, 224, 265
Ascension, 112, 120–21, 129–34
Assent, 47–48, 57, 62n20, 78, 90–91, 215, 259n21

Athanasius, 42
Atheism, 2n1, 9n7, 12n14, 18, 55, 99n37, 113m 188n70, 163n47, 220–22
Augustine, 20, 70, 104, 108n53, 158, 193n40
Aumann, Jordan OP, 79n58

Bach, 245
Bacon, Francis, 103–4
Balthasar, Hans urs, 81n63, 113–14, 139n37, 231n27
Barber, Michael, 30n16
Barth, Karl, 127–28n14
Bates, Matthew, 103n41, 214–16, 227n19
Beatitude, 151
Beatitudes, The, 3, 78
Beauty: 7, 13, 31–32, 36, 45, 57, 76, 89, 98, 106, 109n56, 118, 142, 147n11, 193, 200, 222, 224, 228n21, 230; way of, 239–66
Belief, "ironic," 217–38, 260
Benedict, St., 31, 191n36, 266
Berry, Wendell, 186
Biocentrism, 187
Boethius, 142
Bonaventure, 171, 202
Buddhism, 55, 250

Caravaggio, 244
Cardinal Virtues, 148
Caritas, 39n11, 44n27, 67, 70n34, 104n43, 143–68, 173–80, 184, 188–89, 251n15

279

280   INDEX

Catechism of the Catholic Church, 25, 27, 57n8, 58n10, 68, 102n38, 160, 173n4, 244
de Chardin, Fr. Teilhard, 108–9, 135n28
Charity, 143–96
Chautard, Dom Jean-Baptiste: 28n14
Chesterton, G. K., 113, 232
Conscience, 37–38, 44n28, 54, 137n31, 174
Congregation for the Doctrine of the Faith (CDF), 34n1, 49
Christ, body and blood of, 111, 153, 213, 261
Colossians (Letter), 111, 255
Common Good, 160, 164, 166, 172, 177n14, 183
Communion, 11, 21, 24n9, 46, 48, 82, 89–90, 106n49, 108, 151, 153, 190, 202, 249
Compassion, 3, 110
Confucianism, 161
Consolation, 76, 115, 142, 207
Contraception, 49, 177, 251–52
Corinthians (First Letter), x, 14, 31, 111, 121, 123, 128, 154, 223, 260
Corinthians (Second Letter), 199
Cottingham, John, 224–28, 258n19
Covenant, 74, 199
Creation, 32, 62, 68n31, 106–109, 118, 126n11, 127n14, 128, 135n28, 140, 150n18, 154–56, 169, 173, 178–80, 183–93, 222, 242n5, 256
Credo, 73
Cross, 3, 41, 43, 69–70, 107, 111–12, 115, 119, 142, 153–54, 226, 252, 254, 265
Crossan, John Dominic, 258
Crucifixion, 41, 111, 119

Dark Night of the Soul, 62, 212
Deposit of revelation, 47–48, 75
Descartes, René, 4
Diakonia, 159
Dialogue of action, 177
Dignity, human, 48, 78n53, 150, 157, 164–66, 172–75, 180, 184, 187, 190, 251, 257
Dionysius the Areopagite, 242
Disciple/discipleship, 8, 50, 53, 117–19, 129, 131, 141, 153, 202–204, 220, 226, 236, 240, 247, 254, 260, 265

Divine nature, 23, 60
Divine Pedagogy, 66–67, 200
Divinization (*theosis*), 18, 21–25, 31, 35, 40–44, 106n50, 108–11, 133, 135n28, 150, 154, 187, 190, 193
Domestic church, 30n18
Dostoevsky, Fyodor, 12, 118n70
Doubt, 7, 9, 30n17, 59, 62–64, 69, 72, 132, 141, 192n38, 205, 207, 211, 218, 224, 258–63

Easter, 118, 140–41
Ecclesiastes (Book of), 67, 208–11
Ecological spirituality and virtues, 181–85
Ecology: cultural, 183; human, 173–80; integral, 169–96
Eleutheria, 40
Enns, Peter, 198, 204–15
Environment, 109, 159, 170–92, 245
Ephesians (Letter), 152, 251
Epistemology, 10, 96, 139, 198, 200–203, 226
Eros, 54n3, 145–55
Esolen, Anthony, 138n33,
Eternal life, 45, 101, 103–109, 115, 122, 126n12, 128–29, 135–36, 141, 161, 261, 264n26
Eucharist, 19, 106–108, 139, 153–54, 190, 213
Evolution, 11n10, 40, 104, 106n50, 108, 123, 126n11, 135n28, 136, 179n18, 188, 191
Exegesis, 25, 75–76, 116, 123–24, 132, 143n2, 221n9
Existentialism, 1, 7, 11–14, 47, 60, 71–72, 96, 114, 116, 122, 125, 131, 140n38, 205–207, 217, 240, 258n19, 266
Exodus, 67, 71–72, 89, 148

Faith/belief, 53–99
Family, 99, 145, 149, 152–53, 157–58, 162, 167, 174, 178, 180, 183, 224, 251–58
Faust, 140–41
Faustina, 59
Fee, Gordon, 14n16
Fiduciary framework, 231–32
Fortitude, 148
Francis of Assisi, 26, 41, 63n21
Freedom, 33–52

INDEX

de Gaál, Emery, 12
Galatians (Letter), 23, 40–41, 80–81, 206n19, 214
Genesis, 150n18, 152, 179, 188, 198–99
Goethe, 140
Golden Rule, 161
Good Friday, 118–19
Gregory the Great, 79

Hail Mary, The, 27
Heaven, 3–4, 18, 26, 63n21, 103n41, 105–106, 118, 129–34, 139, 148, 186, 224, 257, 262
Hebrew, 74–75, 102, 116, 147, 198–99, 206
Hell, 3–4, 59, 112–25, 129–34, 137–40, 245, 253
Hemianopia, 200
Hermeneutic, 34n1, 123, 200–201, 221n10, 234
Hevel, 209
Hinduism, 55–56, 250, 258
Holiness, 6–7, 17–32, 35, 56–59, 200, 212, 223n13, 244, 247–48, 258n19, 265
Holy Saturday, 112–19, 122, 129
Holy Spirit, 23, 50, 92, 151, 156, 251
Hope, 100–142
Hugh of Saint-Victor, 25
Humanism, 2n1, 9n7, 99n37, 118n70, 156
Hume, David, 262–63
Humility, 24, 41, 60–61, 64, 69, 93
Hypocrisy, 3

Integral human development, 44, 155–59, 174
Integrity, 48, 89–90, 176, 205, 241, 247
Isaiah (Book of), 74, 227, 254
Islam, 55–56, 189n32, 250
Israel, 41, 66–68, 153, 198, 201, 207, 210

Jacob, 67–68, 236
James (Book of), 82n66
James, St., 63, 82
Job (Book of), 69–70, 209–11
John of the Cross, 21–22, 27, 62, 79n58, 189–90, 212

John of Damascus, 24
John (First Letter), 31, 143, 161
John (Gospel), 44, 50, 63, 111, 128, 153, 249, 257, 261
John Paul II, 131n20, 150–53, 156, 160–63, 166, 170, 172–77, 242
Johnson, Dru, 198–204
Joy, x, 2–3, 25, 46, 50, 57, 71, 83–84, 102, 105, 131–32, 154, 185, 247–48, 250–56
Judaism, 82n66, 115n65, 201, 214
Judas, 139n34, 230
Judgment, 72, 113n63, 134–35, 215
Judges, 201
Justice, 82, 126, 134–38, 148, 156–57, 167, 191n37

Kant, Immanuel, 13, 136n29, 161
Kardiatheology, 226
Kerygma, 159
Kierkegaard, Søren, 12, 229–30

Last things, 103n4, 113, 129, 137, 142
Laudato Si', 109, 160, 169, 172–76, 181–92
Lectio Divina, 25–30
Leo XIII, 165–66
Leo the Great, 24n9, 90
Leviticus (Book of), 154, 160
Lewis, C.S., 30, 481, 113, 130–33, 136, 139, 145n7, 146n7, 209, 242, 261–63
Liberation theology, 34n1
Liberalism, economic, 166
Liturgy: 25, 30–32, 66n26, 85–86, 108–109, 153, 159, 190n34, 211, 213, 242, 256
Logos, 86, 96, 157
de Lubac, Henri, 2n1, 9, 77, 99, 118n70, 135n28
Luke (Gospel), 64
Lumen Fidei, 11n12, 37n6, 48, 53n1, 57–60, 63, 71, 75–79, 87–90, 118
Lumen Gentium, 50, 56, 110, 213, 258n19
Luther, Martin, 81, 245

MacIntyre, Alasdair, 229–32, 265–66
Madden, James, 126n11

Magisterium, 37, 47–50, 58, 87, 89–90, 92, 203–204, 236
Marcel, Gabriel, 12n14
Mark (Gospel), 161, 201
Marriage, 7, 24, 99, 147, 151–53, 157, 172, 174, 180n19, 206, 251–53, 261, 263
Martin, Ralph, 139n37
Martyria/martyrdom, 41–42, 63, 159, 247
Marx, Karl, 34, 104, 106, 263n26
Marxism, 166
Mary (Mother of God), 64–65, 112, 132n21, 210n29
Materialism, 104, 125n10, 142, 163, 264n27
Matthew (Gospel), 3, 23, 70, 82, 115, 139, 163, 201, 261
Maximus the Confessor, 108n53
Meconi, David, 108n53
Meditatio/meditation, 26, 29–31, 42n20, 131–33
Menssen, Sandra Lee, 227n21
Mercy, 20, 24, 101–2, 137–39, 148n13, 192–93, 255
Merton, Thomas, 12–13, 212
Messiah, 63
Metaphysics, 130, 158, 161n45
Mission, 41–42, 50, 118, 155, 159, 169
Morality, 80–81, 127n13, 172, 240, 244
Mormonism, 56
Moser, Paul, 226–27
Muhammad, 55n5
Mystical body of Christ, 31, 89, 185
Mysticism, 62, 79, 83–84, 89, 92, 105–6, 109, 133, 153–54, 185, 189–90, 212

Neo-paganism, 188–89
Newman, John Henry, 44, 47–48, 62n20, 78n54, 91n14, 203n14, 215, 259–60
New Testament, 40, 124, 125n10, 140n38, 153, 161, 198, 207, 223
Nietzche, Friedrich, 1–19, 32, 34, 47, 49, 53–58, 76, 79, 83–84, 87, 98–99, 112, 117–18, 136, 142, 144, 149, 151, 169, 200–201, 240–41, 261–66
Nichols, Aidan, 6n5

Nihilism, 3, 5, 10, 135–36, 260–63
Nostra Aetate, 56n6
Nussbaum, Martha, 225–26

Obedience, 33–52, 81, 84–99, 210, 228n21, 231n27, 264n26
O'Connor, Flannery, 245
Old Testament, 40, 115, 147n11, 150, 207
Our Father, The, 27

Pantheism, 188–89
Pascal, Blaise, 72, 226–27, 259, 262
Passion(s), 3, 39, 41, 48, 69, 110–11, 115, 151, 154, 245, 247
Patristics, 23–24, 42, 67, 108, 115, 242
Paul, St., 13–14, 35, 42, 79–82, 88, 101, 106, 111, 121, 123, 190, 199, 216n41, 223, 232, 251, 253, 255, 260, 264
Paul VI, 49, 158, 160n41, 165, 177, 252n16
Penner, Myron, 96n29, 228–37, 257, 260
Peter, St., 7, 36
Peterson, Jordan, 97n35, 179n18, 118n70
Philia, 145–46
Philippians (Letter), 43, 72
Philippe, Jacques, 242
Philosophy, 4–5, 12n14, 19, 38, 95, 123–26, 161, 198, 200–202, 217, 219, 224–29, 233, 237, 258n19, 263n26, 266
Pinckaers, Servais, 36–39, 44–45, 80–81, 145n4, 219
Pistis, 198, 206, 215–16
Pius XII, 12n14
Plantinga, Alvin, 200n4, 264n26
Plato, 147, 152n22, 241
Polyani, Michael, 201
Pontifical Council for Culture, 242–43
Pontifical Council for Interreligious Dialogue, 177
Postmodernism, ix, 96n29, 117, 136n30, 205n17, 265
Prayer, 17–19, 25–32, 43, 58, 66–69, 79n58, 139, 185, 212–13, 242, 246n9
Protestantism, 56, 199, 203
Prudence, 148, 191

Psalms (Book of), 29–30, 211, 254
Purgatory, 137–38

Rahner, Karl, 13, 106
Ramage, Matthew, 26n11, 30n17, 80n59, 86n2, 102n40, 115n65, 124n8, 134n27, 140n38, 202n9, 209n26, 210n28, 216n41, 239n1, 263n26
Raphael, 245
Rausch, Thomas S.J., 6n5, 11, 90n13, 103n41, 126n12
Relativism, 37n8, 44, 176, 182, 257n18
Resubstantiation, 108, 190
Resurrection, 22, 63, 112, 115, 118–29, 132n21, 133–35, 137, 217–18, 221–22, 224, 226–27, 236, 240, 249–61
Revelation (Book of), 106, 115
Revelation, Divine, 13–14, 45, 47–48, 57, 66, 85, 86n2, 116, 158, 189, 202–3, 211, 228–29, 241, 259n20
Romans (Letter), 24, 35, 78, 91, 106, 11, 190, 232, 260
Rorty, Richard, 233
Rousseau, Jean-Jacques, 87
Rowland, Tracey, 6n5, 48n36
Rziha, John, 58n12

de Sales, Francis, 26, 28, 105, 146n8
Scripture, fourfold sense of, 25–26
Second Vatican Council, 19, 41, 50, 56, 90, 110, 124, 213, 258
Secularism, 4–16, 197, 217–20, 237
Secularity, 9–10
Seewald, Peter, 61n18, 65n24
Self-denial/sacrifice, 3
Self-mortification, 110
Sentimentality, 79, 156
Skepticism, 2, 10, 32, 36, 47–48, 53, 55, 63, 141, 170, 262
Smith, James, 9, 218–24
Smith, Janet, 49

Socialism, 161, 166
Social justice, 156
Solidarity, 159–68, 183
Spadaro, Fr. Antonio, 62n20, 172n3, 205n17
Spiritual body, 123, 128
Stewardship, 177, 184
Stump, Eleonore, 200, 225–26, 259n20
Subsidiarity, 159–68, 183
Suffering, redemptive, 109–121, 133, 253–63
Sullivan, Thomas, 227n21
Sunday, 19–20, 22, 25, 118, 211

Taoism, 96
Taylor, Charles, 9, 141, 219
Temperance, 148
Ten Commandments, 20, 23
Teresa of Calcutta, 59, 212
Thérèse of Lisieux, 59, 184, 192
Thomas (Apostle), 9, 63–64, 218
de Tocqueville, Alexis, 4
Tolkien, J.R.R., 113, 119
Torrell, Jean-Pierre O.P., 60n15
Totalitarianism, 164
Transubstantiation, 103–112

USCCB, 49, 191n37

Via pulchritudinis, 239–66
Vocation, 156, 158, 188, 244, 251, 254

Welfare State/Social Assistance State, 164–67
Works of Mercy, 192–93
Worship, 85n2, 108, 134, 213–14, 223, 245, 264n26

Xavier, Francis, 41

Yada, 199–201
Yahweh, 201, 210
Young, Julian, 53n1

The Experiment of Faith: Pope Benedict XVI on Living the Theological Virtues in a Secular Age was designed in Arno and composed by Kachergis Book Design of Pittsboro, North Carolina. It was printed on 55-pound Natural and bound by Maple Press of York, Pennsylvania.